T0291188

# Healthcare Infrastructure, Resilience and Climate Change

This book highlights the vulnerability of healthcare buildings in the context of climate change–triggered extreme weather events (EWEs) and the case for mitigation. With a concise discussion on climate change and its consequences in the form of such events, a cost model and equations that register losses and help quantify them are then presented. The model can be used to estimate the significant potential loss that might occur during an EWE and help healthcare facilities prepare for them.

The book analyses cases of major EWEs in India over the last two decades and collates the data available into various categories. Through this research the authors have developed a framework which assists healthcare facilities with a detailed calculation of value losses, both tangible and intangible. The framework can be used to assess the impacts on healthcare buildings in terms of disruption of services so that appropriate decisions related to the resilience in healthcare planning can be taken into consideration. Thus, the book is useful for directing planning and design processes aimed at continuity of service and building resilience to perform in the face of natural disasters and extreme weather.

The purpose of this book is to prompt facilities planners and healthcare facilities to prepare to respond to EWEs through the planning and design process in a rational manner. Built infrastructure professionals such as architects and engineers, policy makers, and academics with an interest in disasters, risk and climate change will all find this book to be key reading.

**Virendra Kumar Paul** is faculty at the Department of Building Engineering and Management at the School of Planning and Architecture, New Delhi. Associated with the department since 1985, his areas of interest in research and academia include construction project management and fire safety in buildings. His research is also focused on the study of the impact of disasters and vulnerability and advocacy for safe design practices. He is a well-published author in renowned high-impact journals from publishers such as Springer, Taylor & Francis and UGC Care and other peer-reviewed journals. He has served on numerous committees steering the development of public healthcare and educational campuses.

**Chaitali Basu** has served at the School of Planning and Architecture, New Delhi, since 2016 before she moved to the University of the West of England, Bristol, UK, to serve as a senior lecturer in quantity surveying and construction technologies. She is an alumna of BITS Mesra, SPA Delhi, Oxford Brookes, UK, and a BHAVAN scholar (Michigan State University, USA). Her academic interests include building performance evaluation, building surveying, and construction project management.

**Abhijit Rastogi** is faculty at the Department of Building Engineering and Management, School of Planning and Architecture, New Delhi. Having been a part of academia for more than eight years, Dr Abhijit is extensively involved in research and teaching. His areas of academic research include construction management, risk management, building materials, and skill development.

**Sumedha Dua** is a research scholar who has been associated with healthcare infrastructure and educational projects. Her areas of interest include energy efficiency, disaster management, resilient healthcare design and development, construction management, and sustainability. She is pursuing academic research in risk assessment of healthcare infrastructures in extreme weather events.

# Healthcare Infrastructure, Resilience and Climate Change

Preparing for Extreme Weather Events

**Virendra Kumar Paul, Chaitali Basu,
Abhijit Rastogi and Sumedha Dua**

LONDON AND NEW YORK

Designed cover image: © Virendra Kumar Paul

First published 2023
by Routledge
4 Park Square, Milton Park, Abingdon, Oxon OX14 4RN

and by Routledge
605 Third Avenue, New York, NY 10158

*Routledge is an imprint of the Taylor & Francis Group, an informa business*

© 2023 Virendra Kumar Paul, Chaitali Basu, Abhijit Rastogi and Sumedha Dua

*British Library Cataloguing-in-Publication Data*
A catalogue record for this book is available from the British Library

ISBN: 978-1-032-49306-0 (hbk)
ISBN: 978-1-032-48891-2 (pbk)
ISBN: 978-1-003-39310-8 (ebk)

DOI: 10.1201/9781003393108

Typeset in Times New Roman
by Apex CoVantage, LLC

The book is dedicated to the conviction and commitment of academia and research fraternity pursuing the cause of climate change and its mitigation that can have an impact on extreme weather events to render healthcare facilities useful to society with a limited need for resilience.

# Contents

*Prologue*                                                                          *xiv*
*Acknowledgements*                                                                  *xvii*
*List of figures*                                                                   *xviii*
*List of tables*                                                                    *xix*
*List of boxes*                                                                     *xx*
*List of abbreviations*                                                             *xxi*

**1  Extreme weather events and critical infrastructure**                           1

   *1.1  Overview  1*
   *1.2  Structure of the chapter  1*
   *1.3  Background  2*
   *1.4  Anthropogenic effects and climate change  3*
   *1.5  Development versus environmental paradox  3*
   *1.6  Defining extreme weather events  4*
   *1.7  Extreme weather events and weather anomalies  5*
      *1.7.1  Typology of extreme weather events  5*
      *1.7.2  Nexus of climate change and extreme
           weather events  7*
      *1.7.3  Impact of climate change on EWEs
           across the world  8*
      *1.7.4  Intensifying disasters  9*
      *1.7.5  Adaptive capacity of communities  10*
   *1.8  Defining critical infrastructure  11*
   *1.9  Critical infrastructure and its challenges  12*
   *1.10  Extreme weather events and challenges
      in infrastructure development  13*
   *1.11  Success milestones and challenges of
      sustainable development  14*
      *1.11.1  Sustainable Development Goals of the UNDP  15*
      *1.11.2  The global scenario  15*

*1.11.3  SDGs: the Indian picture  17*

*1.11.4  Challenges for achieving the SDGs in India  19*

*1.11.5  SDGs and working towards a transformational agenda  21*

*1.11.6  Implications of the unfinished agenda of the SDGs  21*

*1.11.7  Vulnerability of healthcare as a critical infrastructure  21*

*1.12  Summary  22*

## 2   Healthcare infrastructure and extreme weather events       26

*2.1  Overview  26*

*2.2  Structure of the chapter  26*

*2.3  Responses to climate change: India's efforts  27*

*2.4  Experts' opinion on EWE and healthcare infrastructure vulnerability  28*

*2.4.1  Reviews on EWE vulnerability  29*

*2.4.2  Reviews on healthcare projects' shortcomings  29*

*2.4.3  Reviews on resilience intervention  30*

*2.4.4  Reviews on enhancing awareness  31*

*2.5  Importance of healthcare facilities  32*

*2.6  Health and hazards scenario in India  32*

*2.7  Vulnerability of health infrastructure: status of research in India  33*

*2.8  Role of government in making healthcare resilient  34*

*2.9  Guidelines in India for hospital safety  35*

*2.10  Hierarchy of public healthcare (primary and secondary) in India  36*

*2.11  Status of resilience in the healthcare infrastructure in SDMPs  36*

*2.12  Disaster management and preparedness in public hospitals in India  37*

*2.13  Case examples of lack of performance of hospitals in the face of EWEs  38*

*2.13.1  Chennai floods, 2015  38*

*2.13.2  Jammu and Kashmir floods, 2014  39*

*2.14  Findings from case examples of the impact of EWEs on the healthcare infrastructure  40*

*2.15  Resilience and challenges in infrastructure  42*

*2.16  Need to supplement knowledge  44*

*2.17  Need for capacity building for competence development  45*

*2.18  Summary  45*

**3 Impact of extreme weather events on the critical infrastructure** 49

3.1 *Overview 49*

3.2 *Structure of the chapter 50*

3.3 *Inclusion of critical infrastructure in climate change
response initiatives 50*

3.4 *Impact of extreme weather events on critical
infrastructure 50*

    *3.4.1 Kerala floods (2018–2019) 51*

    *3.4.2 Cyclone Fani (2019) 53*

    *3.4.3 Kotrupi landslide (2017) 54*

    *3.4.4 Mumbai floods (2017) 54*

    *3.4.5 Chennai floods (2015) 55*

    *3.4.6 Cyclone Hudhud (2014) 56*

    *3.4.7 Cyclone Phailin (2013) 58*

    *3.4.8 Delhi floods (2013) 59*

    *3.4.9 Uttarakhand floods (2013) 59*

    *3.4.10 Ladakh flash floods (2010) 61*

    *3.4.11 Bihar floods (2008–2020) 62*

3.5 *Impact of climate change and EWEs on healthcare
infrastructure 62*

    *3.5.1 Impact on human health 63*

    *3.5.2 Impact on healthcare structures 64*

3.6 *Status of response to disasters and EWEs in India 66*

    *3.6.1 Disaster management reform in India 66*

    *3.6.2 Robustness of disaster management and response
mechanism in India 67*

    *3.6.3 Quick response flow chart: NIDM 67*

    *3.6.4 Agencies authorised to issue warnings 68*

    *3.6.5 National disaster response policies review: status of
disaster response 68*

3.7 *The need to place resilience over response 70*

3.8 *Summary 71*

**4 Public health systems and the impact of extreme weather events** 73

4.1 *Overview 73*

4.2 *Structure of the chapter 73*

4.3 *Public healthcare systems 74*

4.4 *National Health Policy 2017 74*

4.5 *Mapping of the healthcare sector in India 75*

    *4.5.1 Health infrastructure in India 76*

4.5.2 Access to healthcare in India  77
4.5.3 Role of government in public health  79
4.5.4 Challenges in healthcare in India  79
4.6 Adverse living conditions holding back health  80
4.6.1 Limited access to healthcare and quality of care  80
4.6.2 Absence of manpower in healthcare  81
4.6.3 Affordability or the cost of healthcare  81
4.6.4 Current status of public healthcare in India  81
4.6.5 EWEs and the position of disadvantage in the
healthcare system in India  82
4.7 Infectious diseases  82
4.7.1 Upsurge in infectious diseases because of climate
change  83
4.8 Healthcare delivery systems in India  83
4.8.1 Public healthcare infrastructure: modes of delivery  84
4.9 Impact of EWEs on the healthcare infrastructure  86
4.9.1 Risks to the healthcare system due to climate change
and EWEs: impacts on human health and health
facilities  87
4.10 Summary  88

5   The case for resilience in healthcare facilities                    91

5.1 Overview  91
5.2 Structure of the chapter  91
5.3 Disruption due to uncertainty of events  92
5.3.1 Disruption in healthcare facilities  92
5.4 Stages of disruption  93
5.4.1 The first rescue stage: disruption of the initial
emergency response  93
5.4.2 The second rescue stage: disruption of the
infrastructure critical to public health and welfare  93
5.4.3 The recovery stage: short-term and long-term public
health concerns  94
5.5 Impact of disruption on the health of victims  95
5.6 Resilience in structures  96
5.7 Redundancy in structures  97
5.8 Objective: continuity of services  98
5.8.1 Density of healthcare services  98
5.8.2 Redundancy of healthcare services  99
5.8.3 Mitigation of the impact of disruption on healthcare
services  99
5.9 Summary  99

**6  The theory of resilience and risk in healthcare facilities**          101

   *6.1  Overview  101*

   *6.2  Structure of the chapter  101*

   *6.3  Resilience, reduction, and safety  102*

      *6.3.1  Defining resilience  102*

      *6.3.2  Need for resilience  103*

      *6.3.3  Resilience versus redundancy  104*

      *6.3.4  Domain of disaster resilience and reconstruction  104*

      *6.3.5  Defining risk reduction  105*

         *i  Current DRR governance frameworks  105*

         *ii  Mainstreaming DRR into the health sector  106*

      *6.3.6  Defining safety  106*

   *6.4  Risk during EWEs/hazards  107*

      *6.4.1  Risk assessment  107*

      *6.4.2  Risk identification  108*

      *6.4.3  Risk estimation  108*

      *6.4.4  Risk probability  109*

      *6.4.5  Risk quantification  109*

      *6.4.6  Risk analysis  110*

      *6.4.7  Risk management framework  110*

         *i  Resources  110*

         *ii  Establishing internal communication and reporting mechanisms  111*

         *iii  Establishing external communication and reporting mechanisms  111*

         *iv  Implementing the framework for managing risk  111*

      *6.4.8  Risk evaluation  111*

      *6.4.9  Acceptable risks  112*

   *6.5  Resilience in relation to critical infrastructure  112*

      *6.5.1  The concept of resilience in critical infrastructure systems  113*

      *6.5.2  Factors determining the resilience of critical infrastructure  114*

      *6.5.3  Factors determining robustness  115*

      *6.5.4  Factors determining recoverability  115*

      *6.5.5  Factors determining adaptability  115*

      *6.5.6  Observations  116*

   *6.6  The concept of resilience in healthcare  116*

      *6.6.1  The need for resilience in healthcare systems in the face of climate change  117*

      *6.6.2  Features of a resilient health system  117*

      *6.6.3  Climate-smart healthcare  119*

*6.6.4 Indicators for healthcare resilience  120*

*6.7 Loss potential  121*

*6.8 Summary  121*

**7  The economics of resilience**                                                 124

*7.1 Overview  124*

*7.2 Structure of the chapter  124*

*7.3 Impact of natural disasters/EWEs on the economy of
the country  125*

    *7.3.1 Effects of natural disasters/extreme weather events at
different levels of development  126*

*7.4 Financing resilience  128*

*7.5 International cost models that calculate loss potential  129*

    *7.5.1 Hospital Safety Index  129*

    *7.5.2 Interpretation of results  130*

    *7.5.3 The global context of safety index and loss
potential  131*

*7.6 Defining economic resilience  131*

*7.7 Defining value losses  132*

*7.8 Defining tangible and intangible losses due to EWEs  133*

*7.9 Summary  134*

**8  Cost model for calculating tangible and intangible value losses**     136

*8.1 Overview  136*

    *8.1.1 Loss estimation approach  137*

    *8.1.2 Quantification of dimensions of resilience  138*

        *8.1.2.1 Analysing and measuring disaster
resilience  139*

        *8.1.2.2 Quantifying disaster resilience  139*

    *8.1.3 Quantification of vulnerability  141*

     *i Global Focus Model  141*

     *ii Prevalent Vulnerability Index  142*

    *8.1.4 Value-based or value-driven healthcare system  142*

*8.2 Value losses quantification approach  143*

*8.3 Measuring indirect losses using econometric analyses  143*

*8.4 Application of the cost model  149*

*8.5 Summary  150*

**9  Conclusion and a way forward**                                             151

*9.1 Background  151*

*9.2 Project evaluation and realisation process  154*

*9.3 Tasks ahead 154*

    *9.3.1 Risk mapping 160*

    *9.3.2 Risk index for a specific facility: hazard potential, areas of improvement, and establishing benchmarks 160*

    *9.3.3 Identify risk mitigation strategies 161*

        *i Risk reduction by direct resource input to current facility 162*

        *ii Create a supplementary facility 162*

        *iii Risk transfer to alternate facility 163*

    *9.3.4 Risk mitigation framework (RMF): objective of RMF consistent with overall objective 164*

    *9.3.5 Implementation of mitigation measures 164*

        *i Resilience resource generation 165*

        *ii Rework mitigation framework and review index: propose revised RRG 166*

    *9.3.6 Demonstrate social cost benefit and define risk sensitivity (failure risk) 166*

    *9.3.7 Risk-sensitive implementation plan 167*

    *9.3.8 Reiteration of objectives as achievements 168*

**10 Annexures** 169

    *10.1 Experts' opinions on EWEs and healthcare infrastructure vulnerability: transcripts 169*

*Index*      *177*

# Prologue

Extreme weather events (EWEs) have been recorded to cause massive destruction, especially owing to their non-predictability in most cases. While natural disasters are a function of hydrological and geological phenomena, EWEs are distinctly uncertain and variable in severity. Critical infrastructure is significantly impacted in the event of an EWE, disrupting mobility, accessibility, built infrastructure damages, continuance of services, and engineering utilities. This disruption is most pronounced in healthcare-related facilities at a macro level and infrastructure at the level of a hierarchical system.

The role of the healthcare infrastructure is of momentous importance, since it provides the necessary emergency and medical services, in addition to serving as a shelter. However, not all healthcare facilities have the endurance to sustain impacts of EWEs. Some structures give way, owing to various circumstances, such as structural stability, age of the structure, height from mean sea level, intensity of EWE, etc. It is therefore important to be able to determine losses to strategize mitigation. This exercise needs to be carried out especially in the feasibility, design and pre-construction stage to minimise the impact of such events. At the outset, let there be no dispute that the reality of climate change is concomitant with EWEs. Hence, the impacts of such events are a contextually responsible academic perusal.

EWEs have been recorded to affect critical infrastructure considerably. However, the focus on healthcare infrastructure merits specific attention, especially in countries where availability and access to such infrastructure are much lower than required. This book highlights the vulnerability of healthcare buildings in the context of climate change–triggered EWEs and the case for mitigation. With a succinct discussion on climate change and its consequences in the form of EWEs, a detailed account of risks, resilience, and case studies is presented, followed by proposal of a cost model that enlists value losses to facilitate in quantification of the same. This model will estimate the quantum of the losses that might occur during an EWE, which would help healthcare facilities develop and implement their preparedness plans to avoid losses in case an EWE occurs.

The initial section of the book presents the experiences of the authors in the areas of healthcare planning and disaster mitigation, especially as they relate to EWEs. The concern for a rational approach to resilience needs to be incorporated in the development of critical infrastructure. The general understanding of critical infrastructure highlights the issues involved in dealing with resilient planning and risk reduction. Further, the subject of resilient planning in healthcare buildings as critical infrastructure is elaborated further in this book through sustained research undertaken by the authors.

One of the learnings from experience in EWE and domain knowledge of healthcare infrastructure is the nexus between these two areas being completely absent in the process of carrying any construction forward from the inception stage through to completion. In reality, when one finds that the services of a particular healthcare facility have suffered, causing disruption during an impact, it is largely because of an absence of analysis from the standpoint of disruption. It is possible that while the general appreciation might have existed for mitigation of an uncertain disruption in some cases, the tools and templates did not exist for undertaking such a mitigation exercise. Thus, the book aims to bridge this gap for the application in practice as well as impart the nuances of extreme weather impact and healthcare planning.

The book presents an understanding of the issues related to occurrence and impacts related to EWEs. A framework is proposed to assess the impacts in healthcare buildings in terms of cost towards disruption of services. This can help to undertake appropriate decision-making related to resilience in healthcare planning and preparedness.

The purpose of this book is to prompt facilities planners and healthcare facilities into a thinking process that helps prepare a response to EWEs through planning and design in a rational manner. With the occurrence of EWEs being unpredictable, the appropriate response is required in terms of preparedness and the criticality of the infrastructure in serving societal needs without causing disruption of services. The book analyses cases of major EWEs in the country in the last two decades to assess the losses and impacts on various sectors and infrastructure typologies. It was found during the analysis that the details of the data for losses available for most cases was not sufficient and did not assign a fair importance to healthcare facilities. As a result, the framework proposed in the book has been evolved to assist healthcare facilities with a detailed quantitative analysis of tangible and intangible value losses.

Tangible value losses are directly associated with the costs and utilisation of finances. Intangible value losses focus on the perception and usefulness of the costs of intangible factors. The intangible value losses have a notion of subjectivity for arriving at the quantification and thus are taken as notional inputs aggregating a set of variables into a quantifiable value. The cost model includes the value loss of disruption of services in healthcare facilities for the duration that the infrastructure is rendered non-functional pending restoration. The cost model proposed in the book for the purpose of assessment of value loss, therefore, takes data from the users, where the data is a subset of basic inputs. The proposed cost model can be adapted to fit the requirements of the number of beds or for generic hospital configurations, typical district hospitals, tertiary hospitals, and typical hospitals attached to medical colleges. The outcome of the book, in the form of a generic value loss cost model, is a versatile framework that can be tailored to suit categories other than tertiary care.

The proposed cost model, therefore, offers the healthcare planners and facilitators an easily accessible set of equations that helps pre-determine the kinds of losses and the quantum of these losses that may occur in case an EWE strikes their region or community. While the book helps in creating preparedness of the medical facility in terms of financing, funding and safeguarding of assets, it also provides an opportunity to the designers and planners to ensure resilience in the structure. It is understood that certain losses may not be avoidable; however, it can be ensured in the design and pre-construction stage, with design innovations and techniques, that a healthcare facility does not get adversely affected by an EWE.

Careful, cohesive, and comprehensive designing in terms of architecture, services, and structure can safeguard the structure against collapse or inundation, thereby also evading problems such as non-functionality, temporary or permanent closure of institution, shifting of patients, unemployment, excessive tangible or intangible losses, and asset damage.

This book is expected to benefit planning and design professionals involved in ensuring the continuity of service, beyond creating an infrastructure with appropriate resilience to perform in spite of uncertainties associated with EWEs in the emerging climate change scenario. The book is also in alignment with the roles of physical planners, urban and regional planners, environmental planners, built-infrastructure professionals (architects and engineers), and healthcare planners. Most importantly, it equips healthcare facilities and building professionals in contributing towards public policy meaningfully.

# Acknowledgements

The motivation for the book came from the UGC-UKIERI project on Decision-Support System (DSS) Framework for Disaster Resilience Infrastructure Planning, wherein the potential of a need for knowledge sharing and new insights into resilience in healthcare was realised. The authors duly acknowledge the UKIERI team colleagues from UWE Bristol for undertaking to work on this important area.

The authors acknowledge the contribution of other project colleagues for creating a holistic thinking on the subject which has been carried forward and collated in the form of this book.

While the subject matter of the book was the realisation and conviction of the authors instrumental in creating this useful resource, it would not have been possible without the inputs obtained from the professionals associated with the EWE and healthcare facilities planning and design sector. Gratitude is expressed to various experts from healthcare and infrastructure projects, academia, healthcare professionals, construction professionals, architects, and designers.

It is hoped that the aspirations of developing the area of EWE in respect of resilience in healthcare facilities has been duly justified and presented in the book.

The support from the colleagues, namely Associate Professor Mr. Sushil Kumar Solanki, Assistant Professor Mr. Salman Khursheed, and Assistant Professor Mr. Luke Judson, has been immense for participating in numerous brainstorming sessions and helping us to crystallise our thoughts. Their support is duly acknowledged with gratitude.

For completion of this task during COVID-19 pandemic times, the support of our family members cannot go unrecognised, who stood by our commitment and were supportive of the limited and constrained movement that we had to undertake for discussions and review of the work.

In any case, blessings of our family members in particular, and friends in general, always bear fruit at the end of work carried out with the right earnestness.

# Figures

1.1  Process of incorporating resilience: establishing the premise
     of an existing dynamic.                                                   1
1.2  Structure of Chapter 1.                                                   2
2.1  Process of incorporating resilience: lack of rational resource
     allocation for incorporating resilience.                                 26
2.2  Structure and overview of Chapter 2.                                     27
3.1  Process of incorporating resilience: losses to infrastructure
     in the absence of rational resource allocation.                          49
3.2  Structure and overview of Chapter 3.                                     50
3.3  Pathways by which climate change affects health.                         63
3.4  Impacts of climate change on infrastructure and access to care.          65
4.1  Process of incorporating resilience: losses to healthcare
     due to lacking resilience.                                               73
4.2  Structure and overview of Chapter 4.                                     74
5.1  Process of incorporating resilience: curtailing disruption
     through rational resource allocation.                                    91
5.2  Structure and overview of Chapter 5.                                     92
6.1  Process of incorporating resilience: instituting the approach of
     risk reduction and resilience.                                           101
6.2  Structure and overview of Chapter 6.                                     102
6.3  Building blocks of health systems that promote climate resilience.       118
6.4  Intersection of sustainable healthcare and resilience.                   119
7.1  Process of incorporating resilience: through project-specific
     resource allocation and rational financing.                             124
7.2  Structure and overview of Chapter 7.                                     125
8.1  Process of incorporating resilience: value loss quantification
     in the case of an EWE occurrence.                                        137
8.2  Loss estimation process.                                                 138
8.3  Components of losses due to disaster.                                     144
9.1  Conventional process of project realisation and evaluation.              155
9.2  Methodology flowchart.                                                    159

# Tables

| | | |
|---|---|---|
| 1.1 | SDGs and their relevance/impact on EWE and infrastructure | 16 |
| 3.1 | Agencies authorised to issue warning in case of disaster: NDRP, 2001 | 68 |
| 6.1 | Climate change resilience indicators for healthcare facilities | 120 |
| 8.1 | Hyogo Framework of Action | 139 |
| 9.1 | Overall objective and outcome of the study and steps to achieve the objectives | 153 |
| 9.2 | Incorporating resilience strategies in conventional project development processes | 156 |
| 9.3 | Linkage of risk mapping with healthcare and work already done and the outcome of the identified objective | 160 |
| 9.4 | Linkage of risk index with healthcare and work already done and outcome of the identified objective | 161 |
| 9.5 | Linkage of risk mitigation strategies with healthcare and work already done and outcome of the identified objective | 161 |
| 9.6 | Linkage of direct resource input to current facility with healthcare and work already done and outcome of the identified objective | 162 |
| 9.7 | Linkage of supplementary facility with healthcare and work already done and outcome of the identified objective | 163 |
| 9.8 | Linkage of risk transfer to alternate facility with healthcare and work already done and outcome of the identified objective | 163 |
| 9.9 | Linkage of risk mitigation framework with healthcare and work already done and outcome of the identified objective | 164 |
| 9.10 | Linkage of implementation of mitigation measures with healthcare and work already done and outcome of the identified objective | 165 |
| 9.11 | Linkage of resilience resource generation with healthcare and work already done and outcome of the identified objective | 165 |
| 9.12 | Linkage of rework and review with healthcare and work already done and outcome of the identified objective | 166 |
| 9.13 | Linkage of social cost benefit with healthcare and work already done and outcome of the identified objective | 166 |
| 9.14 | Linkage of risk-sensitive implementation plan with healthcare and work already done and outcome of the identified objective | 167 |
| 9.15 | Linkage of reiteration of objectives with healthcare and work already done and outcome of the identified objective | 168 |

# Boxes

1.1   Implications of climate change                                                    7
1.2   State of extreme weather events data in India                                      8
1.3   Climate vulnerability ranking of India                                             9
1.4   Need for action against climate change                                            13
1.5   Relevance of SDGs to healthcare infrastructure                                     18
1.6   Relevance of SDGs to the healthcare infrastructure                                 19
1.7   Role of SDGs in India                                                              20
4.1   Monitoring progress of health indicators                                           76
4.2   Improvements in India's healthcare system                                          79
4.3   Efficiency of healthcare infrastructure after disruption due to disasters          86
6.1   India's efforts in DRR                                                            105
6.2   Benefits and opportunities from resilient infrastructure                          112
6.3   Designing climate-resilient infrastructure                                        113
6.4   Planning to improve the resilience of healthcare facilities                       116
7.1   Economic impacts of EWE on healthcare                                             127
7.2   Diversification away from disaster risk                                           132

# Abbreviations

| | |
|---|---|
| **ADB**: | Asian Development Bank |
| **AMRI**: | Advanced Medical Research Institute |
| **ART**: | Anti Retroviral Therapy |
| **ATM**: | Automated Teller Machines |
| **BIS**: | Bureau of Indian Standards |
| **BMS**: | Basic Minimum Services |
| **CHCs**: | Community Health Centres |
| **CGE**: | Calculable General Equilibrium |
| **CI**: | Critical Infrastructure |
| **CoBRA**: | Community-Based Resilience Analysis |
| **DBT**: | Direct Benefit Transfers |
| **DCGI**: | Drug Controller General of India |
| **DCI**: | Disaster Control Infrastructure |
| **DFID**: | Department for International Development |
| **DRM**: | Disaster Risk Management |
| **DRR**: | Disaster Risk Reduction |
| **EAG**: | Empowered Action Group |
| **ESI**: | Environmental Sustainability Index |
| **EVIN**: | Electronic Vaccine Intelligence Network |
| **EWE**: | Extreme Weather Events |
| **FAR**: | Floor Area Ratio |
| **FEMA**: | Federal Emergency Management Agency |
| **FRU**: | First Referral Unit |
| **GAD**: | General Anxiety Disorder |
| **GDI**: | Gender-Related Development Index |
| **GDP**: | Gross Domestic Product |
| **GFM**: | Global Focus Model |
| **GIS**: | Geographic Information System |
| **GoI-UNDP**: | Government of India and United Nations Development Programme |
| **GRIHA**: | Green Rating for Integrated Habitat Assessment |
| **HDI**: | Human Development Index |
| **HEA**: | Household Economy Approach |
| **HEP**: | Hydroelectric Power |

| | |
|---|---|
| **HFA**: | Hyogo Framework for Action |
| **HFL**: | Highest Flood Level |
| **HRTC**: | Himachal Road Transport Corporation |
| **ICU**: | Intensive Care Unit |
| **IDNDR**: | International Decade for Natural Disaster Reduction |
| **IDRN**: | India Disaster Resource Network |
| **IMD**: | India Meteorological Department |
| **IPCC**: | Intergovernmental Panel on Climate Change |
| **IPD**: | In-patient Department |
| **IS**: | Indian Standard |
| **JNNURM**: | Jawaharlal Nehru National Urban Renewal Mission |
| **MDGs**: | Millennium Development Goals |
| **MGNREGA**: | Mahatma Gandhi National Rural Employment Guarantee Act |
| **MHA**: | Ministry of Home Affairs |
| **MMR**: | Maternal Mortality Ratio |
| **MNP**: | Minimum Needs Program |
| **MoHFW**: | Ministry of Health and Family Welfare |
| **NACP**: | National AIDS Control Programme |
| **NAPCC**: | National Action Plan on Climate Change |
| **NDMA**: | National Disaster Management Authority |
| **NDMP**: | National Disaster Management Plan |
| **NGO**: | Non-Governmental Organization |
| **NHP 2017**: | National Health Policy 2017 |
| **NIDM**: | National Disaster Management Guidelines |
| **NRHM**: | National Rural Health Mission |
| **NUHM**: | National Urban Health Mission |
| **OCHA**: | UN Office for the Coordination of Humanitarian Affairs |
| **OPD**: | Out-patient Department |
| **OT**: | Operation Theatre |
| **PAHO**: | Pan American Health Organization |
| **PDCA**: | Plan-Do-Check-Act |
| **PHCs**: | Primary Health Centres |
| **PMJDY**: | Pradhan Mantri Jan Dhan Yojana |
| **PTSD**: | Post-Traumatic Stress Disorder |
| **PVI**: | Prevalent Vulnerability Index |
| **RMF**: | Risk Mitigation Framework |
| **RNTCP**: | Revised National Tuberculosis Control Programme |
| **ROMS**: | Risk and Opportunity Management Methodology |
| **RRG**: | Resilience Resource Generation |
| **RWSS**: | Rural Water Supply and Sanitation |
| **SAPCC**: | State Action Plan on Climate Change |
| **SDGs**: | Sustainable Development Goals |
| **SDMA**: | State Disaster Management Authority |
| **SDMP**: | State Disaster Management Plan |
| **SES**: | Socio-ecological Systems |
| **SFDRR**: | Sendai Framework of Action for Disaster Risk Reduction |

| | |
|---|---|
| **SOP**: | Standard Operating Procedure |
| **TERI**: | The Energy Research Institute |
| **TFR**: | Total Fertility Rate |
| **ULB**: | urban local bodies |
| **UN**: | United Nations |
| **UNDP**: | United Nations Development Programme |
| **UNDRR**: | United Nations Office on Disaster Risk Reduction |
| **UNFCCC**: | United Nations Framework Convention on Climate Change |
| **UNISDR**: | United Nations International Strategy for Disaster Reduction |
| **USAID**: | United States Agency for International Development |
| **WHO**: | World Health Organization |
| **WMO**: | World Meteorological Organization |

# 1 Extreme weather events and critical infrastructure

## 1.1 Overview

This chapter establishes the premise of extreme weather events and the rapid increase in their occurrences in the past two decades. Existing infrastructure and buildings are typically designed to follow code provisions and bylaws to withstand the natural hazards to which they are exposed in accordance with their location. However, a general lack of resilient interventions in design, construction, and functioning have been observed in the existing building stock. Figure 1.1 builds from this premise and unfolds the process of incorporating resilience in the subsequent chapters.

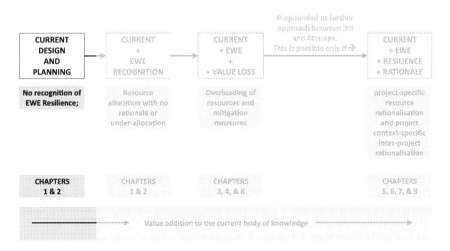

*Figure 1.1* Process of incorporating resilience: establishing the premise of an existing dynamic.

## 1.2 Structure of the chapter

The chapter lays the foundation of concepts of extreme weather events (EWEs), critical infrastructure (CI), Sustainable Development Goals (SDGs), resilience, and

DOI: 10.1201/9781003393108-1

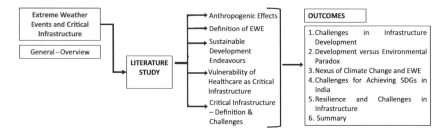

*Figure 1.2* Structure of Chapter 1.

vulnerability. Additionally, it introduces the vulnerability of the healthcare infrastructure to EWEs and climate change. Through a literature study, the nexus of climate change and EWE, and the paradox of development versus environment, is established. This leads to a discourse on resilience and the need to reduce vulnerability. Figure 1.2 explains the structure and outcome of this chapter.

## 1.3   Background

This book explores the theme of impacts of EWEs with a focus on the healthcare infrastructure, the most critical of all typologies of infrastructure, due to its dual purpose of acting as an emergency and healthcare service structure and as a place of refuge during a disaster.

Healthcare in India has significantly developed over the decades by way of an increase in the number of healthcare centres, proposed typologies to service different sections of the society, medical education and institutions, quality of treatment and healthcare provided, and the invested interest of the governments to maintain the upkeep of the physical and mental health of the society. However, even as strong structures of the hierarchy have been strategized by the government, officials, medical practitioners, and healthcare planners, only a small fraction of the same has been implemented to its full capacity on the ground. The majority of healthcare planning remains only on paper and, when implemented, does not operate to its full capacity or efficiency. Further, healthcare structures often lack the structural stability and disaster-proof designs, which results in the dysfunction of the entire structure, thereby disrupting the services, and forces patients to be moved to other healthcare services.

Disruption of healthcare infrastructures and services has also been observed to cause momentous losses to patients, staff, and hospitals alike. While the disruption might be due to uncertainty of the occurrence of the disaster in terms of timing and preparedness, the structure is expected to be designed to withstand the impact. Further, backup for electricity, medicine, and medical services is expected to be accounted for and made available whenever needed. However, these buildings lack processes to arrest disruptions of the structure, thereby facing severe consequences and shifting of patients, unemployment of staff, renovation and retrofitting of the structure, and loss of economic activity for the duration of the dysfunction. This demands a resilience and redundancy strategy for these healthcare structures, with an objective to maintain the continuity of services.

## 1.4    Anthropogenic effects and climate change

Climate change and the consequential EWEs have been observed to escalate sharply in recent decades. While climate change and EWEs are triggered by numerous factors, the major contributors are carbon emissions and global warming. Various strategies are being derived to reduce the escalation of climate change and EWEs, for instance, the Intergovernmental Panel on Climate Change, World Climate Programme, the United Nations Environment Programme, the United Nations Framework Convention on Climate Change, and the SDGs. These programmes are directed at curbing and reducing climate change and EWEs, due to their destructive impacts on society and infrastructure. EWEs and climate change not only cause heavy losses to the built infrastructure but also wipe out populations, cause massive fatalities, and lead to severe injuries and trauma, thereby affecting the life, the fabric of the communities and the economy.

Climate change can largely be attributed to human activities, or anthropogenic changes, which cause global warming. Due to an increased consumption of fossil fuels over the centuries, the atmospheric concentration of carbon dioxide has increased exponentially in the atmosphere. This, in turn, causes the greenhouse effect, which further results in global warming. The warming of the Earth's atmospheric temperature is thereby a driver of climate change, which results in higher temperatures than in previous centuries. Climate change, or global warming, has resulted in the melting of glaciers, leading to a rise in sea levels. In addition to this, deforestation and increased reclamation of land, which push the oceans farther back, have resulted in increased pressure on natural resources and water bodies.

Increase in global temperatures and greater pressure on natural resources have also resulted in an increase in the frequency and intensity of EWEs, such as extreme precipitation, flooding, cyclones, and droughts. In the urban context, where critical infrastructure is of immense significance for smooth operation and functioning of the cities, these occurrences of EWEs cause disruptions in critical functions and trigger haphazard movements, thereby adding to casualties and impact.

## 1.5    Development versus environmental paradox

The paradox of development-environment suggests that

> within the structure of contemporary global capitalism, economic growth has been identified as both a prerequisite prosperity on the one hand and a harbinger of ecological damage on the other. The paradox claims that our contemporary reality – as expressed in existing political economic structures and their corresponding social relations – is fundamentally unsustainable,

because in attempting to improve the quality life today by pursuing economic growth we erode the foundations upon which future life depends.

(Rosene, 2016)

Various factors have been pointed by Tyagi (2018) to highlight the precise paradox that exists between development and the environment. Developing countries are often struggling to work and improve conditions of poverty and the battle for survival. Hence, they cannot have similar concerns as developed countries. Nevertheless, pollution and depletion of natural resources are rampant in developing countries as well and cannot be ignored.

While developed and industrialised countries can shift the focus on sustainability and green issues, they may cause an obstruction in the development and industrialisation of the developing countries. Even so, the process of development must encompass environmental care and social justice and security holistically, in addition to industrialisation and overall development of the country; any nation that does not pursue these in conjunction holds back its economic growth (Tyagi, 2018).

Further, even as a population exerts excessive pressure on all types of resources, primarily originating from natural assets, which further causes degradation, it is also the population that is a significant source of and harbinger for development for any country. However, population continues to be a key contributor to degradation of the environment when it tends to cross the threshold of the support systems (Tyagi, 2018).

Industrialisation has also been observed to cause severe socio-economic impacts. While necessary for economic growth, it has also been recorded to throw the ecology off balance, in terms of contamination of air, water, and land. Further, industrialisation has also led to social disturbances like displacement, migration, loss of livelihood, deforestation, etc. (Tyagi, 2018).

Urbanisation has been unplanned and rapid, thereby neglecting development in villages. Due to a lack of amenities and opportunities in rural areas, people in the villages are forced to move to urban setups, causing further stress on the limited resources, and consequentially the local environment (Tyagi, 2018).

Lastly, these concerns are more relevant to the vulnerable sections of society and conflict with the interests of the privileged class: "their assertions against contradictions and complexities imposed by power elites". This baseline fact acts as a stimulus to the environment versus development debate and continues to drive the same (Tyagi, 2018).

## 1.6   Defining extreme weather events

An extreme weather event has been defined by Seneviratne et al. (2012) as

The occurrence of a value of a weather variable above (or below) a threshold value near the upper (or lower) ends ("tails") of the range of observed values of the variable.

Weather events, even if not extreme statistically, can lead to extreme conditions or extreme impacts, nevertheless. This can occur either by a critical threshold being crossed in an ecological, social, or physical system or when these weather events occur simultaneously with other events. Depending on when and where the events occur, they can have varying impacts. For instance, a weather event such as a cyclone can have extreme impacts depending upon the location, duration, and time of the day of its landfall. On the other hand, not all EWEs lead to severe impacts. Some climate extremes, for example, droughts and floods, may occur because of the accumulation of climate or weather events, which may not be extreme individually, but their accumulation may become extreme (Seneviratne et al., 2012).

Most EWEs and extreme climate events (ECEs) are the result of variations in the natural climate, *and natural decadal or multi-decadal variations in the climate provide the backdrop for anthropogenic climate changes.*

The increased frequency and intensity of EWEs can be attributed to exponential increases in carbon emissions, global warming, and consequential climate change. Models have predicted that the 21st century is likely to experience an intensification in the frequency and magnitude of warm daily temperature extremes and decreases in cold extremes on a global scale. Further, the frequency of heavy precipitation has also been predicted to increase in various regions over the 21st century. Similarly, higher coastal water levels, and thereby coastal erosion floods, are very likely to increase due to a rise in the mean sea levels. EWEs also include extreme winds (resulting in cyclones), heat waves, glacial retreat, droughts, and landslides (Seneviratne et al., 2012).

## 1.7   Extreme weather events and weather anomalies

Weather anomalies denote the "departure of an element from its long-period average value for the location concerned". For instance, a temperature anomaly is the variation from a baseline or average temperature. The baseline temperature is normally calculated by computing the average of 30 or more years of temperature data. A negative anomaly shows that the temperature under observation was cooler than the baseline, while a positive anomaly shows that the temperature under observation was warmer than the baseline. Anomalies are also useful in minimising problems when stations are removed, added, or found missing from the monitoring network (National Centers for Environmental Information, 2020).

While anomalies can be understood as outliers in 30 years of average data, EWEs are single events that are likely to cause destruction and are often repetitive. However, various studies find the cause of both to be anthropogenic changes and global warming.

### *1.7.1   Typology of extreme weather events*

**i)    Heat wave**

According to the WMO Commission for Climatology Task Team, a heat wave has been defined as "a period of marked unusual hot weather (maximum, minimum and daily average temperature) over a region persisting at least three consecutive days during the warm period of the year based on local (station-based) climatological conditions, with thermal conditions recorded above given thresholds."

Heat waves may result in agricultural losses, wildfires, health-related risks, fatalities, power outages, damage to ecosystems, and damage to water sources (WMO Commission for Climatology Task Team, 2018).

ii) **Drought**

From a meteorological perspective, drought is defined as a *prolonged absence or marked deficiency of precipitation*, in the international meteorological vocabulary. From a hydrological application perspective, drought is defined as "a period of abnormally dry weather sufficiently prolonged to give rise to a shortage of water as evidenced by below normal streamflow and lake levels and/or the depletion of soil moisture and a lowering of groundwater levels".

Droughts are different from other EWEs. While EWEs such as floods and cyclones are detectable immediately and can be prepared for in terms of response, recovery, and resilient infrastructure, droughts develop at a slow pace, thereby making their onset and ending prediction difficult. The complexity in their determination and consequential unpreparedness is one of the major reasons that droughts cause extreme devastation, thereby affecting society, agriculture, infrastructure, economy, and ecosystems (WMO Commission for Climatology Task Team, 2018).

iii) **Dust storms**

A dust storm or sandstorm is "a meteorological phenomenon, which refers to the erosion, transport and deposition of dust and soil particles in the atmosphere by strong wind currents".

Dust storms can cause a reduction in visibility, health hazards, accidents (air and land bound), air pollution, and deposition of dust/sand (Ghosh & Pal, 2014).

iv) **Cold wave**

The WMO Commission for Climatology Task Team defines a cold wave as "marked and unusual cold weather characterized by a sharp and significant drop of air temperatures near the surface (maximum, minimum and daily average) over a large area and persisting below certain thresholds for at least two consecutive days during the cold season. 'Cool spell' refers to persistently below-average temperature conditions occurring during the warm season".

Cold waves have been observed to cause hazardous weather leading to frost bite, death due to cold, hypothermia, severe impacts on human health, and high heating costs (WMO Commission for Climatology Task Team, 2018).

v) **Tropical cyclones**

Tropical cyclones are "warm-cored, intense cyclonic, atmospheric vortices that develop over the warm tropical oceans", which have a horizontal scale typical of 100–1000 km and extend throughout the depth of the troposphere.

An intense mature tropical cyclone usually consists of an eye with a weak subsidence near its centre. The centre is surrounded by rapid swirling flow, where a deep convective ring slopes radially outward with height (Wang, 2012).

Recurring cyclones have been recorded to cause a significant number of fatalities, loss of private and public buildings, loss of livelihood opportunities, and severe damage to infrastructure (Arya, 2010).

vi) **Extreme precipitation**

An extreme precipitation event is defined as "a marked precipitation event occurring during a period of time of one to several days (usually less than a week) with daily total precipitation exceeding a certain threshold defined for a given location (station based)".

The occurrence of events of extreme precipitation is a significant hazard. It has been observed to lead to floods, landslides, significant infrastructure damage, and agricultural losses, in addition to causing fatalities and major economic losses (WMO Commission for Climatology Task Team, 2018).

vii) **Floods**

Floods occur when "an overflow of water submerges land that is usually dry. Floods are often caused by heavy rainfall, rapid snowmelt or a storm surge from a tropical cyclone or tsunami in coastal areas".

Floods have been recorded to cause massive devastation, fatalities, and significant destruction to personal property and critical public health infrastructure. People living in floodplains with non-resilient homes and buildings, lacking warning systems and awareness of flood occurrences and protection measures, are most vulnerable when floods strike (World Health Organisation, 2020).

viii) **Landslides**

The term landslide describes "downhill earth movements ranging from rapidly moving catastrophic rock avalanches and debris flows in mountainous regions to more slowly moving earth slides".

While some landslides are gradual in their movement and damage capacity, others are rapid moving and can destroy property, livelihoods, and lives unexpectedly.

Landslides can be triggered due to erosion, freezing and thawing, poor construction practices, heavy rainfall, earthquakes, and volcanic eruptions. They are usually linked with periods of heavy rainfall and rapid snowmelt and have been observed to worsen the impacts of flooding. Areas that have been subject to forest and bush fires are significantly prone to landslides (Disaster Center, 2020).

### 1.7.2   Nexus of climate change and extreme weather events

---

**Box 1.1   Implications of climate change**

Climate change has been recorded to shift the intensity and frequency of hazards, such as heavy rainfall, heat extremes, high sea levels, droughts, and possibly cyclones, with direct implications for disaster risks (IPCC, 2007).

---

Changes in climate can lead to changes in the intensity, duration, frequency, spatial extent, and timing of climates, thereby leading to unprecedented weather extremes. Even when extreme events related to climate and weather are not extreme statistically, they can still cause damage depending on the consequential events socially, ecologically, or in the physical system.

Changes in the mean climate can also be directly linked to changes in extremes, since in some variables, mean future conditions are projected to lie within the tails of present-day conditions. Natural climate variability, including phenomena such as El Niño, can lead to various climate and weather extremes. The anthropogenic climate changes also ensue from natural decadal or multi-decadal variations in the climate (Seneviratne et al., 2012).

### 1.7.3    *Impact of climate change on EWEs across the world*

It has been well established in literary sources that the increase in frequency and intensity of EWEs in recent decades can be significantly linked to climate change, due to an enhanced carbon footprint and greenhouse gas emissions. Some of the changes in EWEs have also been associated with anthropogenic climate changes, which include decrease in cold temperature extremes, increase in warm temperature extremes, increase in the quantum of heavy precipitation events, and increase in coastal surges arising in many regions.

Even as the occurrence of some of the EWEs can be predicted and the authorities can ensure preparedness, their intensity may or may not be predictable, especially with constantly varying geophysical variables. Such conditions worldwide are described below, as adapted from an article by Kundzewicz (2016).

---

**Box 1.2    State of extreme weather events data in India**

In the previous two decades, artificial intelligence interfaced machine-learning models and machine-learning simulations have provided hazard scenario assessments and comprehensive climate variability for both the mid-term (2050) and long term (2100) (IPCC, 2017). However, information on short-term effects cannot be obtained from these meteorological and climatological analyses. They lack hazard sensitivity indexing since they do not account for historical events. In India, since its inception, the IMD has been the record-keeper of observational climate data. While IMD has recorded specific data from several observatory stations on various climatic variables in a gridded format, a synchronised repository of historical data on climate events is not available. Even as availability of data is a significant challenge, further complications in the scenario arise from a lack of consensus internationally on best practices for mining and collating the data ((UCL)-CRED, 2015). At the local level, informed planning is hindered by the unavailability of data, specifically due to a lack of information and details on climate variable attributions and evidence that can be interpreted and explained visually. The scale of damage and losses can therefore be reduced by employing comprehensive, risk-proof planning, informed by localised risk assessments (Mohanty, 2020).

a. The occurrence of extremely high temperature in the patterns of February (such as 20°C) is not likely to cause any intense events directly. However, if vigorous vegetation growth commences for this reason, which is later interrupted by a severe frost, then damage is likely to arise.
b. Extreme natural phenomena in Poland relate to temperature (very low or very high), fog, strong wind, intense rainfall, flooding, landslides, icing, snow avalanches, mudslides, extreme snow cover (or an extreme lack of snow cover), forest fires, drought, seismic phenomena, and lightning.
c. A spell of heavy rain in late May and early June 2016 caused destructive flooding in many European countries (primarily Germany and France, in addition to Austria, Belgium, Moldova, The Netherlands, Romania, and the UK), due to which more than 20 deaths were recorded.
d. Starting in the southwest of Fort McMurray, Alberta, a major wildfire was recorded in Canada in May 2016. The community was swept away due to the wildfire, destroying almost 2400 houses and structures and forcing the greatest wildfire evacuation in the history of the region. Forest areas were consumed in the fire, and operations in the Athabasca oil sands were affected, as the fire spread across northern Alberta and into Saskatchewan. It was concluded that the climatic background was a trigger to this event – the fire risk index was found to be very high due to hot and dry antecedent weather conditions (Kundzewicz, 2016).

### 1.7.4   *Intensifying disasters*

In recent decades EWEs have escalated substantially, thereby increasing the consequential economic damages. Further, impacts of EWEs are critical to the communities that rely directly or indirectly on agriculture for their livelihoods, which comprise 70% of the total population of the Indian subcontinent. Various communities reside in areas of low resource productivity and high ecological vulnerability. Additionally, these communities have unsecured and limited rights over the productive natural resources. A combination of these factors acts as a major force contributing to the vulnerability of communities to natural disasters and EWEs.

The Indian subcontinent has been subject to recurrent damages due to successive monsoons, droughts, and unpredictable flooding. Further, intensifying monsoons and changes in precipitation patterns also continue to cause land degradation and severe floods. This may eventually foster far-reaching consequences for the country's economy (UNDP, 2017a).

---

**Box 1.3   Climate vulnerability ranking of India**

India has witnessed more than 478 EWEs between 1970 and 2019, most of which have occurred after 2005. According to the Climate Risk Index, 2018, India jumped nine places in climate vulnerability rankings and was ranked the fifth-most climate-vulnerable country in the world (Mohanty, 2020).

---

For instance, the state of Odisha has experienced floods in 49 of the last 100 years, in addition to droughts in 30 years and cyclones in 11 years. It is not unusual for the state to experience the occurrence of floods, droughts, and cyclones in a single year.

Presently, more than 12% of the Indian landmass is flood-prone and 68% is drought-prone. While there is an increase in the number of villages in the country experiencing droughts, rising temperatures due to global warming are observed to cause the snowlines of glaciers to melt and reduce further, thereby increasing the downstream volume of water into the mainland and enhancing the risk of floods during the monsoon season.

The coastline, about 7516 kilometres long, is characterised by a shallow continental shelf, flat coastal terrain, and high population density, having extreme vulnerability to cyclones and associated hazards such as high-velocity winds, storm tides, and heavy rains. About 8% of the area in India is prone to tropical cyclones and related disasters. Even though the frequency of tropical cyclones in the North Indian Ocean is the lowest in the world, including the Arabian Sea and Bay of Bengal, their impact is comparatively more devastating on the east coast of the country. Further, a 10% increase per decade has been reported in the number of storms exceeding 100 millimetres of rainfall in a day (UNDP, 2017a).

The frequency, intensity, and duration of heat waves have also been observed to increase in various regions across the globe, leading to increased mortality and morbidity, with impacts varying with people's age, location, health status, and socio-economic factors. It can therefore be inferred that EWEs and extreme consequences due to EWEs can be segregated as two separate entities, with the latter depending on damage potential, exposure, and vulnerability.

### 1.7.5   *Adaptive capacity of communities*

Depending upon the efficiency of a community to adapt or cope with climate change and consequential EWEs, the impacts of such events are felt disparately. This can be understood as the adaptive capacity of a community. Adaptive capacity is defined by the IPCC as "the ability of a system to adjust to climate change (including climate variability and extremes) to moderate potential damages, to take advantage of opportunities, or to cope with the consequences" (Joint Global Change Research Institute and Battelle Memorial Institute, Pacific Northwest Division, 2009).

A special research report commissioned by the National Intelligence Council in 2009 found through detailed vulnerability assessments that compared to most countries, India is ranked as more vulnerable to climate change. Further, adaptive capacity is higher in the northwest and southern parts of the country but is lowest along the Indo-Gangetic Plain. To arrive at an overall comparative measure of vulnerability, when adaptive capacity and sensitivity are considered, only five Indian states have been ranked higher than the global average, and small mountainous northern inland states tend to be ranked higher than coastal states.

In the special research report, a summation of an index of climate sensitivity under exposure with the district-level index of adaptive capacity was applied to assess the vulnerability. The districts with the highest or lowest sensitivity were found not necessarily to be the least or most vulnerable. For instance, many districts in southern Bihar were found to exhibit medium sensitivity to climate change but were highly vulnerable due to their low levels of adaptive capacity. In contrast, many districts in northern Punjab were found to exhibit very high sensitivity to climate change but were found to be only moderately vulnerable due to their high levels of adaptive capacity (Joint Global Change Research Institute and Battelle Memorial Institute, Pacific Northwest Division, 2009).

## 1.8    Defining critical infrastructure

The term infrastructure has been defined by Gheorghe & Ionut (2008) as "the underlying foundation or basic framework (as of a system or organization)".

In a report from 1997, addressed to the U.S. president, infrastructure is defined as "a network of independent, mostly privately-owned, man-made systems and processes that function collaboratively and synergistically to produce and distribute a continuous flow of essential goods and services".

Infrastructure and infrastructure systems are essential to the highly developed society, wherein the citizens have become progressively reliant on the ease of availability of infrastructure. Specific types of infrastructure play vital roles in underpinning the economy, security, and way of life.

Although CI has varied and differing definitions among different countries, its significance for the efficient functioning of societies is extensively recognised. Specifically in the case of highly industrialized societies, which are greatly reliant on the smooth operation of infrastructure services, such as electricity and telecommunications technology, the interconnected infrastructure networks ensure facilitation of operations of systems such as health, transport, and sewage treatment (Bach et al., 2013). CIs are primarily categorised by the following characteristics:

a.  Organisations/systems/facilities that have a significant role in the functioning of societies
b.  The breakdown of such facilities could cause momentous disruption to the daily functioning and lifestyle of societies

CI can also be categorised into socio-economic and physical systems. While physical CI systems include basic services such as transport, water supply, wastewater management, electricity, telecommunication, and information technologies, socio-economic CI systems encompass facilities such as schools, hospitals, disaster management services, public administration, and recreational areas. CI may exist in private or public sectors, depending on their type of ownership, management, and regulation. In some cases, shared competencies between public and private sectors manage the CI (Lenz, 2009).

## 1.9   Critical infrastructure and its challenges

CI can be identified as a well-connected and comprehensive system, with the individual sectors and sub-sectors acting as its sub-systems, composed of discrete elements. These elements may be structural or the necessary equipment. It is therefore vital that the CI establish and maintain a high level of security and reliability. Consequently, these CI systems must also have high resilience against the effects of internal as well as external threats (Rehak et al., 2019).

The management of CI should be interwoven into a country's governance system, owing to its significance for public good. This is highlighted in the Target D of SFDRR, or the Sendai Framework of Action for Disaster Risk Reduction, which calls for the development of infrastructure resilience by 2030 to ensure a reduction in damage induced by disasters and EWEs, in addition to a diminution of disruption of the basic services dispensed by these CI systems. Further, it emphasises on the need to take national as well as local action to ensure that the CI remains effective, safe, and operational before, during, and after the occurrence of a disaster event (UNDRR, 2015).

Asia and the Pacific have achieved notable progress in poverty reduction and economic growth in the past five decades. Investment in infrastructure played a major role in the advancement of economic and social development. According to a recent study conducted by the Asian Development Bank (Meeting Asia's Infrastructure Needs, 2017), an additional USD 22.6 trillion needs to be invested in infrastructure by Asia and the Pacific between the period of 2016 and 2030. However, the additional investment required to achieve resilience against future changes in climate and weather patterns is not included in this amount. At the same time, a considerable surge in the impacts of changing climate and weather patterns is anticipated in the regions under scrutiny, such as heat waves, droughts, floods, and tropical cyclones. Major geophysical shocks, including earthquakes and tsunamis, are also being recorded in this time for the regions. The uncertain nature of climate change is expected to alter the intensity, frequency, duration, extent, and timing of EWEs and is likely to cause unprecedented extremes (ADB, 2017).

Natural disasters and extreme events in the past indicate a trend of disruption in services and CI – primarily in the power sector – thereby resulting in significant economic losses. The report has pointed out 24 cases of failure in the power sector in India due to floods since 1974. The largest blackout in a power sector in the world was recorded in India in 2012 that caused disruption and distress to more than 600 million people across 22 states, thus bringing to light the vulnerability of the power sector to drought. Further, states such as Odisha and Andhra Pradesh, which are prone to multi-hazards, have encountered enormous damages to their power infrastructure. It is therefore evident that the power sector in India needs robust inputs necessary to embed the inherent as well as acquired resilience into the sector (Mohanty et al., 2020).

Disaster control infrastructure (DCI) refers to infrastructure assets that are designed and developed specifically to protect populations and assets in hazard-prone regions from the effects of the hazard event. DCI encompasses structures such as storm surge barriers, sea walls, river embankments, cyclone shelters, dikes, etc. These DCIs are designed and developed based on patterns of past hazards and expected return periods of EWEs. However, the design of these structures faces challenges due to several uncertainties associated with the manifestations of climate change at the local level (IWRI, 2018).

EWEs pose challenges to CI in terms of the physical attributes of natural disasters, i.e., destructiveness, which is determined by the destructive force of the disaster and the possibility of proliferation in the affected territory. There is a strong correlation of the intensity of disasters with the vulnerability of the community affected by the disaster. (For instance, an earthquake of a certain severity may not cause the same degree of destruction to a rural community with crumbling earthen houses as compared to an urban setup with concrete multi-storey structures.) Therefore, it is imperative to consider the physical attributes of natural disasters to implement mitigation strategies against the impacts of the natural disasters (Mijalković & Cvetković, 2013).

## 1.10  Extreme weather events and challenges in infrastructure development

---

**Box 1.4   Need for action against climate change**

Globally, India is the fifth-most vulnerable country. While the frequency and intensity of extreme events are increasing, we are left with less than a decade to adhere to the Sendai Framework; course correction needs to have a razor-sharp focus on curtailing the compounded impacts of climate extremes. There is no denying that the climate is changing, and it is changing fast.

– Abinash Mohanty, Programme Lead with
the Risks and Adaptation, CEEW

---

EWEs can be defined as "events in which a measured climate property exceeds either upper or lower thresholds compared to what was previously recorded at that location; these thresholds apply to either event frequency or event intensity" (Chow, 2018). While an EWE is a consequence of global warming, climate change, and natural variations in climate over decades, the potential that it holds to cause extreme damage and loss to property and life is immense.

Climate and weather extremes, for example, cold snaps, droughts, heat waves, tropical cyclones, heavy precipitation events, and wildfires, have become increasingly common in their appearance in recent years globally. Due to the increase in direct exposure to climate and consequent vulnerability of the urban residential system to damage, EWEs have been observed to modify and affect urban resilience directly. This has also been observed to occur due to an additional reduction in adaptive and coping capacities (which are primarily managed by municipal policies). Hence, the resilience of settlements is likely to diminish, depending on the intensity and frequency of the EWE and whether these extreme events are taken account of during urban planning and development (Chow et al., 2007).

The definition of CI puts this into focus:

> Tightly coupled asset, network, system, or part thereof located in states and subject to multiple hazards which is (perceived as) essential and provides non-substitutable services to maintain vital societal functions, health, safety, security, economic or social well-being of people. The disruption or destruction of these infrastructures for an extended period may have cascading effects across scales.
>
> (Ruiten et al., 2016)

Since the frequency and intensity of EWEs are changing and, therefore, unpredictable, they pose serious threats, known and unknown, to the built infrastructure. The operational hours and procedures of the infrastructure are affected, in addition to structural damage. Further, CI is seen to be interdependent, therefore causing loss of access to each other in case one or more fails to respond. The unpredictability of the severity and scale of EWEs account for more risks to CI.

## 1.11   Success milestones and challenges of sustainable development

Sustainable development can be understood as a viable and balanced methodology of usage of natural resources that not only meets the needs of humankind in the present but also focuses on preserving the environment and resources for future generations. In the Indian context, sustainable development entails a multiplicity of development schemes in the fields of clean technology and social and human resource segments and has gained importance in both public and private sectors (Thakare, 2011).

Post-liberalisation growth in India in the 1990s was a watershed moment leading to a significant surge in the demand of natural resources and energy. The ambitious goal thus set the country on a development trajectory and initiated an unprecedented consumption of natural resources such as oil, coal, energy, and water. Some of the consequences of this enlarged resource consumption were greater waste generation, increased carbon emissions and air pollutants, excessive discharge of wastewater, etc., which continue to increase manifold to this day. The resulting ecological imbalance and worsening health implications led to a realisation of the need for sustainable growth embedded in sensitive urban planning and design. This includes measures such as usage of environmentally friendly construction materials, low embodied energy processes, and low operational costs, among others. As a landmark move, it was made mandatory for all new government buildings of public-sector undertakings to acquire minimum specified green ratings. The buildings are required to comply with at least a three-star rating under the GRIHA scheme by The Energy Research Institute (TERI) (Das & Kumar, 2011).

### 1.11.1    *Sustainable Development Goals of the UNDP*

The SDGs were an initiative of the United Nations Conference on Sustainable Development, held in Rio de Janeiro in 2012. The primary objective of the SDGs was to formulate a set of universal goals that attempt to encounter the urgent environmental, economic, and political challenges being faced across the world. SDGs replace the MDGs, or the Millennium Development Goals, that were devised in 2000. Establishing measurable objectives which were agreed upon universally, the MDGs were prepared to prevent deadly diseases, tackle extreme poverty and hunger, expand primary education to all children, and other such development priorities (UNDP, 2020).

Some of the major achievements of the MDGs have been:

- Reduction of the number of people living in extreme poverty globally by more than 50% – from 1.9 billion in 1990 to 836 million in 2015
- A nearly 50% reduction in the number of out-of-school children of primary school age – from 100 million in 2000 to 57 million in 2015
- Reduction in maternal mortality rate by 45% globally since 1990
- MDG drinking water target was met by 147 countries; MDG sanitation target was met by 95 countries; both targets combined have been met by 77 countries
- Official assistance from developed countries for development increased by 66% in real terms in the period from 2000 to 2014, reaching $135.2 billion

(UNDP, 2017b)

Also known as the Global Goals, the SDGs adopted by all United Nations (UN) member states in 2015 were envisioned as a "universal call for action for protection of the planet, ensuring peace and prosperity for all people, and ending poverty by 2030". The 17 SDGs identified have been integrated to recognise and acknowledge the importance of striking a balance between environmental, social, and economic sustainability in development and that action taken in one aspect has effects and consequences in other aspects. The relevance of these SDGs and their impacts on healthcare infrastructure have been identified in Table 1.1.

### 1.11.2    *The global scenario*

Since the enforcement of the SDGs in 2016, the UN member countries have taken various proactive measures to achieve their targets on time. Many countries have

*Table 1.1* SDGs and their relevance/impact on EWE and infrastructure

| S. No. | SDG Description | Relevance/Impact on Healthcare Infrastructure |
|---|---|---|
| 1. | **No poverty**<br>End poverty in all its forms everywhere | **Medium Relevance/ Medium Impact** |
| 2. | **Zero hunger**<br>End worldwide hunger, achieve improved nutrition and food security, promote sustainable agriculture | **Low Relevance/Low Impact** |
| 3. | **Quality education**<br>Ensure equitable and inclusive quality education; promote and ensure lifelong learning opportunities for all | **Medium Relevance/ Medium Impact** |
| 4. | **Gender equality**<br>Achieve gender equality; empowerment of all girls and women | **Medium Relevance/ Medium Impact** |
| 5. | **Reduced inequalities**<br>Reduce inequality among and within countries | **Medium Relevance/ Medium Impact** |
| 6. | **Peace, justice, and strong institutions**<br>Promote inclusive societies for sustainable development; build accountable, inclusive, and effective institutions at all levels; provide access to justice for all | **Low Relevance/Low Impact** |
| 7. | **Partnerships**<br>Revitalise worldwide partnerships in sustainable development, strengthen means of implementation | **Low Relevance/Low Impact** |
| 8. | **Life below water**<br>Sustainably use and conserve seas, oceans, and marine resources for benefit of sustainable development | **Low Relevance/Low Impact** |
| 9. | **Good health and well-being**<br>Promote well-being and ensure healthy lives for all at all ages | **High Relevance/High Impact** |
| 10. | **Clean water and sanitation**<br>Promote sustainable management and ensure availability of clean water and sanitation for all | **Low Relevance/Low Impact** |
| 11. | **Affordable and clean energy**<br>Ensure access to reliable, clean, affordable, modern, and sustainable energy for all | **Low Relevance/Low Impact** |
| 12. | **Decent work and economic growth**<br>Promote sustainable and inclusive economic growth, complete and productive employment, decent work for all | **Medium Relevance/ Medium Impact** |
| 13. | **Industry, innovation, and infrastructure**<br>Promote sustainable and inclusive industrialisation, build resilient infrastructure, foster innovation | **High Relevance/High Impact** |
| 14. | **Sustainable cities and communities**<br>Ensure safety, sustainability, and inclusivity of human settlements and cities | **High Relevance/High Impact** |
| 15. | **Sustainable consumption and production**<br>Ensure sustainable production and consumption patterns | **Medium Relevance/ Medium Impact** |
| 16. | **Climate action**<br>Ensure urgent action towards combatting climate change and its impacts | **Medium Relevance/ Medium Impact** |
| 17. | **Life on land**<br>Manage forests sustainably; protect from desertification; halt biodiversity loss; halt and reverse land degradation; promote, protect, and restore terrestrial ecosystems | **Low Relevance/Low Impact** |

ratified the Paris Agreement on climate change, in addition to developing policies to address urbanisation. Further, extreme poverty and under-five mortality have been observed to be reduced. To reduce disaster risk and losses in lives, livelihoods, and health, the UNDP member countries prepared various frameworks. The Sendai Framework, which is essentially the successor to the Hyogo Framework for Action, is a voluntary, non-binding agreement for member states of the UN. Yokomatsu & Hochrainer-Stigler (2020) highlight the dimensions that separate disasters and resilience following the matrix approach based on the Sendai Framework. The authors further elaborate on the challenges to create a balance between scientific, conceptual, and case studies. The Sendai Framework presented four priorities for Disaster Risk Reduction 2015–2030:

- Priority 1: Understanding disaster risk
- Priority 2: Strengthening disaster risk governance to manage disaster risk
- Priority 3: Investing in disaster risk reduction for resilience
- Priority 4: Enhancing disaster preparedness for effective response and to "Build Back Better" in recovery, rehabilitation, and reconstruction

(Yokomatsu & Hochrainer-Stigler, 2020)

While a large number of countries have worked to support sustainable production and consumption, some challenges are persistent. Ocean acidification has been observed to have risen, posing the risk of extinction to millions of species of flora and fauna. People's access to health services and learning outcomes of children need improvement. Various organisations, including private sectors, civil societies, development organisations, academia, government, and citizens, are making efforts towards the acceleration of achievement of these goals collectively (NITI Aayog, 2019).

### *1.11.3   SDGs: the Indian picture*

India's key development programmes, resource allocation, and policy focus, when observed at a macro level, align with the SDGs. For instance, the largest health protection scheme globally, i.e., the Ayushman Bharat (Pradhan Mantri Jan Arogya Yojana), covers over 500 million people and closely aligns with SDG 10 (reduced inequalities) and SDG 3 (health and well-being).

The International Solar Alliance saw the comprehensive climate action agenda and leadership presented by India to align with the goals of SDG 7, i.e., clean and affordable energy. The Aspirational Districts Programme developed by India aims to bring about holistic development to 112 relatively backward districts, which further contributes to regional equality. This aligns with the essence of SDG 10 of reducing inequalities (NITI Aayog, 2019).

The Parliament of India has organised many forums, which also include the South Asian Speakers' Summit, February 2017, to focus on gender equality, climate change, elimination of poverty, and resource mobilisation for SDGs. In addition to this, as a part of reinforcing the country's commitment to the national development agenda and SDGs, the Speakers' Research Initiative was launched to provide insights related to SDGs to the members of Parliament.

---

**Box 1.5   Relevance of SDGs to healthcare infrastructure**

**SDG 1: No poverty**

To end poverty in all its forms everywhere, a resilient healthcare infrastructure is needed to serve all sections of society.

**SDG 3: Quality education**

To ensure equitable and inclusive quality education and promote and ensure lifelong learning opportunities for all, a healthcare infrastructure can provide a robust platform to provide quality learning and education.

**SDG 4: Gender equality**

To achieve gender equality and empower all girls and women, the healthcare infrastructure can act as an institution of knowledge as well as employment for female-oriented upliftment.

**SDG 5: Reduced inequalities**

To reduce inequality among and within countries, the role of the healthcare infrastructure in providing equal work and education opportunities to promote equality is significant.

**SDG 9: Good health and well-being**

To promote well-being and ensure healthy lives for all people at all ages, an evenly distributed resilient healthcare infrastructure is necessary to serve all sections of society.

---

The organisation NITI Aayog plays a significant role in strengthening the countrywide communication process currently in progress, both informally and formally. It also promotes sharing of inter alia good practices and new knowledge among various regions to encourage and accelerate growth and implementation of SDGs across the country. The organisation therefore plays a significant role in achieving the SDGs in an expedient manner.

Civil society organisations also play an important role to understand and resolve the SDG-related issues ranging from the grassroots level to national level. Operating independently as well as in collaboration with other agencies and government organisations, these organisations work towards creating awareness, offering feedback and providing inputs on SDG-oriented work (United Nations High Level Political Forum, 2017).

Corporate-sector organisations and industry associations have undertaken consultations and initiated actions in various areas. These actions include innovative climate action, environmental sustainability, and all-encompassing development schemes on various subjects. They have also worked in conjunction with the communities, civil societies, and government in order to formulate and apply inventive and original solutions and courses of action in addition to working within the industry and related sectors (United Nations High Level Political Forum, 2017).

---

**Box 1.6 Relevance of SDGs to the healthcare infrastructure**

**SDG 12: Decent work and economic growth**
To promote sustainable and inclusive economic growth, complete and pro-
ductive employment, and decent work for all, healthcare facilities can
provide work and education opportunities to promote economic growth.
**SDG 13: Industry, innovation, and infrastructure**
To promote sustainable and inclusive industrialisation, build a resilient infra-
structure, and foster innovation, a resilient healthcare infrastructure can
help with easy recovery and relief in times of EWEs and other hazards.
**SDG 14: Sustainable cities and communities**
To ensure safety, sustainability, and inclusivity of human settlements and cities, resilient healthcare can help achieve easy recovery and relief in times
of EWEs and other hazards.
**SDG 15: Sustainable consumption and production**
To ensure sustainable production and consumption patterns, sustainable utilisation within the healthcare infrastructure is needed to help reduce the
load on resources.
**SDG 16: Climate action**
To ensure urgent action towards combatting climate change and its impacts,
sustainable healthcare services are necessary to help reduce the load on
resources.

---

The Government of India has launched various programmes in order to implement and execute the SDG agenda. One of these is the Pradhan Mantri Jan Dhan
Yojana (PMJDY), the world's largest financial inclusion programme. A cumulative
amount of INR 1.6 trillion (USD 25 billion at INR 64 per USD) was disbursed
by the government by leveraging the PMJDY. This financing helped 329 million
beneficiaries using direct benefit transfers (DBTs). State governments are working at different phases of their 15-year programs, including vision and stratagem
roadmaps, at the sub-national level. The strategic insights (from the 2030 agenda
and national development agendas) of most of the state governments have been
observed to be matching with their own specific priorities and contexts. To facilitate
the process of SDG implementation, the state planning and development departments are also functioning as focal points by providing the necessary information
and support (United Nations High Level Political Forum, 2017).

*1.11.4    Challenges for achieving the SDGs in India*

The achievement of SDGs may encounter several challenges, such as inefficient
leadership, insufficient investments, lack of coordinated partnerships and implementation, and lack of indicators with effective data collection. Institutions and

processes that directly and indirectly impact health in the context of globalised trade, migration, environment, and security need to have an increasing interface with the global governance for health for the success of SDGs. Also, in relation to policy reform, regulation, funding, implementation, activism, and public representation, leadership is necessary for progress and development (Singh, 2016).

A profound transformation is needed to address the upcoming challenges of sustainable development, and all countries need to recognise this, to adopt a universal development agenda (post-2015), with sustainable development at the core. These transformations include shifts to sustainable methods and patterns of consumption and production in an economic manner, along with renewed global partnerships, effective governance, and means of implementation (Singh, 2016).

---

**Box 1.7   Role of SDGs in India**

In the past few years, the Indian subcontinent has directed its progress and development pathways to achieve its priorities in terms of economic growth, employment, water, food and energy security, poverty reduction and alleviation, and disaster resilience. In addition, the country also aims at adoption of robust and transparent governance along democratic lines and restore its natural capital. However, upcoming challenges in terms of increasing inequities, impacts of climate change, and struggling human development indices have been realised and recognised by both the government and the citizens. An opportunity to integrate and revitalise the efforts to achieve national as well as global aims and aspirations has been found in the framework provided by the post-2015 UN Sustainable Development Agenda (Bhamra et al., 2015).

---

Ineffective social inclusion, widespread regional disparities, gender inequality, and rural-urban gaps are also some of the other challenges encountered when implementing the agenda. A major challenge is to set an unbiased and meaningful standard worldwide for the basic needs. These are adequate sanitation, nutrition, access to potable and sustainable water sources, primary health services, and access to infrastructure, which includes roads, electricity, and communication. Additionally, greater challenges to the prosperity and peace to the society worldwide are events such as violent conflicts; loss of biodiversity; climate change; degradation of drylands, forests, and water bodies; and a worldwide economic downturn. These challenges threaten to reverse the accomplishments that have been achieved until now and jeopardise any possible benefit (Singh, 2016).

Even as the SDGs are widely accepted, there has also been criticism for them being excessive in number and wide in scope. It is challenging to develop and sustain advocacy, mobilisation, continuity, and public awareness for 169 targets across 17 goals in the SDGs. This has been compared to the MDGs, where the goals were 8 in number, along with 18 targets that were simpler to understand and were considered to be more pragmatic for adoption worldwide by businesses, civil societies, and governments (Singh, 2016).

### 1.11.5    *SDGs and working towards a transformational agenda*

The goal of achieving the SDGs by 2030 creates opportunities to collaborate with determination, hard work, and dedicated leadership, as well as a commitment to mutual development, supported by strengthened use of science and technology. It offers an opportunity for healthcare practitioners and planners to throw light on the interdependence between development, energy, health and education, governance matters and to make health a precondition for a sustainable society and advancement towards prosperity (Singh, 2016).

The cohesive design of the SDGs not only makes them complex but also exhibits additional benefits from explicit objectives and goals. For instance, clean drinking water and sanitation will not only improve health and reduce water-borne diseases but will also contribute to improved well-being and nutrition. To ensure that health remains fundamental to post-2015 SDGs, the social, environmental, and economic aspects of sustainable development need to be omnipresent. The advent of this new paradigm of sustainability provides an unprecedented opportunity (Singh, 2016).

Multi-stakeholder alliances that involve governments, international and private organisations, civil society, parliaments, trade unions, local authorities, research, and educational institutions offer an incentive to support the transformative endeavours of the post-2015 development agenda. To ensure accountability and transparency, the efficacy of such associations depends on assigning specific roles and responsibilities (Singh, 2016).

### 1.11.6    *Implications of the unfinished agenda of the SDGs*

In the global competitive landscape, as the development trajectory continues to flourish, the consequences of the unfinished agenda often manifest themselves in greater magnitude. The critical infrastructure will continue to be vulnerable unless the SDGs and goals of other synergetic actions globally outperform the impact paradigm. This needs a parallel action plan to make critical infrastructure, in our case the healthcare infrastructure, resilient to the impacts of EWEs.

### 1.11.7    *Vulnerability of healthcare as a critical infrastructure*

Climate change and EWEs have been found to undermine the social determinants of health, threaten the viability of several environmental advantages provided by natural ecosystems, and thereby have a direct impact on health. They can worsen the health outcomes significantly owing to various hazards that interact with pre-existing vulnerabilities. The strength of the health systems and their capacity to adapt to and manage climate-sensitive health risks moderate almost all of the health impacts (World Health Organisation, 2020).

The health risks of climate change can be observed in the increasing intensity or frequency of storms, heatwaves, and floods, in addition to observations through gradual changes in average conditions. This variability is particularly alarming, since it is less predictable than changes in mean conditions. These variabilities have the potential to debilitate not only social systems but also health facilities and CI, and they may consequentially cause irreversible changes (World Health Organisation, 2020).

It is therefore imperative to better understand the processes of improvement and protection of resilience in public health systems to such EWEs, given their implications. In addition, it has been argued in previous research on the subject of facilities management that older structures have often been seen as undervalued resources in various sectors, including health, and that the profession of facilities management is itself at risk.

Even as newly constructed buildings could be relatively more resilient to external factors and forces, the existing healthcare infrastructure may be less resilient, thereby highlighting the specific need to develop strategies for adaptation and resilience to extreme weather or external risks. As an example, many hospitals located in floodplains have recently been observed to collapse and get infiltrated due to the pressure exerted on the structure by floods. This also damages several services and equipment, which were typically located in basements that are usually prone to inundation. Moving flood water can pose major risks during extreme weather and can damage the foundations and roads. During storms, the high winds that accompany them can damage wall coverings and roofs and can even blow the entire structure down. Further, in high-speed wind circumstances, the flying debris can pose a significant danger to people and property (Loosemore et al., 2014).

In contrast, extreme temperatures during heat waves can cause the temperature tolerances of heat management technologies and many existing construction materials to exceed their limit, which may result in their breakdown and under-/non-performance. In the case of healthcare, this can pose a serious risk, since several patients' health depends on specifically controlled humidity levels and controlled temperature conditions. During the occurrence of EWEs, electricity, water, and gas supply and infrastructure are likely to suffer damage or outages, thereby posing major risks to the hospitals that are heavily dependent on critical infrastructure (Loosemore et al., 2014).

Many facilities related to healthcare, such as community health services, old-age care centres, primary care clinics, and rural nursing posts, form a part of healthcare infrastructure for a community, in addition to the hospitals. "These facilities form a complex set of relationships which need to work collectively for an effective response to climate and EWEs" (McGeorge et al., 2011).

## 1.12    Summary

To achieve the overall objective of the book, it has been divided into nine chapters, each of which is a step with sub-objectives that help achieve the overall objective. Each chapter uses information from the literature to arrive at outcomes and inferences that support the following chapters. Case examples are used in each chapter as references to scenarios that either need to be avoided or need to be exemplified.

Climate change, because of anthropogenic activities leading to excessive resource consumption, greenhouse effect, and carbon emissions, has offset the upsurge in the intensity and frequency of EWEs. While international and national attempts are perceived as a response to combat climate change, it is essential to note that sustainable development need not draw sufficient attention towards the disruption and destruction caused by the consequential extreme weather. The chapter highlights this through the demonstration of challenges faced by critical infrastructure and the vulnerability of the healthcare infrastructure. Healthcare facilities serve as the backbone during and after an EWE, owing to their capability to extend services beyond healthcare, towards shelter, rescue, and nutrition in the aftermath of a disaster. It is therefore crucial to shift the focus from response to resilience and risk reduction in the case of EWEs and climate change. Resilience in healthcare infrastructure not only saves lives but also reduces the socio-economic losses; saves reconstruction; and reduces the need for evacuation, rescue, and recovery. Often, financial resources in the budget allocated to resilience and risk reduction may get diverted towards other developments, since the need or results of investments in disaster management may not be visible for an unknown period. This, however, does not alleviate the attention from the fact that EWEs are uncertain, sporadic, and sudden. Investment in resilience, therefore, is identified as a critical step to save not only lives and resources but financial implications in the future as well.

## References

ADB. (2017). *Region at Risk: The Human Dimensions of Climate Change in Asia and the Pacific*. Manila: Asian Development Bank.

Arya, A. S. (2010). *Mainstreaming Disaster Risk Reduction in the Housing Sector*. New Delhi: National Institute of Disaster Management.

Bach, C., Gupta, A. K., Nair, S. S., & Birkmann, J. (2013). *Critical Infrastructures and Disaster Risk Reduction – Training Module*. New Delhi: National Institute of Disaster Management.

Bhamra, A., Shanker, H., & Niazi, Z. (2015). *Achieving the Sustainable Development Goals in India: A Study of Financial Requirements and Gaps*. New Delhi: United Nations Development Programme; Ministry of Environment, Forest and Climate Change, Government of India.

Chow, J., Darley, S., & Laxminarayan, R. (2007). Cost effectiveness of disease interventions in India. *Resources for the Future Discussion Paper*, 07–53.

Chow, W. T. (2018). The impact of weather extremes on urban resilience to hydro-climate hazards: A Singapore case study. *International Journal of Water Resources Development*, 510–524.

Das, B. K., & Kumar, A. (2011). Green buildings: An approach towards sustainable habitat. In *National Conference on Sustainable Development of Urban Infrastructure* (pp. 9–13). Nagpur: Dattsons Nagpur.

Disaster Center. (2020, October 13). *Disaster Center*. Retrieved from http://disastercenter.com/New%20Guide/Landslides.html

Gheorghe, B., & Ionut, B. G. (2008). *Critical Infrastructure Interdependencies*. Romania: Universitatea Națională de Apărare, Carol I.

Ghosh, T., & Pal, I. (2014). Dust storm and its environmental implications. *Journal of Engineering Computers & Applied Sciences*, 30–37.

IPCC. (2007). *Climate Change 2007: Synthesis Report*. Geneva: Intergovernmental Panel on Climate Change.

IPCC. (2017). *IPCC Special Report on Global Warming of 1.5°C*. Malmo: Intergovernmental Panel on Climate Change.

IWRI. (2018). *International Workshop on Disaster Resilience Infrastructure*. New Delhi: IWRI.

Joint Global Change Research Institute and Battelle Memorial Institute, Pacific Northwest Division. (2009). *India: The Impact of Climate Change to 2030*. Washington, DC: National Intelligence Council.

Kundzewicz, Z. W. (2016). Extreme weather events and their consequences. *Papers on Global Change*, 59–69.

Lenz, S. (2009). Vulnerabilität Kritischer Infrastrukturen, BBK (Bundesamt für Bevölkerungsschutzund Katastrophenhilfe-bonn). *Forschungim Bevölkerungsschutz*.

Loosemore, M., Chow, V. W., & McGeorge, D. (2014). Managing the health risks of extreme weather events by managing hospital infrastructure. *Engineering, Construction and Architectural Management*, 4–32.

McGeorge, D., Chow, V. W., Carthey, J., & Loosemore, M. (2011). Modelling the impact of extreme weather events on healthcare infrastructure using rich picture diagrams. In *Procs 27th Annual ARCOM Conference* (pp. 973–981). Bristol: Association of Researchers in Construction Management.

Mijalković, S., & Cvetković, V. (2013). Vulnerability of critical infrastructure by natural disasters. In *The Academy of Criminalistic and Police Studies, Belgrade* (pp. 91–102). Belgrade: The Academy of Criminalistic and Police Studies, Belgrade.

Mohanty, A. (2020). *Preparing India for Extreme Climate Events*. New Delhi: Council on Energy, Environment and Water (CEEW).

Mohanty, S. K., Chatterjee, R., & Shaw, R. (2020). Building resilience of critical infrastructure: A case of impacts of cyclones on the power sector in Odisha. *Climate 2020*, 1–17.

National Centers for Environmental Information. (2020). *National Centers for Environmental Information*. Retrieved from www.ncdc.noaa.gov/monitoring-references/dyk/anomalies-vs-temperature

NITI Aayog. (2019). *SDG India: Index and Dashboard 2019–20*. New Delhi: NITI Aayog.

Rehak, D., Senovsky, P., Hromada, M., & Lovecek, T. (2019). Complex approach to assessing resilience of critical infrastructure elements. *International Journal of Critical Infrastructure Protection*, 125–138.

Rosene, R. K. (2016, July 26). *The Growth-Environment Paradox: An Illustrated Guide*. Retrieved from http://ryankatzrosene.blogspot.com/: http://ryankatzrosene.blogspot.com/2016/07/the-growth-environment-paradox.html

Ruiten, K. V., Bles, T., & Kiel, J. (2016). EU-INTACT-case studies: Impact of extreme weather on critical infrastructure. In *FLOODrisk 2016–3rd European Conference on Flood Risk Management*. E3S Web of Conferences. https://www.e3s-conferences.org/articles/e3sconf/abs/2016/02/e3sconf_flood2016_07001/e3sconf_flood2016_07001.html

Seneviratne, S., Nicholls, N., Easterling, D., Goodess, C. M., Kanae, S., Kossin, J., . . . Rahimi, M. (2012). Changes in climate extremes and their impacts on the natural physical environment. In S. I. Seneviratne (ed.), *Managing the Risks of Extreme Events and*

*Disasters to Advance Climate Change Adaptation* (pp. 109–230). Cambridge; New York: Cambridge University Press.

Singh, Z. (2016). Sustainable development goals: Challenges and opportunities. *Indian Journal of Public Health*, 247–250.

Thakare, K. R. (2011). Sustainable development of urban infrastructure: Problems and recommendations. In *National Conference on Sustainable Development of Urban Infrastructure* (pp. 37–46). Nagpur: Dattsons Nagpur.

Tyagi, A. (2018). Development-environment paradox: An experience of Odisha, India the human factor of environmental emergencies. *Journal of Environmental Research and Development*, 529–535.

(UCL)-CRED, L. (2015). *EM-DAT: The Emergency Events Database*. Universite catholique de. Université catholique de Louvain, Brussels, Belgium.

UNDP. (2017a). *Mainstreaming Disaster Risk Reduction & Climate Change Adaptation in District Level Planning*. New Delhi: United Nations Development Programme.

UNDP. (2017b, April 17). *The Millennium Development Goals Report 2015*. Retrieved from www.undp.org/content/undp/en/home/librarypage/mdg/the-millennium-development-goals-report-2015.html

UNDP. (2020). *Sustainable Development Goals*. Retrieved from www.undp.org/content/undp/en/home/sustainable-development-goals.html

UNDRR. (2015). *Sendai Framework for Disaster Risk Reduction*. New York: United Nations.

United Nations High Level Political Forum. (2017). *Voluntary National Review Report on Implementation of Sustainable Development Goals*. New York: The High-Level Political Forum on Sustainable Development.

Wang, Y. (2012). Recent research progress on tropical cyclone structure and intensity. *Tropical Cyclone Research and Review*, 254–275.

WMO Commission for Climatology Task Team. (2018). *Guidelines on the Definition and Monitoring of Extreme Weather and Climate Events*. Geneva: World Meterological Organisation.

World Health Organisation. (2020, October 13). *World Health Organisation*. Retrieved from www.who.int/health-topics/floods#tab=tab_1

Yokomatsu, M., & Hochrainer-Stigler, S. (2020). *Disaster Risk Reduction and Resilience*. Singapore: Springer.

# 2 Healthcare infrastructure and extreme weather events

## 2.1 Overview

Healthcare infrastructure and services subject to natural hazards and EWEs tend to suffer losses owing to their overwhelmed functioning and operations, in addition to their vulnerability characteristics. This chapter entails these vulnerability attributes and their consequences as observed in examples of affected cases. Figure 2.1 illustrates the existing lack of resilient measures necessary to mitigate the vulnerability characteristics of the healthcare infrastructure.

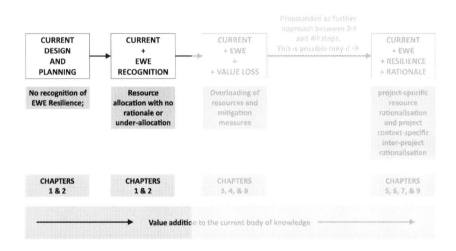

*Figure 2.1* Process of incorporating resilience: lack of rational resource allocation for incorporating resilience.

## 2.2 Structure of the chapter

This chapter highlights the significance of the healthcare infrastructure during the occurrence of EWEs and the lack of research and resilience in this area in the literature as well as in practice. The Indian guidelines and role of government are discussed. Using case examples of instances when the healthcare infrastructure

DOI: 10.1201/9781003393108-2

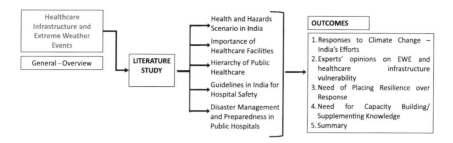

*Figure 2.2* Structure and overview of Chapter 2.

failed in the aftermath of an EWE, inferences have been derived and the need for strengthening and updating the guidelines and infrastructure are highlighted. Figure 2.2 explains the structure and outcome of this chapter.

## 2.3   Responses to climate change: India's efforts

Some of the notable initiatives launched by the Government of India in order to address the challenges faced due to climate change are as follows:

- *The National Action Plan on Climate Change (NAPCC)* – To initiate climate change adaptation and mitigation actions across the country
- *State Action Plan on Climate Change (SAPCC)* – Emerging from NAPCC, eight national-level missions have been formulated that address the environmental and socio-economic concerns arising from climate change
- National flagship programmes such as Mahatma Gandhi National Rural Employment Guarantee Act (MGNREGA), Jawaharlal Nehru National Urban Renewal Mission (JNNURM), etc., also include measures and actions that address climate change–related issues

(United Nations Development Programme, 2017).

The NAPCC involves India's vision of evolving as an ecologically sustainable development and lists the measures that can be taken to implement and achieve this vision. This initiative is founded on the awareness of the interlinkage of various domains, such as energy, water, urban spaces, forests, agriculture, industry, and the fragile mountain environment, and acknowledges the need for simultaneous attention to these domains to ensure effective climate change mitigation and adaptation actions. The SDGs adopted by the UN also recognise this need for inter-related policies and coordinated action (Saran, 2019).

The national missions are on solar energy, enhancing energy efficiency, creating a sustainable urban habitat, conserving water, sustaining the fragile Himalayan ecosystem, creating a green India through expanded forests, making agriculture sustainable, and creating a strategic knowledge platform for serving all the national missions.

The NAPCC also acknowledges the fact that energy security is co-existent with climate change; that India made a strategic shift from its long duration of dependence on fossil fuels to renewable and cleaner sources of energy, such as solar energy, hydro power, and nuclear energy; and is making headway towards a pattern of economic activity based on such progressive sources. This shift is expected to not only help the country combat climate change but also enhance the energy security. Hence, India's climate change strategy is motivated by a co-benefit approach. While India's response to climate change has evolved according to the viability of its own resources, as constituted in the NAPCC, it is also recognised that the response is closely related to the parallel multi-lateral effort to establish a global climate change regime, based on the provisions and principles of the UNFCCC (Saran, 2019).

## 2.4   Experts' opinion on EWE and healthcare infrastructure vulnerability

The discussion in the foregoing sections has underlined the significance of impact mitigation of EWEs on the healthcare infrastructure and the need to build resilience into the planning and design approach from a rather academic perspective. However, practical application is quite different from the scholarly perspective. Any advocacy of the approach, particularly considering rational resilience, therefore, would have to consider such challenges and variables that are not part of routine discourse. In view of this, it is felt prudent that before we further delve on the subject, the views of experts may also be solicited. To this end, two expert groups were identified, namely, one from the domain specialisation of environment and weather phenomenon, and the other from the professional background involved in the planning and design of the healthcare infrastructure. The experts are prominent stakeholders in the planning, design, and management processes of healthcare delivery projects and have an autonomous-specific outlook on the domain of knowledge structured in this book.

The research questions are as follows:

i.   **EWE vulnerability**: Opinion on the vulnerability of the healthcare infrastructure to surge in EWEs in the wake of current global climate change.
ii.  **Healthcare projects' shortcomings**: What shortcomings do you find existing in practice in the tendering, design, construction, and estimation processes of the healthcare infrastructure?
iii. **Resilience intervention**: What steps can be taken by designers/architects to ensure incorporation of region-specific resilience in their designs?
iv.  **Enhancing awareness:** Often, designing of critical infrastructure, specifically healthcare, has been found to lack awareness, or understanding, and knowledge. How do you think this can be augmented to increase awareness among practitioners?

The experts were asked these four questions, and their subjective opinion on each of these was sought. Most of the experts believed that global warming and climate change have affected weather conditions and have a significant impact on all infra-structure, especially healthcare and other critical infrastructure. The experts had autonomous and specific outlooks on each of these questions, and their reviews augmented the direction and structure of the book, as well as helped in validating the need and subject of the study.

### 2.4.1   Reviews on EWE vulnerability

It was commonly observed that along with climate change and a surge in EWEs, urban planning, design, and construction practices are also held responsible for the failure or non-performance of the healthcare infrastructure on account of an extreme weather occurrence. Interfering human activities such as disruption of natural drainage patterns, reclaiming of land from the sea, over-construction, industrialisation, and over-utilisation of natural resources also cause infrastructure, including healthcare facilities, to disrupt and fail.

Further, healthcare facilities in rural areas and smaller towns and districts are irregular and not available sufficiently, which makes the existing facilities even more vulnerable. The imbalance of mapping the healthcare infrastructure propor-tionately with their geographic location and connectivity (physical and digital) makes the medical facilities as well as the populations highly vulnerable to EWEs.

The healthcare infrastructure does not exist or function independently; all types of infrastructure are co-dependent, and failure/non-performance of one type of infrastructure impacts all others. While medical facilities are responsible for pro-viding first aid, emergency services, and shelter services and continue to treat the OPD and IPD patients already in the hospital, any failure in energy, water, trans-port, or IT infrastructure puts the healthcare infrastructure also at risk.

Further, the process of curbing global warming and controlling climate change is slow, but the impact of these on EWEs, and thereby, on the healthcare infra-structure is evident and only increasing. It is therefore important that the medical facilities are resilient and undisrupted in terms of function and are designed to be climate smart.

### 2.4.2   Reviews on healthcare projects' shortcomings

There was a common outlook about designers, practitioners, and clients being uninformed about the vulnerability of healthcare facilities to such extreme events, especially these being an outcome of climate change. Many are not aware that cli-mate change is the cause and that EWEs are a consequence that further affect infra-structure. As a result, the tendering processes and selection of consultants reduces to merely an achievement of the maximum number of beds, lowest bid, and highest built-up area.

This also emphasises the fact that there have been massive medical, technological, and construction technique advancements, which are not progressively encouraged in the Indian construction industry. Advancement of medical knowledge and health-care, as well as construction practices and planning ideologies, can help healthcare facilities become more efficient, resilient, and better prepared for any EWE occurrences. However, the lack of competent medical practitioners in medical facilities, especially in rural areas, where even the design, planning, and operation of infrastructure is in a pathetic state, leads to poor functioning of such facilities.

Absence of healthcare mapping in the country due to lack of resources and fitting guidelines, authorities, and approvals leads to poor distribution of healthcare facilities and increases the pressure, and consequently vulnerability, of the healthcare infrastructure in urban areas.

Healthcare infrastructure is the most important among critical infrastructure, due to its function and emergency service. Even if the country has the technical know-how and knowledge to design and erect structures that are resilient, the authorising parties, clients, consultants, and doctors may or may not be supportive. The idea of making the most out of limited availability of land area, finances, and providing the maximum number of beds leads to uninformed decision-making, and in turn, leads to vulnerability of the healthcare infrastructure in the absence of investments in resilient construction and design practices.

### 2.4.3    *Reviews on resilience intervention*

Most of the experts were of the opinion that design and construction of the healthcare infrastructure is an area of expertise, and therefore, must involve the consultation of a hospital expert as well as a disaster manager. A hospital consultant's inputs would be beneficial for functionality, space flow and movement, sterile zones, management, etc. A disaster manager's inputs would help understand the vulnerability of the healthcare infrastructure under study and assist decision-making and investment needs to make the structure and operation safe, resilient, and undisrupted. Further, the medical facility may also begin to include a disaster management wing/department, which is aware, prepared, and equipped to deal with any natural hazard/EWE/disaster occurrences.

Another significant recommendation for planners and designers is to increase sensitisation towards land use classification and mapping of infrastructure. The location of healthcare facilities should be as less exposed to potential natural hazards as possible. This further leads to suggested micro-zonation for hospitals such that the facilities are safer at certain 'safe-zone' locations.

Structural designers and architects must also ensure the quality and safety compliance with codes and standards. However, it must also be ensured that if the disaster management plans and standards are not updated, the designers and disaster managers should nevertheless ensure safe design and planning that are resilient to hazards.

A brief estimation of the tangible and intangible losses to the healthcare facility during the process of inception, design development, and construction is a useful route to ensure that the hospital is aware and prepared to face the consequences and has the opportunity to invest in the facility to reduce its vulnerability and enhance resilience and preparedness. The use of a vulnerability index, loss potential, hazard potential, and resilience index in such cases is positively advantageous.

### 2.4.4   Reviews on enhancing awareness

Involvement of suitable consultants and specialists, development of detailed project briefs before the tendering process, simulations of scenarios that involve the healthcare infrastructure and its performance in the occurrence of specific hazards, and development of a sensitised design towards the needs and safety of consumers are some of the recommendations by the experts reviewed in this survey.

A commonality in all the reviews was intense consultation with specialists. While various types of consultation techniques exist, it is also important to get the best suitable and experienced persons on board. For a typology of infrastructure that is highly sensitive in terms of its service as well as the structural and social vulnerability, it is imperative to involve specialised consultants who also understand what critical infrastructure is and that the facility they are working in is a critical facility. Further, different grades of consultation, including the ones who are running the facilities, should be interacted with to ensure awareness and preparedness for all levels of hierarchy in the organisation.

Medical care is one of the most essential services in the duration and aftermath of any disaster/EWE. The healthcare infrastructure is expected to serve and provide emergency medical attention for trauma, injuries, and fatalities, and even shelter, if needed. It is therefore crucial that the healthcare facility remains safe and functional in terms of structure, equipment, service, staff, management, finances, accessibility, and social availability. The hospital also has to continue treating the existing patients and offer urgent medical services to the new patients and those affected due to the disaster/EWE.

In a country like India, which is disaster prone, is subject to recurrent small and medium disasters, and is high-density and resource-stretched, it is important to have a robust healthcare infrastructure. This is critical for the long-term recovery benefits as well as effective response and relief. These factors have an impact on both health outcomes and the health infrastructure. (Krishnan & Patnaik, 2018).

However, it has been observed and explored in this section that medical facilities often malfunction in the country, which has a heavy impact on the existing and inbound patients as well as OPD. Disrupted functioning of the healthcare facilities can increase the human vulnerability to the EWE due to increased influx and reduced capability of the facility to function, during and post EWE. Through the observations made in this section, it is safe to say that the healthcare infrastructure in India is not adequate to serve in case an EWE strikes; rather, medical facilities have often been found to be failing in the advent of EWE. Designers may sometimes be oblivious and negligent about the safety and continuity of healthcare services during EWEs and design to exploit FAR and the number of beds. Rather, the designers need to work in conjunction with disaster managers and healthcare specialists to achieve medical, management, structural, financial, and functional safety during and after EWEs.

As the frequency and intensity of EWEs increase due to global warming and climate change, the solution is to make the healthcare infrastructure climate smart, resilient, and prepared, instead of designing with negligence and unawareness. The following sections explore the works of various authors on research and observations made on the functioning and responsiveness, or the lack thereof, of the medical facilities in India.

## 2.5    Importance of healthcare facilities

It is crucial that healthcare facilities and hospitals always remain safe and functional. Hence, all levels of the health infrastructure and facilities need to be paid special attention, and it must be ensured that they continue to provide treatment to in-patients, as well as treating the people injured by EWEs. Ideally, prevention and promotion programmes of the hospitals must also not be suspended, such as haemodialysis and prenatal care, which may place added strain on the organisation. Therefore, in order to ensure continuity of medical services in the event of disaster/EWE, it is critical for the healthcare facility to devise and implement formal disaster management and risk mitigation plans to navigate in the event of such occurrences. In addition, the structural and architectural design of the building must be responsive and continue to function, and the equipment must also maintain serviceability. While disaster management and mitigation plans are formulated by many hospitals, where the significance of these requirements is realised and recognised, prevention needs to be incorporated in these plans as well so as to ensure that the disaster risk management system is strengthened and operative (Nia & Kulatunga, 2017).

## 2.6    Health and hazards scenario in India

More than 50% of India's landmass and geography are susceptible to more than one hazard (i.e., multiple hazards) of high intensity. In the duration between 1970 and 2015, the number of disasters recorded in the Indian subcontinent were 614, which included earthquakes, floods, drought, landslides, storms, and extreme temperatures. These disasters led to over 198,000 deaths and affected over 2 billion people across the country. The losses recorded were more than USD 93 billion ((UCL)-CRED, 2015).

In addition to the consistently high positioning of the Indian subcontinent on the ranking of fatalities due to natural disasters, the economic and infrastructure losses have also been observed to rise sharply. The fragility of the Indian healthcare infrastructure and medical service systems has been highlighted in the previous decade. Some of these incidents have been presented in this section to indicate the magnitude of the losses. The floods of 2018 in Kerala caused significant damage to a hospital that was 125 years old and served 350,000 people (Stalin, 2018). Similarly, the Chennai floods of 2015 caused the death of 18 patients owing to a power failure. The annual urban flooding of Mumbai also poses a high risk of infections (Barnagarwala, 2017).

The earthquake that occurred in Gujarat in 2001 caused 172 fatalities and has been recorded as a notably tragic instance of the level of impact that a disaster inflicted on a healthcare facility. A civil hospital of 281 beds collapsed in this incident. This disaster led to the enhancement of earthquake resistance in buildings using the technology of base isolation. This was later included in the revised Indian Seismic Code IS 1893: 2002 for Criteria for Earthquake Resistant Design of Structures. A pan-India review of the seismic vulnerability of 1.6 lakh public healthcare facilities revealed that more than 54% of these healthcare facilities fall in moderate- to very high-risk zones (Krishnan & Patnaik, 2018).

## 2.7    Vulnerability of health infrastructure: status of research in India

The interlinkage between disasters and public health emergencies is a sparsely researched discipline in India. Most of the reports that are available publicly study the impacts from specific disaster events, individual health conditions, or evaluation of existing policies in the domain. The melioration of this research involves the evolving policy discourse of disasters and EWEs in the country, which is augmented and amended with the occurrence of major disasters (Krishnan & Patnaik, 2018).

Some of the most common research subjects for their impacts on human health are the Odisha super cyclone (1999), the Gujarat earthquake (2001), and the Indian Ocean tsunami (2004).

i.    **Impact of vector-borne diseases** – The impact of vector-borne diseases has been studied by various authors, such as leptospirosis by the WHO (2000) before the super cyclone and cholera outbreaks by Sur et al. (2000). A study on psychiatric disorders in survivors of the Latur earthquake in 1993 was conducted by Sharan et al. (1996). The earthquake was graded VIII on the Mercalli intensity scale and caused more than 10,000 deaths (Krishnan & Patnaik, 2018).

ii.   **Non-communicable diseases** – Since 2000, the epidemiological transition of the country from communicable to non-communicable diseases was studied in detail. Rastogi et al. (2004) and Shah & Mathur (2010) studied the threats of chronic diseases and cardiovascular diseases; hypertension, cancers, and diabetes were studied by Ghaffar et al. (2004), Reddy et al. (2005), Misra et al. (2011), and Patel et al. (2011). Khandelwal et al. (2004) conducted a study on the impact of disasters and mental health priorities (Krishnan & Patnaik, 2018).

iii.  **Epidemic** – Myers et al. (2000) conducted research on the epidemic preparedness in public health. It also focused on the disease surveillance methods, environmental forecasting, and promotion of epidemic prevention control (Krishnan & Patnaik, 2018).

iv.   **Mental health** – Various studies were prompted by the Odisha super cyclone of 1999 that had an impact on over 10,000 people. The studies conducted by Sharan et al. (1996) and Kar et al. (2004) examined the subjects of post-traumatic stress disorder (PTSD) and mental health vulnerability (Krishnan & Patnaik, 2018).

v.  **Infectious diseases** – Diseases that were typically vector- and water-borne
    and a consequence of flooding, such as diarrhoea, leptospirosis, and chikungu-
    nya, were studied in detail, in addition to the general challenges of managing
    infectious diseases (Krishnan & Patnaik, 2018).

The evolution of disaster policies in the Indian context was studied by Jha et al.
(2016). The policies were aimed to ensure reduction of the mortality rate due to a
disaster through improved evacuation systems and early warning systems.

## 2.8   Role of government in making healthcare resilient

Management of health during EWEs and natural disasters is also covered under
the larger umbrella of public health. In India, the growth and inclusion of public
health, healthcare infrastructure safety, and risk mitigation in disaster management
guidelines and standards have been slow but steady.

The Model Public Health Act, developed in 1955 and revised in 1987, placed a
focus on encouraging a preventive public healthcare ecosystem through regulation,
monitoring, and inspection. However, the act did not gain enough leverage to be
accepted by the states. It laid emphasis on single-focus health schemes for rampant
health problems such as leprosy, malaria, tuberculosis, and high mortality among
children and mothers through curative medical services. This overshadowed the
importance of preventive public health measures, thereby leading to its low acceptance (Krishnan & Patnaik, 2018).

The Disaster Management Act of 2005 was a significant governance response
to manage natural disasters in the Indian subcontinent. However, its foremost focus
was to direct efforts towards rescue and relief operations, especially until the early
2000s. A clear mandate was not received on the roles and responsibilities of healthcare institutions or facilities in risk reduction or impact mitigation. The National
Disaster Management Authority (NDMA), formed under the Ministry of Home
Affairs (MHA), held the responsibility of managing the developmental, economic,
and environmental issues related to natural and other disasters. Being a signatory
to the Sendai Framework for Disaster Risk Reduction, India was among the first
countries to devise a National Disaster Management Plan in 2005 (NDMP). The
primary goal of NDMP 2005 was to achieve a significant reduction in disruptions to critical infrastructure and services, in addition to disaster risk mitigation
(Krishnan & Patnaik, 2018).

In the years following 2005, the NDMA has developed various standards on
risk mitigation and construction practices for specific hazards and disasters. The
minimum standards of relief and management of hazards and disasters have been
provided in detail in these guidelines. These hazards/disasters include earthquakes,
floods, cyclones, tsunamis, droughts, urban flooding, nuclear emergencies, and
chemical disasters. Additionally, the guidelines include sections on mass casualty
management and medical preparedness in case of occurrence of these disasters. The
NDMA has also published comprehensive guidelines on psychosocial health; the
guidelines for hospital safety were released in 2016 (Krishnan & Patnaik, 2018).

## 2.9   Guidelines in India for hospital safety

The Disaster Management Act makes it a requisite for all state governments to define and formulate independent State Disaster Management Plans (SDMPs) that entail the articulation of preparation, mitigation, response, and recovery from disasters. A significant component of these SDMPs is mass casualty management and medical preparedness. They recommend that the state may provide services and healthcare according to the standards defined by the National Authority (Part II, point 24(d)). It is prescribed by the Disaster Management Act that every hospital needs to have an emergency disaster management plan, which must be apprised and updated on a regular basis with mock drills and periodic checks (Krishnan & Patnaik, 2018).

These management guidelines for specific hazards, formulated by the NDMA, furnish details on effective and appropriate preparedness in terms of medical services and efficient healthcare delivery systems and health facilities to manage diseases, injuries, and conditions concomitant with the specified hazard. It also allocates responsibilities to departments in the district, state, private hospitals, urban local bodies, and state health departments to enable multi-agency collaboration.

For earthquakes, the guidelines outlined by NDMA recommend retrofitting of lifeline structures and selective seismic strengthening in earthquake-prone regions. These guidelines are applicable for tertiary care centres, all health facilities, and all major and minor hospitals. The hospitals also need to be informed and updated on the India Disaster Resource Network (IDRN) database. The involvement of the corporate sector is recommended in the guidelines for urban flooding, for improvement of delivery of relief measures. Minimum standards of relief have also been published by the NDMA for people affected by disasters. These include provisions for food, water, sanitation, shelter, health, rehabilitation, and special attention to more vulnerable groups (Krishnan & Patnaik, 2018).

Further, guidelines for hospital safety were laid down by the NDMA in 2016 for mainstreaming disaster preparedness, mitigation, prevention, and response activities within the healthcare sector. The document of the NDMA guidelines is an amalgamation of disaster response, relief and reduction fundamentals, and mitigation measures from a spectrum of standards from national (Bureau of Indian Standards, National Building Code, Indian Public Health Standards, Clinical Establishment Act) and international (World Health Organization, Pan American Health Organization) sources. Further improvement and elaboration of the NDMA guidelines, to develop frameworks for implementation, involved the empanelment of several domain experts. The guidelines discuss in detail some of the parameters of disaster safety and disaster management for hospitals and are listed here:

- Awareness generation for hospital safety
- Hospital disaster preparedness
- Licensing and accreditation
- Fire safety
- Design and safety of hospital buildings

(Krishnan & Patnaik, 2018)

## 2.10    Hierarchy of public healthcare (primary and secondary) in India

The National Action Framework for Hospital Safety underlines five areas of priority for action, in addition to drawing attention to the gaps, recommending interventions, assigning work to relevant agencies, and estimating a timeline. The priority areas are as follows:

- Capacity building
- Risk mitigation
- Response, recovery, and preparedness
- Education, advocacy, and awareness generation
- Strengthening of institutional mechanisms

However, in practice, a gap has been found in terms of compliance with state and national guidelines and building codes, lack of preparedness and planning, and varying quality of healthcare facilities. It was found that there was no statutory provision for the regulation and standardisation of disaster response plans devised for hospitals. Consequentially, disaster management plans are not maintained and updated in hospitals. In a survey, only 26% of the healthcare facilities providing trauma care had a disaster management plan that was well-documented (Joshipura, 2008; Mehta, 2006). In an on-site survey conducted in a flood-prone district, the primary health facilities lacked basic utilities for response-related activities, such as backup of power facility, equipment, and standard operating procedures. The states and their subordinate administrative units hold the responsibility of monitoring these aspects of hospital management (Phalkey et al., 2012).

## 2.11    Status of resilience in the healthcare infrastructure in SDMPs

In the event of a calamity or natural hazard, the SDMP is responsible to provide guidelines that help shield the vulnerabilities of the state, outline the measures for mitigation and prevention of natural and man-made disasters, promote capacity building, and assign responsibilities to various departments. Hospitals have been identified as critical or lifeline facilities. In a detailed study conducted by Krishnan & Patnaik (2018), in their working paper "Health and Disaster Risk Management in India", the authors found that the SDMPs did not entail a sufficient level of detail in proportion with the disaster vulnerability of the state or the quantum of healthcare facilities that were at risk. These plans were outdated, and even as they are required to be updated annually (as facilitated by the law), only eight states had updated their plan up to 2016. Further, it was found that these plans dedicated a significant portion of the sections to disaster response rather than preparation for a disaster in their standard operating procedures (SOPs). Even though the formulation of plans does not ensure the quality of response of the state to disasters, the lack of a detailed plan would result in lack of implementation of response and resilience practices, or poorly implemented practices, in the event of limited resources and time. The SOPs for relevant departments define elaborate steps for response and rehabilitation, and the SDMPs focus primarily on the response phase. As compared to frameworks devised globally, the indicators for the functional and non-structural resilience of the healthcare infrastructure were found to not have been covered appropriately in the SDMPs (Krishnan & Patnaik, 2018).

As pointed out by the authors of the working paper, the SDMPs detailed the structural indicators and are mentioned in 75% of the documents. However, the documents address non-structural indicators the least. Lengthy checklists have been drafted for response-related activities, which include medical equipment, furniture, and backup facilities, but do not include action points. Functional indicators were mentioned in 75% of the documents. The SDMPs of all states recommend that hospitals prepare a mass casualty management plan, a medical preparedness plan, and checklists for training of health workers during emergency situations. One of the fundamental requirements that enable the functional continuity of healthcare facilities of the state is to prepare lists of all health facilities available, along with their supporting services, such as ambulances, power stations, police stations, etc. However, this nature of information pertaining to health facilities in the state was included only in 50% of these SDMP documents. SDMPs for the states of Odisha and Assam include details of the population under service. The SDMP for Odisha includes provision of a high-tension power line dedicated for the district headquarter hospitals in order to ensure uninterrupted communication with the health control room. Most of the SDMPs, except for the one developed by the state of Meghalaya, do not include functional indicators pertaining to mental health and post-disaster psychosocial support. Other indicators such as media management, mobile hospitals, SOPs, and district-level data are well addressed. Sixteen states mention the utilisation of the IDRN. The online portal of the IDRN maintains a database of medical equipment and healthcare professionals to accelerate decision-making during a disaster (Krishnan & Patnaik, 2018).

## 2.12   Disaster management and preparedness in public hospitals in India

A study conducted by Sharma et al. (2016) in their article "Are our hospitals prepared for disasters? Evaluation of health-care staff vis-à-vis disaster management at a public hospital in India", administered a cross-sectional questionnaire at a multi-speciality hospital located in North India, namely Government Medical College and Hospital-32, that serves a population of around 11 lakhs. The study group under review includes the healthcare personnel employed in the emergency services of the hospital. The first part of the questionnaire focused on evaluating the awareness and basic knowledge of the study group in terms of disaster management, with the use of closed-ended questions. The second part of the questionnaire assessed the study group's attitude towards disaster management processes and response activities. The final part of the questionnaire assessed the general and specific practices followed by the healthcare facility vis-à-vis training of the personnel in disaster management.

The results of the questionnaire and the study conducted showed low awareness of the fundamentals of disaster management among the officials employed in the hospital, despite the technicians and administrative staff having been employed and working at the facility for a long duration. Nevertheless, the study also showed that the majority of the officials and staff in the hospital had a positive attitude and enthusiasm towards disaster preparedness activities. This can be interpreted as a positive indication for policy makers to organise and implement disaster preparedness and capacity-building programs in hospitals (Sharma et al., 2016).

Currently, the pressure of demand on resources and facilities in hospitals is immense. However, hospital management and policy makers need to realize that training and continuous education of hospital officials is indispensable and is an essential requirement to prevent catastrophic losses in the wake of any disaster. The study conducted by Sharma et al. (2016) revealed that almost 70% of the officials and employees of the hospital were not aware of any disaster drills being conducted in the facility.

Regular training of hospital staff in addition to a well-documented disaster management plan is essential for disaster preparedness, which is a dynamic process. However, disaster preparedness and safety response procedures cannot be ensured in a healthcare facility without regular drills aligned with the disaster management plan for the hospital. The Joint Commission on Accreditation of Healthcare Organizations has made it mandatory for healthcare facilities to subject their disaster management and emergency plans to examination twice a year, which includes at least one community-wide drill. These drills can be conducted in the form of physical disaster drills, computer simulations, and table-top exercises (Sharma et al., 2016).

## 2.13   Case examples of lack of performance of hospitals in the face of EWEs

This section highlights some of the EWE occurrences in India in the past decade and how the healthcare facilities not only failed to provide shelter and medical aid but also collapsed and caused further damage.

### 2.13.1   Chennai floods, 2015

The occurrence of the Chennai floods of 2015 caught the hospitals off-guard, including both public and private facilities, and these hospitals were found to be severely unprepared and highly vulnerable. The Tambaram Taluk Hospital in Chromepet had to be evacuated and patients transferred to other hospitals, and the out-patient services had to be operated from a wedding hall for two days. The ground floor of ESIC Hospital in KK Nagar was inundated and patients had to be shifted to upper floors. In addition, at least 13 primary health centres in Kancheepuram and Tiruvallur districts were drastically affected (Krishnan, 2015).

With the rise in water levels, most systems associated with urban life failed abysmally – the communication networks went under, roads caved in, sewage pipelines were damaged and wrecked, houses collapsed, and carcasses floated on roads.

Among the worst affected healthcare facilities was the MIOT Hospital, where 18 patients who were on ventilator support died on December 2 and 3, as stated in the health secretary's press release. A case was registered against the hospital under section 176 of the Criminal Procedure Code.

A need for stricter planning, drafting, and implementation of disaster management, preparedness, and safety standards for hospitals is brought forth as a significant observation from the impacts of these floods. The issue with safety standards and the lack thereof was previously raised after the occurrence of the Advanced Medical Research Institute (AMRI) fire tragedy, where the basement of a seven-storey hospital in Kolkata encountered a fire in December 2011. It was found that 90 patients had choked to death by morning at the hospital. A policy document was prepared months before the incident of the AMRI fire by Kavita Narayan, a disaster management expert, trained by the Federal Emergency Management Agency (FEMA), along with experts in the field of structural engineering, medicine, and hospital design. The policy document extensively detailed the duties and emergency actions of non-medical and medical employees in case a disaster strikes. The document entailed comprehensive instructions for the doctors, nurses, and management on planning and evacuation in case of an emergency due to natural or any other disaster. It has been established that in an ideal case situation, the response procedures must begin as soon as the danger is identified, such as a rise in water levels or the start of spread of fire (Krishnan, 2015)

The private sector of healthcare facilities caters to almost 40% of the in-patient services and 60% of out-patient services in Tamil Nadu, as identified by the State Health Department. Minimum standards to be followed for hospital functioning and safety have been enacted by the central government in the form of the Clinical Establishments (Registration and Regulation) Act, 2010.

The government of the state of Tamil Nadu has been relatively inactive in terms of the Tamil Nadu Private Clinical Establishments (Regulation) Act, 1997. The act came into force in April 1997, but the rules for its implementation still have to be determined. The state government is required to implement one of three options, which are enactment of the state act, adoption of the central act, or modifications in the existing act governing healthcare and clinical establishments. It has been found that the state has not implemented any of these options (Krishnan, 2015).

Expert Kavita Narayan stated that the Indian subcontinent lacks even minimal standards for hospital safety in case of disaster occurrences, and the enforcement of disaster preparedness plans is a far cry in the country. It was also mentioned by the expert that specific rules were incorporated in the draft hospital safety document. Since India currently does not have a policy for this, these documents and guidelines are not mandatory to be followed (Krishnan, 2015).

### 2.13.2   *Jammu and Kashmir floods, 2014*

The floods of 2014 occurred due to a breach of dykes by river Jhelum in the state of Jammu and Kashmir. The floods caused crippling damage to major hospitals in the cities within a few hours, with the patients, doctors, and attendants trapped inside. The following hospitals suffered disruptive damages:

- SMHS Hospital
- Bone and Joints Hospital
- Lala Ded Maternity Hospital
- Children's Hospital
- Jhelum Valley Medical College Hospital
- Gousia Hospital

The inundation in the hospitals was observed to follow similar patterns of impact: electricity was the first to get disrupted, followed by failure of diesel generators. Water filled the kitchens and drug stores, and most of the diagnostic equipment in basements were rendered useless and inaccessible. It was claimed by the healthcare officials that restoration of normalcy in services took almost a month (Hussain, 2014).

Even as rescue operations had commenced, first responders and rescue personnel did not reach many patients, staff, and attendants who needed to be evacuated. At Children's Hospital, three doctors managed to salvage eight oxygen cylinders, which helped some new-born children to survive for one more day. Due to a shortage of food supplies, the attendants were offered dextrose, and later, a dry mix of sugar and rice was offered as meals. Rescue and relief operations did not reach the Children's Hospital for more than 50 hours. This hospital was the first one to sink. By the time it received help from army rescuers, 14 babies had died, as claimed by attendants and doctors (Hussain, 2014).

A major gynaecological hospital of Kashmir suffered extensive loss and damages to patients and infrastructure. Doctors fled without tending to surgery and critical patients. Some of the patients were evacuated when youth rescue teams accessed the hospitals in boats and rafts. The Sher-i-Kashmir Institute of Medical Sciences Medical College (SKIMS) saw a major influx of serious cases, since it was the only tertiary-care hospital that remained unaffected by the floods (Hussain, 2014).

With the collapse of the main healthcare setup, the state of Kashmir relied on peripheral hospitals to manage patients at district levels. As many as 577,595 patients were recorded to report to the OPDs in all district hospitals in Kashmir, and 34,577 of them were admitted, as claimed by the Director of Health Saleem-ur-Rehman. This happened in the duration of 16 days, during which 1435 surgeries were also conducted (Hussain, 2014).

## 2.14   Findings from case examples of the impact of EWEs on the healthcare infrastructure

In the previous four decades, India has put in place various frameworks, guidelines, and standards to ensure the preparedness, resilience, and 'build-back-better' schemes, in addition to the recovery and relief measures during and after a natural disaster/EWE strikes. However, these frameworks and guidelines have been observed to lack updating, technological advancements, inclusion of internationally applied concepts, and ideations – but most of all, the Indian system has not been able to implement many of these frameworks and guidelines in a strict fashion. Most papers, journal articles, and newspapers highlight this lack of enactment and persistence in the Indian healthcare delivery systems.

Various government health policies have been drafted and applied to protect and ensure easy access and economical treatment to large sections of the society. However, most of these policies remain on paper and are not put into practice. A significant reason that has been observed in the literature and examples earlier for this is the absence of a safe, suitable, and operational infrastructure that would act as a medium of healthcare delivery to the public. Similar observations were made by an expert, who was subject to the questionnaire in this book, about the lack of any legitimately usable services in the rural and local areas. Only a very small fraction of hospitals in urban areas have been found to function as per guidelines and standards; however, the medical care dispensing in such facilities is financially beyond the reach of most of the population of this developing country. Even if the facilities were affordable, it would not be possible for these few healthcare facilities to cater to the pressure of the massive populace.

While public healthcare infrastructure in the urban setup fulfils the standards and code provisions measurably, the waiting times for treatments at these hospitals can extend up to months due to a limited number of beds and equipment, medical practitioners, and space. However, it is quite evident from the examples studied that the structures severely lack any mindful and measurable service provision and operation in rural areas and towns. Most of these facilities are barely making ends meet in terms of their healthcare delivery processes, and almost all of these facilities in rural areas do not have a medical practitioner and a usable tangible structure in place. This adds pressure on the functioning public healthcare facilities in urban areas, thereby increasing the waiting times and pressure on resources and staff. A major reason for such pressure, therefore, is inadequate healthcare infrastructure mapping through the country. Hospitals and medical delivery centres are not located in proportion to the need and population numbers of the areas and districts.

Another substantial contributor to the 'poor health' of the healthcare infrastructure is the lack of strict implementation of standards and code provisions which clearly state the need and methods to apply resilient and substantial construction practices. The National Building Code, Indian Standards, and National Health Policy clearly outline the details of the loads, design details, and resilient practices corresponding to all hazards/EWEs. These, however, are not employed appropriately and are often overlooked during planning, design, and construction of hospitals and medical centres, thereby making them extremely vulnerable to EWEs and numerous other hazards such as earthquake and fire. Most medical facilities exist in a pathetic state; some are even non-existent, despite having been earmarked at locations.

The study also finds the sudden occurrence of EWEs and their unanticipated intensity and frequency as a reason for the unpreparedness of the healthcare infrastructure. Climate change and global warming have affected the frequency and intensity of EWEs, and there has been an increased number of such occurrences that have caught the medical infrastructure off-guard. While the standards do include preparedness measures in their guidelines, most institutions and medical facilities tend to overlook these measures due to the uncertainty of these events. A healthcare structure has a probability to never face EWEs in its lifetime; however, it is this uncertainty that needs to be designed for, to safeguard the hospital's structural and financial interests, in addition to the safety of staff and patients. In the chain of deterioration of facilitation, even the government programmes have been observed to divert finances occasionally from such uncertainties to other programmes that need urgent attention. A significant reason for such diversion is the unsure returns and the longer time periods where the effects of implementation of resilience and preparedness practices and associated funds can be recognised and brought to the front.

The research and studies in India are also not significantly aimed at the losses and lacking nature of the healthcare infrastructure in the wake of EWEs/hazards. While studies focus on healthcare delivery systems, EWEs, and resilience, very few of them look at these aspects in conjunction. Many research projects speak of reconstruction and build-back-better, yet very few of them understand, evaluate, and highlight that resilience is the need of the hour. Only a handful of research projects comprehend and conduct studies on impacts of EWEs on healthcare infrastructure, even fewer on the quantum of losses and how to control these losses. Many studies develop indices of safety, vulnerability, and loss, yet there are not enough studies that delve deeper into the precise quantum of these losses preceding EWEs and methods to avoid such losses.

Some private organisations and NGOs acknowledge this and try to implement resilient practices in vulnerable areas. However, these are carried out at the community level and focus more on the local housing instead of healthcare and other infrastructure. Implementation and operation of such resilience mechanisms on a larger scale are possible when they are ensured publicly, with the active involvement of healthcare infrastructure specialists and disaster managers.

Having pointed out the lack in healthcare infrastructure and implementation of basic resilient practices, it becomes imperative for this book to provide a platform for recognition and calling out such deficiencies in the system. The cost model and loss framework proposed in this book are one of the many firsts and aim to trigger awareness and processes that begin to make hospitals and other medical delivery centres prepared and resilient.

## 2.15   Resilience and challenges in infrastructure

Organisations and policies have often been observed to exhibit a tendency to use resilience as a nebulous concept, paradigm, or inspiration. Policy documents such as those from the Asian Development Bank (ADB), European Union, the government of Netherlands, and the UK Environment Agency refer to resilience as 'something to pursue'. International agreements in three post-2015 agendas, such as the Sendai Framework for Disaster Risk Reduction, SDGs, and the UNFCCC, all call for resilience (Bruijn et al., 2017).

The risk management approaches which are currently being utilised pay less attention to recovery rate and capacity and mostly have a sectoral focus. Yet, the conventional risk management approaches are being fundamentally challenged by not only climate change but also by the changes in society. This calls for a more comprehensive and wide approach for risk management and may be facilitated by the concept of resilience. UNISDR (2009) defines resilience in the context of disaster risk reduction as "the ability of a system, community or society exposed to hazards to resist, absorb, accommodate to and recover from the effects of a hazard in a timely and efficient manner, including through the preservation and restoration of its essential basic structures and functions" (Bruijn et al., 2017).

Various researchers highlighted the lack of integration, persistently isolated knowledge, and practices to manage disaster risks. Yokomatsu & Hochrainer-Stigler (2020) stressed the need for a multi-disciplinary, multi-stakeholder approach in integration with measurement, tools, techniques, and institutional structures that can realistically support comprehensive risk assessment and management across multiple hazard landscapes (Yokomatsu & Hochrainer-Stigler, 2020).

Risk is often perceived as a conjunction of the probability of a hazard and its consequences. These consequences are typically affected by the exposure of people, property, infrastructure, and communities and their vulnerability to a hazard/EWE. The risks posed by these hazards/EWEs are usually expressed in terms of the (average) expected annual damage, or the (average) expected annual number of casualties, with the management of the hazards/EWEs mostly being risk-based.

Hence, the reduction of these risks posed by EWEs needs adoption of measures that would either decrease the probability of the EWE or ease the consequences. Performing a cost-benefit analysis on the economics of risk reduction can provide some insight into the effectiveness of the proposed measures. It has been noted that even as the cost of investment towards risk reduction can be determined relatively easily, the benefits of these investments or the measures adopted, and the risk reduction accomplished, are sufficiently difficult to establish and mostly contain considerable uncertainty. Also, certain relevant potential impacts of measures may not be easily expressed monetarily, mostly in the case of intangible factors such as loss of life or damage to cultural heritage.

Five principles were proposed by Bruijn et al. (2017) to augment the resilience and coping abilities of communities that are vulnerable to EWEs. These principles help consider the aspects that are often lacking in the risk management approaches. These principles are:

a) Looking at beyond-design events
b) Adopting a systems approach
c) Increasing recovery capacity by paying attention to financial and social capital
d) Building and preparing infrastructure according to the 'remain functioning' principle
e) Remaining resilient in the future

(Bruijn et al., 2017).

## 2.16    Need to supplement knowledge

While there has been extensive discourse about EWEs and climate change both in literature and international development goals alike, much less has been implemented on the ground. The knowledge areas around EWEs, climate change, and critical infrastructure, along with their interconnections and impacts, have been widely discussed in various journal articles, reports, and conferences. Similarly, resilience, disaster risk reduction, and reconstruction find a strong ground for dialogue and theory and have well-established policies, procedures, and guidelines to be followed to achieve resilience and the like.

However, through the discourse offered in this book, it has emerged that only a small fraction of these guidelines, protocols, and safety codes have been implemented on the ground. Focusing on healthcare facilities as one of the most critical infrastructures, there are several instances of incomplete implementation of these policies and guidelines. At a national level, where public healthcare is the primary source of healthcare in rural and sub-urban regions, it has often been found that the public health facilities are dysfunctional or non-performing. Further, even as the new structures may be resilient to the EWEs in their respective regions, the existing healthcare structures are observed to severely lack resilience or the awareness thereof. As a result, when a weather calamity strikes, these structures are highly likely to get severely destroyed or inundated, thereby becoming non-functional and causing massive tangible and intangible losses. Additionally, the reconstruction of these structures, if provided, does not follow resilience guidelines either.

It is therefore evident that even as the attempts of the central and state governments to improve healthcare facilities and curb the spread of diseases have been phenomenal, the status quo of the progress in healthcare infrastructure, especially in case of achieving resilience towards EWEs, is not satisfactory. In addition to the non-proactivity of the implementing authorities and practitioners, the lack of awareness and knowledge of the loss potential in these structures in case an EWE strikes are also nominal or inexistent. The tangible and intangible losses are not accounted for, before or during the planning/design/construction stages, thereby resulting in far more losses than anticipated, including trauma and loss of life.

This book evolves out of the need to serve the purpose to supplement the industry, as well as the literature, of the knowledge and ideology of knowledge, awareness, and expertise to determine overall and specific losses, both tangible and intangible, for a healthcare facility. The determination of losses from a practical viewpoint not only helps enhance awareness and knowledge but also provides a robust and usable framework that uses nominal inputs from the user to point out the losses that the health facility may face in case an EWE strikes. This not only aids the facility to decide to save as much as possible and have a contingency plan in addition to the emergency plan but also helps the healthcare planners and designers to ensure minimal losses by designing structures keeping in mind the reduction of loss numbers.

## 2.17    Need for capacity building for competence development

Critical infrastructure, especially healthcare infrastructure, is a sensitive typology that needs extensive design and functionality inputs. At the outset of EWEs and global climatic change that this book discusses, it becomes evident that the health-care infrastructure can be extremely vulnerable to EWEs and pose severe danger and unexpected repercussions as a result. It is therefore of significance to design-ers, clients, and authorities alike to make these structures resilient to EWEs so as to cause minimum damage and losses. However, this kind of rational resilience can be achieved only in the presence of efficient domain knowledge and awareness in the realm of vulnerabilities and operational significance.

However, it has been noted that there is not enough domain knowledge to sup-plement understanding of the criticality of the vulnerabilities to consultants, as a result of which, the consultants may not be found competent enough to produce resilient outputs for the critical infrastructures. This can also be attributed to the lack of awareness (besides the lack of knowledge) of the severity of the EWEs. While global warming and climate change are widely known and discussed, the consultants may not be aware of the outcomes of lacking designs and how the infrastructure may perform in case of an EWE.

In the construction industry, where focus as well as financial investments are often lifted from an uncertain event that may or may not happen throughout the service life of the building (such as fire, earthquake, flood, and other EWEs) and directed towards other additional facilities and new technologies, it is unlikely for the clients and stakeholders to incorporate region-specific resilience or multi-event resilience in the infrastructure.

The practitioners therefore need sufficient domain knowledge to supplement their awareness and competence to be able to apply the capacity building of the infra-structure towards EWEs and climate change. It is important that the nexus of the knowledge and applicability through the literature and practical channels is made available to the practitioners to enable them to integrate their structures with requisite resilience, rather than waiting for a massive change in the form of norms or code pro-visions. This book offers a medium that culminates knowledge through various lit-erature on EWEs, climate change, and sustainability and helps with understanding its impacts on the critical infrastructure in general and the healthcare infrastructure spe-cifically. The book then proceeds to propose a template that helps with understanding the loss potential of these infrastructures and the kind and degree of losses that the hospital buildings may face in the event of a natural hazard due to extreme weather.

Hence, the book offers a baseline for development of domain knowledge and a platform for assessment of detailed vulnerabilities, which would further supple-ment the understanding of designers, architects, and other consultants to enable them to competently apply rational resilience in practice.

## 2.18    Summary

The response, recovery, and relief of communities and societies in the aftermath of an EWE is significantly dependent on critical infrastructure. The healthcare infrastructure is expected to function efficiently during and after an extreme event strikes. However, these healthcare facilities are prone to damage and disruption and can pose a threat to the medical relief and rescue processes. Further, the medical facilities have been observed to malfunction in the country, thereby jeopardizing the injured and existing patients' lives and safety.

Even as the government has formed specialised organisations and various policies and frameworks for disaster management as well as healthcare infrastructure safety, resilience in the healthcare infrastructure has not improved significantly. This also implies that hospital disaster managers encounter major challenges in terms of a lack of coordination, communication challenges, lack of preparedness, and logistic deficiencies.

Additionally, hospital staff and medical practitioners in many facilities have low awareness of disaster management concepts and disaster drills. Mismanagement and unpreparedness of hospitals have been observed through case examples of the Chennai floods, 2015, and Jammu and Kashmir floods, 2014, where hospitals were completely inundated and destroyed, owing to unawareness and lack of relief and rescue activities, in addition to the design failure and absence of resilient planning and measures.

This chapter also includes the reviews from industry experts, whose invaluable inputs to a subjective questionnaire help validate the goal of the study conducted in this book. While the literature is a significant source of authenticated knowledge, expert reviews from a range of professionals in construction, planning, sustainability, and healthcare industries help connect information and learnings in a practical and tangible format.

It is possible that a healthcare facility may never face an EWE in its lifetime; however, the structure and staff need to be aware, be prepared, and have robust mechanisms and drills in place to prevent maximum losses to patients, equipment, and structures.

## References

Barnagarwala, T. (2017). Mumbai rains: Govt hospitals flooded, patients face infection risk. *Indian Express*. Retrieved from https://indianexpress.com/article/cities/mumbai/mumbai-rains-govt-hospitals-flooded-patients-face-infection-risk-4820020/%

Bruijn, K. D., Buurman, J., Mens, M., Dahm, R., & Klijn, F. (2017). Resilience in practice: Five principles to enable societies to cope with extreme weather events. *Environmental Science & Policy*, 21–30.

Ghaffar, A., Reddy, K. S., & Singhi, M. (2004). Burden of non-communicable diseases in South Asia. *British Medical Journal*, 328, 807–810.

Hussain, M. (2014, September 27). Jammu and Kashmir floods: Srinagar hospitals may take a month to restore services. *The Economic Times*. Retrieved from https://economictimes.indiatimes.com/news/politics-and-nation/jammu-and-kashmir-floods-srinagar-hospitals-may-take-a-month-to-restore-services/articleshow/43578885.cms

Jha, A., Basu, R., & Basu, A. (2016). Studying policy changes in disaster management in India: A tale of two cyclones. *Disaster Medicine and Public Health*, 10(1), 42–46.

Joshipura, M. (2008). Trauma care in India: Current scenario. *World Journal of Surgery*, 32(8), 1613–1617.

Kar, N., Jagadisha, Sharma, P., Murali, N., & Mehrotra, S. (2004). Mental health consequences of the trauma of super-cyclone 1999 in Orissa. *Indian Journal of Psychiatry,* 46(3), 228–237.

Khandelwal, S. K., Jhingan, H. P., Ramesh, S., Gupta, R. K., & Srivastava, V. K. (2004). India mental health country profile. *International,* 16(1–2), 126–141.

Krishnan, S., & Patnaik, I. (2018, October 30). *Health and Disaster Risk Management in India.* New Delhi: National Institute of Public Finance and Policy.

Krishnan, V. (2015, December 16). Hospitals unprepared for natural disasters. *The Hindu.* Retrieved from www.thehindu.com/news/national/fix-our-cities-hospitals-unprepared-for-natural-disasters/article7992957.ece

Mehta, S. (2006). Disaster and mass casualty management in a hospital: How well are we prepared? *Journal of Postgraduate Medicine,* 89–90.

Misra, A., Singhal, N., Sivakumar, B., Bhagat, N. J., & Khurana, L. (2011). Nutrition transition in India: secular trends in dietary intake and their relationship to diet-related non-communicable diseases. *Journal of Diabetes,* 3(4), 278–292.

Myers, M. F., Rogers, D. J., Cox, J., Flahault, A., & Hay, S. I. (2000). Forecasting disease risk for increased epidemic preparedness in public health. *Advances in Parasitology,* 47, 309–330.

Nia, S. P., & Kulatunga, U. (2017). Safety and security of hospitals during natural disasters: Challenges of disaster managers. *International Journal of Safety and Security Engineering,* 234–246.

Patel, V., Chatterji, S., Chisholm, D., Ebrahim, S., Gopalakrishna, G., Mathers, C., . . . Reddy, K. S. (2011). Chronic diseases and injuries in India. *Lancet,* 377, 413–428.

Phalkey, R., Dash, S. R., Mukhopadhyay, A., Ranzinger, S. R., & Marx, M. (2012). Prepared to react? Assessing the functional capacity of the primary health care system in rural Orissa, India to respond to the devastating flood of September 2008. *Global Health Action.*

Rastogi, T., Vaz, M., Spiegelman, D., Reddy, K. S., Bharathi, A. V., Stampfer, M. J., . . . Ascherio, A. (2004). Physical activity and risk of coronary heart disease in India. *International Journal of Epidemiology,* 33(4), 759–767.

Reddy, S. K., Shah, B., Varghese, C., & Ramadoss, A. (2005). Responding to the threat of chronic diseases in India. *Lancet,* 366, 1744–1749.

Saran, S. (2019, November 8). *Ministry of External Affairs – Government of India.* Retrieved from www.mea.gov.in: https://mea.gov.in/articles-in-indian-media.htm?dtl/32018/Indias_Climate_Change_Policy_Towards_a_Better_Future

Shah, B., & Mathur, P. (2010). Surveillance of cardiovascular disease risk factors in India: The need & scope. *The Indian Journal of Medical Research,* 132(5), 634–642.

Sharan, P., Chaudhary, G., Kavathekar, S. A., & Saxena, S. (1996). Preliminary report of psychiatric disorders in survivors of a severe earthquake. *The American Journal of Psychiatry,* 153(4), 556–558.

Sharma, S., Koushal, V., & Pandey, N. (2016). Are our hospitals prepared for disasters? Evaluation of health-care staff vis-à-vis disaster management at a public hospital in India. *International Journal of Health System and Disaster Management,* 63–66.

Stalin, J. S. (2018, August 27). 125-year-old hospital, among the best in country, ruined in Kerala floods. *NDTV.* Retrieved from www.ndtv.com/kerala-news/125-year-old-hospital-among-the-best-in-country-ruined-in-kerala-floods-1906970

Sur, D., Dutta, P., Nair, G. B., & Bhattacharya, S. K. (2000). Severe cholera outbreak following floods in a northern district of West Bengal. *Indian Journal of Medical Research,* 112, 178–182.

(UCL)-CRED, L. (2015). *EM-DAT: The Emergency Events Database*. Kerala: Universite catholique de.

UNISDR. (2009). *UNISDR Terminology on Disaster Risk Reduction*. Geneva: United Nations International Strategy for Disaster Reduction.

United Nations Development Programme. (2017). *Mainstreaming Disaster Risk Reduction & Climate Change Adaptation in District Level Planning*. New Delhi: United Nations Development Programme.

WHO. (2000). Leptospirosis, India: report of the investigation of a post-cyclone outbreak in Orissa, November 1999. *Weekly Epidemiological Record*, 75(27), 217–223.

Yokomatsu, M., & Hochrainer-Stigler, S. (2020). *Disaster Risk Reduction and Resilience*. Singapore: Springer.

# 3 Impact of extreme weather events on the critical infrastructure

## 3.1 Overview

With the existing critical and healthcare infrastructure being at significant risk owing to climate change manifestations, including EWEs, the potential losses in value and service can turn out to be momentous. In the absence of a rationale for resource allocation, these facilities might be subject to overloading of resources to encourage mitigation measures, which may or may not be effective. Through case examples studied in this chapter, the value losses faced by various infrastructure sectors have been highlighted. Figure 3.1 recognises the value losses that the existing infrastructure is subject to due to a lack of appropriate resource allocation to ensure mitigation measures.

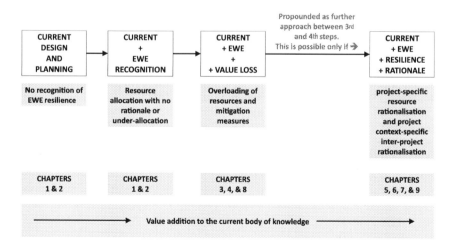

*Figure 3.1* Process of incorporating resilience: losses to infrastructure in the absence of rational resource allocation.

DOI: 10.1201/9781003393108-3

## 3.2    Structure of the chapter

Chapter 3 picks up the discourse on climate change and EWEs and assesses the impact on the critical infrastructure through case examples of the EWEs that occurred in the previous decade. Through the literature, the global and Indian scenarios of the response to EWEs is established. Reforms and disaster management mechanisms used in the country are discussed, which drives the study to determine the need for employing and practising resilience to EWEs over response. Figure 3.2 explains the structure and outcome of this chapter.

*Figure 3.2* Structure and overview of Chapter 3.

## 3.3    Inclusion of critical infrastructure in climate change response initiatives

As has been noted in the previous chapter, the NAPCC initiative incorporates the following aspects in detail:

- Enhancing energy efficiency
- Solar energy
- Conserving water
- Creating a sustainable urban habitat
- Creating a strategic knowledge platform
- Sustaining the fragile Himalayan ecosystem
- Creating a green India through expanded forests
- Making agriculture sustainable

However, it has been observed that the programme does not include the impact and efforts specifically targeted at the healthcare/critical infrastructure. Further, the design/construction aspects have not been incorporated, thereby leaving the theme still unaddressed.

## 3.4    Impact of extreme weather events on critical infrastructure

Built infrastructure, including critical infrastructure (CI), is intertwined with the natural environment, and the health of the infrastructure is closely dependent on the health of the ecology and climate. As a result, it is crucial that the infrastructure, especially CI, is resilient to extreme conditions of the weather/climate.

EWEs pose a severe threat to the built infrastructure, especially due to their changing frequency and intensity. Due to this, the operational resilience of individual CIs encounters complex challenges. Additionally, the infrastructure systems are highly dependent on each other, which poses a significant risk of cascading effects in the case of failure or damage. It is therefore imperative that when mitigation, protection, and adaptation measures are considered, the potential future extreme events and natural disasters must be considered to include predicted and actual instances of CI failures. Hence, when these potential risks due to future disasters are considered, it may be pointed out that the current measures are not sufficient; the CIs need to be protected by implementing different or new measures or by mitigating the impacts of inevitable CI failures (Raikkonen et al., 2016).

The manifestations of climate change have escalated in the previous decades, which have affected the intensity and frequency of natural hazards. These natural hazards and EWEs have only intensified, along with rising sea levels, higher temperatures, varying heat and cold waves, changing rainfall patterns, droughts, and floods. India experiences an extensive variation of EWEs, with a wide spectrum of impacts, owing to the geographical and topographical variations, in addition to varied climates and seasons across the country. The unpredictability of the scale and severity of some of these events poses serious risks to the built infrastructure, especially CI. Even as countries across the world grapple with resisting and reversing climate change, it is nevertheless important that CI be designed and built to incorporate resilience.

Further, maintenance and development costs for CI are high, considering that these infrastructure systems are required to function efficiently under the most challenging circumstances, while also maintaining realistic economic and functional design lives. With increasing scientific evidence indicating a higher likelihood of the frequency and severity of EWEs in the future, the disruption of the functioning and performance of CI is also projected to intensify. Hence, mitigation, protection, and adaptation of CI against EWEs must be ensured simultaneously (Tagg et al., 2016).

A detailed study of various EWEs in India is presented here, convening the intensity of these events, locations, causes of EWEs, and focus on the impacts (direct and cascading) on CI.

The data presented here is collected from various sources and may be approximate. However, the intent is to present the scale and magnitude of the problems.

### 3.4.1    *Kerala floods (2018–2019)*

Heavy monsoon rainfall in the state of Kerala (257% more than usual rainfall) led to a rise in water levels in dams, close to the overflow levels. As a result, most of these dams were opened, causing flooding in the local low-lying areas. Affecting 2 lakh people directly, the floods completely destroyed 2000 houses, partially damaged

15,000 houses, and led to a loss of properties worth Rs. 40000 Cr. Four hundred and fifty people lost their lives, and more than 36,000 people were displaced. Observed impacts on critical infrastructure have been described as follows:

➢ *Transport*

- Public transportation system collapsed in many parts of the state
- Cochin International Airport suspended all flights for two weeks at a loss of 300 Cr
- Kochi Metro Rail suspended services because the metro yard got flooded
- Parts of national highways submerged
- Train services suspended

➢ *Healthcare*

- Many hospitals cancelled routine operations
- Surge in patients
- Some hospitals were waterlogged
- Severe staff shortage
- Most hospitals saw a decline in staff strength by 30% to 35%; bed occupancy increased by 80% to 90%
- Liquid oxygen supply affected due to inaccessible roads

➢ *Telecom/IT*

- The fibreoptic cable was cut
- Base transceiver stations affected
- Services affected in low-lying areas
- Ten per cent of the telecom services of Kerala were impacted

➢ *Water*

- Availability of fresh/drinking water was a major crisis
- Water pumping from major treatment plants was stopped due to a rise in water level or power failure
- Treatment plants were the worst affected, and the drinking water supply was disrupted
- Threat of water-borne illnesses such as cholera, typhoid, hepatitis, and leptospirosis

➢ *Energy*

- Kerala State Electricity Board stopped power generation for a few days because generator turbines were damaged
- Four thousand transformers switched off to avoid mishaps
- Major power outages
- Telecom services affected

➢ *Agriculture*

- Coffee, rubber, cardamom, and black pepper plantations affected

### 3.4.2 Cyclone Fani (2019)

Cyclone Fani was observed to be an unusual occurrence and was recorded as the longest-ever observed lifecycle of a cyclone over the Bay of Bengal. The forecast of its path was revised nine times, and the reported maximum sustained surface wind speed was 175–180 kilometres per hour. The cyclone caused damage to 36,1743 houses, 1031 health facilities, 5735 schools, 107 universities and colleges, 113 monument sites, and 6441 public buildings. Additionally, 48.61 lakh workers were severely impacted, and 19,734 Ha of perennial crops were affected. Six thousand four hundred and forty-one public buildings suffered damage and losses worth Rs. 539 crores. On a macro-economic scale, damage and losses were estimated at 5% of GSDP of the state. Observed impacts on critical infrastructure have been described as follows:

➢ *Healthcare*

- A reported 1031 health facilities affected
- Major damages related to infrastructure, electricity, water, air-conditioning, and communication systems
- Boundary walls and iron grills over boundary walls destroyed
- Standards and codes not followed for public hospital buildings

➢ *Transport*

- Damage to street furniture
- Damage of INR 326.2 crore for all roads including national highways, state roads, rural, and urban local bodies' (ULB) roads

➢ *Energy*

- Damage to transmission system was minor
- Damage to the distribution system: 80,600 km of distribution lines, 202 distribution substations, and 13,400 transformers

➢ *Telecom/IT*

- Telecom infrastructure significantly damaged
- Mobile and internet services disrupted

➢ *Water*

- Rural areas: 1088 piped water supply schemes (49%) suffered damage
- A reported 100,926 (18.9%) toilets constructed under Swachh Bharat Mission (Gramin) partially damaged
- Damage to water supply schemes affecting 337 urban systems
- Overall damages: INR 167.47 Cr
- Losses estimated at INR 28.65 Cr

➢ *Agriculture*

- Horticulture and cash crops were severely affected: 55% of total damage and loss in the sector

- Temporary loss of livelihoods, employment, and agri-income
- Production losses expected to last several years
- Damage and losses to livestock were estimated at Rs. 1206.81 Cr

## ➢ *Housing*

- A reported 3.62 lakh houses (2.96 lakh in rural and 66,040 in urban areas) damaged
- Several women, people with disabilities, and other socially and economically vulnerable groups severely affected

### 3.4.3   *Kotrupi landslide (2017)*

The Kotrupi landslide was the result of slope instability in a region subject to repeated landslides. With the debris of the previous landslides still present in addition to the existence of the fault line, cracks formed on the slope. This allowed the rainwater to percolate into the slope. Further, the cloudburst, which is a recurrent phenomenon (owing to the change in rainfall patterns), caused momentous rainfall. The landslide resulted in 47 fatalities, damaged several hutments, and wiped out an entire village. The flow of Rupi Nullah was blocked after the occurrence and a lake was formed. Observed impacts on CI have been described as follows:

## ➢ *Transport*

- Landslide damaged affected road up to a stretch of 350 metres
- No trace of national highway NH 154 at Kotrupi up to 350 metres
- Several villages cut off from district headquarters due to breaching of road and bridge

## ➢ *Vehicles and equipment*

- Two Himachal Road Transport Corporation (HRTC) buses, a few bikes and vegetable-carrying vehicles buried under the debris

## ➢ *Tourism*

- Disrupted tourism and commercial as well as social activities

### 3.4.4   *Mumbai floods (2017)*

A consequence of extreme rainfall, the Mumbai floods caused 34 fatalities and direct economic damages estimated at almost Rs. 147 Cr. Flood waters caused weakening of foundations, which posed a major risk of collapse to buildings more than 100 years old. Observed impacts on CI have been described as follows:

## ➢ *Healthcare*

- Lower floors of various hospitals were inundated
- Medical staff forced to wade through wards knee-high in filthy water to move patients to the first floor

> *Transport*

- Suburban railway network paralysed
- Central Railway suspended services
- Traffic jams
- Flight operations hit due to extremely poor visibility

> *Energy*

- Power shut off to western and eastern suburbs
- Outages confirmed as preventive measures by power utility firms to prevent electrocutions

> *Housing*

- Societies had more than three-foot-high water levels in the area
- Holes drilled by residents inside houses to allow for faster drainage

### 3.4.5   *Chennai floods (2015)*

The floods in Chennai were attributed to the increased rainfall owing to the inevitable changes in weather patterns as a consequence of climate change. In addition, the encroachment of water bodies and wetlands, development of transportation networks along major water courses, increase in hard-paved areas and concrete surfaces that reduce percolation of water into the ground, decrease in green spaces and open areas, inadequate drainage systems, and heavy siltation along drainage channels added to the enhanced impacts of flooding. The floods caused 324 fatalities, affected more than 4 million people, caused damage to 1 lakh houses, and washed away 10,000 km of roads. Economic damages due to the floods were estimated at around Rs. 20000 Cr. Observed impacts on CI have been described as follows:

> *Healthcare*

- Access affected due to waterlogging
- Interruption of public services, medicine supply, staff and communication due to inundation
- Clinical issues, hygiene, post-flood disease control challenges
- Acute respiratory tract infections, acute gastroenteritis, fever, skin problems

> *Transport*

- Air, road, and rail services remained suspended due to deluge
- Access to health service affected
- Route planning, priority management, implementing mechanisms to mitigate impacts of flooding, coordination with fishermen community, access to fuel affected

> *Energy*

- A total of 50 sub-stations, 16,158 transformers, and 25.6 lakh connections hit
- Losses to infrastructure at Rs. 350 Cr, revenue losses of Rs. 470 Cr.

- Four thousand transformers switched off to avoid mishaps, creating power outages
- Lack of electricity affected telecom services

➢ *Telecom*

- Major IT companies in some areas inundated
- Information and communication technology (ICT) companies halted work

➢ *Water*

- Shortage of safe drinking water
- Lack of sanitation facilities
- No access to water for sanitation
- Poor menstrual hygiene management system
- No waste management

➢ *Agriculture*

- Agriculture crops destroyed
- Damage to agricultural lands due to sand casting and heavy siltation
- Loss of livestock: 9992; 5223 poultry birds died
- Standing crops completely submerged and damaged
- Impact on food supply chains

➢ *Housing*

- A reported 359,171 huts damaged, 65 pucca houses severely damaged, and 13,601 partly damaged
- Rapid deterioration of roofs
- Slum housing schemes submerged: 2,690,660 dwelling units inundated with levels of water ranging up to eight feet

### 3.4.6   *Cyclone Hudhud (2014)*

The formation of high-speed winds over warm ocean basins led to the intensification of Cyclone Hudhud into a severe storm. In Andhra Pradesh, 9.2 million people in over 320 villages in four districts were affected, with 61 casualties. In Odisha, 9657 villages in 151 districts were affected, with three casualties. The affected regions faced massive losses in terms of livelihood, with extensive damage to agricultural and horticultural crops. A reported 752,540 households were severely affected, with the total damages estimated at Rs. 13,263 Cr. Observed impacts on CI have been described as follows:

➢ *Healthcare*

- Shortage of safe drinking water
- Access to health services restricted due to blockage of roads
- Onset of diarrhoea and dehydration and vector-borne diseases
- Injuries: lacerations, broken limbs, water inhalation and ingestion
- Acute respiratory infections, skin infections, diarrhoeal diseases

> *Transport*

- Andhra Pradesh: 3880 km of roads and 53 buildings were damaged
- Estimated loss of Rs. 1111.80 crore.

> *Water*

- Water sources inundated in flooded areas and contaminated
- Extensive damage to pumping equipment, pipes, and tube wells

> *Agriculture*

- Odisha: standing crops extent of loss up to 50%
- Seven hundred and eighteen craftsmen affected because of damage of equipment and raw/finished materials
- Fish farms: 90 hectares damaged
- One hundred and ninety-eight large animals and 472 small animals lost; 39,350 livestock and poultry affected.
- Andhra Pradesh: 237,854 hectares damaged at an estimated loss of Rs. 947.9 Cr.
- Affected horticultural land: 87,984 hectares
- Value of losses: Rs. 1339.23 Cr
- Sericulture: estimated loss of Rs. 1.73 Cr.
- One thousand four hundred and six big animals, 4468 small animals, and 4,634,706 poultry killed

> *Housing*

- Eight pucca (permanent) houses and 883 kutcha (temporary) houses fully damaged
- Nine pucca (permanent) houses and 2749 kutcha (temporary) houses severely damaged
- Three hundred and forty-three pucca (permanent) houses and 40,244 kutcha (temporary) houses partially damaged
- Shelters and houses in low-lying areas waterlogged
- Households experienced loss of or damage to household assets

> *Education*

- State government declared all schools to remain closed for 15 days
- Schools used as relief camps
- Access to schools affected due to subsequent flooding

> *Telecom*

- Land telephone lines disrupted for two days
- Mobile phone networks disrupted for one day
- Seventy-three villages disconnected to communication facilities for two days
- Non-availability of diesel, automated teller machines (ATMs), and lack of right of way

### 3.4.7   *Cyclone Phailin (2013)*

Cyclone Phailin was recorded as the most intense tropical cyclone in the Indian subcontinent (until Cyclone Amphan in 2020) and was categorised as a severe cyclonic storm by the IMD. With the maximum wind speed recorded at 260 kmph, the storm caused 44 casualties and affected 13 million lives. A reported 256,633 rural houses were damaged, and 1,292,967 Ha of crops sustained more than 50% loss. All surface communication systems, power supply, telecommunication, and water supply lines were severely disrupted. The economic loss was estimated at about Rs. 14373 Cr. Observed impacts on CI have been described as follows:

> *Transport*

- Damage to embankments, road shoulders, and pavement caused by rain cuts and inundation
- Road blockage due to falling of trees
- Two hundred and forty-five km of urban roads and 66.6 km of roadside drains destroyed

> *Energy*

- Extensive damage to electrical transmission and distribution networks
- Total damage of US$169 million

> *Water*

- Severely affected existing rural infrastructure
- Crippled access to water and sanitation services
- Three thousand and forty piped water supply systems and 16,2170 tube/bore wells damaged
- Two thousand and five hundred RWSS and 140,000 tube wells damaged due to consequent floods

> *Agriculture*

- Severe crop damage due to submergence of crop fields
- Total crop area affected: 1.3 mha

> *Housing*

- Kutcha (temporary) houses severely damaged due to high-speed winds and associated rainfall
- A reported 256,633 units damaged in rural areas

> *Healthcare*

- Overloading and restricted access to healthcare buildings
- Eight hundred and seventy health centres and hospitals affected

### 3.4.8 Delhi floods (2013)

Floods in Delhi are primarily a consequence of the following factors:

- Change in agricultural land use
- Loss of forest cover
- Massive change in built-up area in watersheds
- Encroachment of flood plains by the Yamuna River
- Poor planning
- Substandard construction of housing structures in high-risk zones
- High population densities

Adding to this, the increase in concrete and hard surfaces led to increased surface run-off, thereby causing flash floods. A huge amount of water was released from the Hathnikund Barrage, flooding the Ring Road at several places. In addition to road and rail traffic being affected, 8000 people and 57 animals had to be shifted to safer places. Observed impacts on CI have been described as follows:

➢ *Transport*

- Increase in travel time

➢ *Water*

- Lack of integrated planning in drainage for storm water
- Encroachment by slum dwellers along the drains caused choking of drains and flooding in the upstream areas due to reduced carrying capacity

### 3.4.9 Uttarakhand floods (2013)

Torrential rains, combined with the probable collapse of Chorabari Lake, triggered major landslides at numerous locations in the state of Uttarakhand. Unprecedented devastation was recorded in Kedarnath shrine and adjacent areas, with extreme losses to life and property. Due to damaged roads, landslides, and debris induced by flash floods, more than 1 lakh people were stranded in different areas for several days. The flash floods caused 169 casualties, with 4021 people reported missing and over 5700 people presumed dead. The economy of the state was impacted significantly owing to a major decline in revenue generated from tourism. A reported 10,171 micro, small, and medium enterprises were affected, with severe unemployment among the populace. Observed impacts on CI have been described as follows:

➢ *Healthcare*

- Nine hundred and thirty household toilets washed away
- A reported 14,526 meters of drains damaged
- No incidence of outbreak of epidemic or infectious disease

- Mass cremation
- Breakdown of potable water supply

➢ *Transport*

- Intense erosion of riverbanks, large sections of roads, and bridges washed away
- Two thousand one hundred and seventy-four roads, 85 motor bridges, and 140 bridle bridges damaged
- Large numbers of vehicles damaged
- Road connectivity to 4200 villages lost
- People remained stranded, disconnected, and isolated for weeks

➢ *Energy*

- Heavy damage to ongoing HEPs and existing power distribution system
- Most parts of these HEP sites washed away
- Major parts of distribution systems damaged
- Distributions substations damaged
- Disruption of power supply to about 3758 villages

➢ *Telecom*

- Breakdown of service communication
- Damaged telecommunication infrastructure
- Disruption in wireless communication

➢ *Water*

- Heavy deposition of silt caused damage to intake wells and treatment plants of the water supply schemes
- A reported 112,000 people affected because of reduced coverage of municipal water supply systems
- Fifty water intake stations and tube wells and 40 km of pipelines severely damaged
- Twenty km of roadside drains washed away
- Water supply and sanitation services in rural areas affected and damaged
- Eight thousand seven hundred and twenty-eight habitations and 1129 million people affected

➢ *Agriculture*

- Agricultural lands eroded mainly on slopes
- Crops damaged due to inundation by flood water
- Siltation in agricultural fields
- Two thousand and ten ha cropped area affected and 1206 ha land washed away
- Total silted land area: 944 ha
- Fishery activities severely affected

### 3.4.10   Ladakh flash floods (2010)

Heavy rains due to cloudburst led to very high discharge in Leh Nallah, with the velocity of gushing water recorded in the range of 7 m/s to 20 m/s. The massive water discharge into the Nallah caused devastating flash floods, affecting more than 9000 people. Seventy-one villages were impacted in Leh, with damage to 1440 houses and 660 ha of crop land area. The value of damage to houses was estimated at Rs. 40.03 Cr, and value of damage to public utilities was estimated to be Rs. 158 Cr. The flash floods caused 234 casualties, along with 64 missing persons, 424 injured, and 1329 animals lost. Observed impacts on CI have been described as follows:

➤ *Healthcare*

- Civil medical and health facilities severely affected
- District civil hospital flooded and filled with debris
- Only two hospitals in the area: the government civil hospital and army hospital; during flash floods, the civil hospital flooded and was rendered dysfunctional

➤ *Transport*

- Road transport severely disrupted
- Roads washed away and blocked with debris
- Major damage caused to 26 different roadways including link roads, airport roads, and internal roads
- Approximately 688.80 km of roads damaged
- A reported 622.34 km of road totally under flood waters
- Twenty-nine bridges damaged, out of which ten completely washed away

➤ *Telecom*

- Main mobile network rendered dysfunctional
- Other mobile networks had limited connectivity
- Radio station transmitter, telephone exchange, mobile phone towers, and various communication systems fully destroyed

➤ *Water*

- Pumping station washed away, which disrupted the water supply
- Large number of toilets were non-functional because they were filled with silt
- Stagnant water, which led to a risk of contamination
- Quality of drinking water deteriorated
- Headworks of most Zamindari khuls/canals destroyed
- Heavy damages to irrigation khuls and footbridges under the Rural Development Department

➤ *Agriculture*

- Impending high risk of food shortage and crisis of hunger and malnutrition
- Food supplies set back due to unpredicted heavy downpour

- Food storage facilities flooded and washed away
- Total crop area affected: 660 hectares

> *Housing*

- Fully damaged kutcha (temporary) houses: 664
- Partly damaged houses – kutcha (temporary) and pucca (permanent): 783
- Number of huts damaged: 458
- Total number of houses damaged: 1447
- Total number of non-residential houses damaged: 458

### 3.4.11   *Bihar floods (2008–2020)*

Floods in Bihar have been observed to occur every year since the previous decade and have wreaked havoc on the lives and livelihoods of the populace, along with the infrastructure and agriculture. More than 3.3 million people were affected in the floods that occurred in 2020, with 434 casualties. The floods displaced 3 million people, and 300,000 houses were destroyed. Observed impacts on CI have been described as follows:

> *Transport*

- Embankment breach caused formation of new streams where no cross drainage works existed
- Flows in excess of design discharge of existing cross drainage structures resulted in collapse of bridges and culverts and severe damage to roads
- One thousand eight hundred and thirty km of roads fully or partially damaged
- One thousand and one hundred bridges and culverts damaged or destroyed
- One thousand six hundred and thirty-five km of rural roads destroyed
- Estimated loss at Rs. 5.7 billion

> *Agriculture*

- A reported 340,000 hectares of crops damaged

## 3.5   Impact of climate change and EWEs on healthcare infrastructure

Weather, climate, and the associated changes affect human health profoundly. EWEs not only cause tens of thousands of fatalities every year but also deteriorate the physical and psychological health of millions of people affected. EWEs such as droughts directly affect the food supply and nutrition, consequently affecting the incidence of diseases linked to malnutrition. Events such as floods and cyclones can trigger outbreaks of infectious diseases in addition to structural and operational damage to the healthcare infrastructure and overwhelming medical services at the most critical times of need.

Climate variability has a significant impact on human health and can cause diseases like malaria and diarrhoea, leading to illness, suffering, and death to millions.

In the long run, climate change may threaten to exacerbate these problems, while also undermining social protection systems, healthcare systems, water supplies, food supplies, and other ecosystems vital for human health in the future (World Health Organisation, 2012).

### 3.5.1   *Impact on human health*

Human health is influenced by psychological, social, and political responses to the changing environment in addition to other factors such as economic changes and changing demographics. These effects on human health can be indirect, such as population displacement leading to undernutrition, as well as direct, such as an increase in temperatures causing heat-related illnesses and death.

As depicted in Figure 3.3, climate change can affect health through three primary exposure pathways, which are:

a)  Direct exposure through weather variables such as storms and heat
b)  Indirect exposure through natural systems such as disease vectors
c)  Pathways significantly mediated through human systems such as malnutrition

The moderating influences mentioned under the section Environmental Conditions in the figure illustrate how exposure pathways of climate change manifest in a particular population. The section Public Health Capability and Adaptation indicates that factors such as socio-economic conditions, adaptation measures,

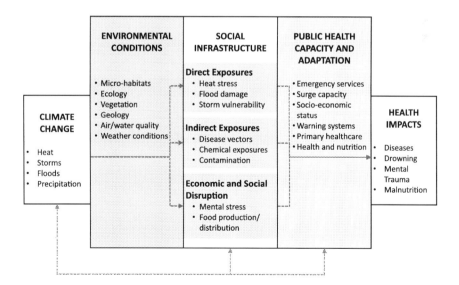

*Figure 3.3* Pathways by which climate change affects health.
Source: Adapted from (Smith et al., 2014)

and background public health moderate the level to which the three types of exposure translate to actual health liability. The arrows at the bottom of the diagram indicate that there may be negative or positive feedback mechanisms between societal infrastructure, public health, climate change, and adaptation measures (Pryor, 2017).

Populations with inadequate or nominal access to basic and essential public healthcare services and medical facilities are more vulnerable to the adverse impacts due to climate variability. The socio-economic and physical conditions of infrastructure that support the well-being of human settlements and populations also have an influence on the health and associated risks in the communities (this includes sanitation facilities, adequate provision of clean water for drinking and washing, adequate supply of power, and waste management systems) (Smith et al., 2014).

### 3.5.2    *Impact on healthcare structures*

An operational framework devised by the World Health Organization (WHO) formulates the strategies for the development of climate-resilient healthcare systems across the globe. The framework states that the guidelines and building code provisions that regulate the construction, development, and maintenance of health facilities must also incorporate the current and predicted climate risks posed to the structures. Resilient healthcare systems have the inherent capacity to adapt to disruptions caused during the occurrence of EWEs, including their vital environmental services, such as drinking water supply and sanitation services (World Health Organization, 2009).

Other manifestations of climate change, such as heat waves, cold snaps, rises in sea level, wildfires, and storms, can cause critical system failures, thereby leading to disruption in services, temporary evacuation, and dysfunction of healthcare facilities. Consequently, health facilities may need to be evacuated and closed temporarily or permanently, further leading to health emergencies for victims, existing patients, and affected communities. Climate threats and the resultant extreme weather conditions have also been observed to cause first-order impacts such as deterioration in air quality, forest fires, or changes in disease vectors, such as mosquitos and ticks. As cascading impacts of such events, patient care and efficient delivery of healthcare services may get disrupted. It can therefore be inferred that healthcare facilities and operations may be subject to varying climatic conditions and loads that the buildings may not have been designed or accounted for (Poitras, 2020).

The normal functioning of hospitals and healthcare facilities can get disrupted temporarily or permanently due to disasters and associated emergencies, thereby significantly diminishing their capacity to deliver immediate medical care for the communities affected. Figure 3.4 indicates the impacts of climate change and disasters on healthcare facilities. Additionally, the extreme events and disasters can also wreak havoc on the physical infrastructure of the health facilities, leading to partial or complete losses in investment towards the operational, functional and

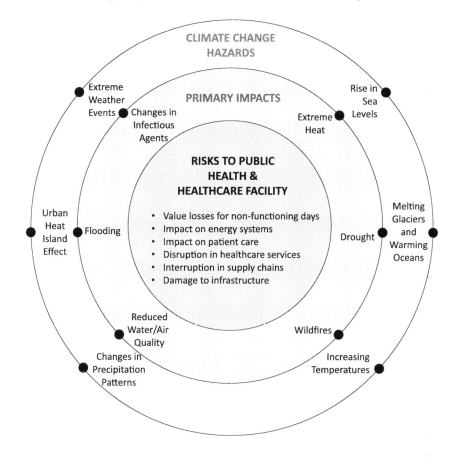

*Figure 3.4* Impacts of climate change on infrastructure and access to care.

*Source:* Adapted from (Aubie et al., 2018)

structural components of the building, including the medical equipment. This further causes severe negative impact to the social and economic development of the affected communities as well as the country's economy and development.

While emergency medical services are usually provided to the affected communities by primary care clinics, community health centres, and rural nursing posts during and after the occurrence of EWEs, most of the acute and critical health services are provided by hospitals. It is therefore essential to develop a process for assessment for the adaptive capacity of hospitals in order to gauge their endurance capacity in the event of an extreme weather condition. This can help develop more suitable facilities management, asset management, and property investment strategies so as to enable the hospitals and administrations to cope with the challenges presented at the time (Loosemore et al., 2011).

Healthcare facilities need to be prepared to cater to the sudden influx of patients and surge in demand in case of emergency, in addition to the challenges of infection control and decontamination of the facility. When a health facility is directly affected due to a catastrophe, the safety of patients, personnel, and staff needs to be ascertained while making the critical decision to evacuate or continue operations. Hence, the healthcare facility also needs to have emergency planning in place to ensure the preparedness of key personnel to perform their roles in case of emergency. Further, the structural and non-structural components and the necessary emergency systems must also be able to bear the surge in demand (Abo, 2008).

## 3.6    Status of response to disasters and EWEs in India

### 3.6.1    *Disaster management reform in India*

At the time when disaster management reforms were not devised, 40 million hectares of the Indian landmass were recorded to be vulnerable to floods, 60% to earthquakes, 68% to drought, and 3.29 million sq. km. to cyclones. Many parts of the Indian subcontinent encountered regular flooding in river plains. High vulnerability and fatalities due to natural calamities were revealed in the records, which triggered the Indian government and scholars to view this domain of public policy with a vigorous sense of urgency, keeping in mind the high vulnerability of the country and the significant devastation caused by disasters (Erramilli, 2008).

Dissemination of the knowledge of best practices and global experience and the exposure thereof gained momentum and resonated with the objectives of disaster management research. The United Nations declared the 1990s the International Decade for Natural Disaster Reduction (IDNDR). A transition from a relief-oriented approach to one based on mitigation and prevention was introduced by the 1994 Yokohama Strategy of the IDNDR. A joint programme for disaster risk mitigation was initiated in 2002 by the Government of India and the United Nations Development Programme (GoI-UNDP), with the assistance of the United States Agency for International Development (USAID) and European Union (EU). Supported by 36 international agencies, such as the USAID, the 17 most disaster-prone states were targeted by the programme for capacity building and the development of climate forecasting systems. Further, India received the largest aid from the World Bank for disaster management programmes in addition to increased exposure to international norms and standards (Erramilli, 2008).

These comprehensively developed disaster management reforms were further revised and refined to integrate prevention and long-term mitigation requirements. The IMD and the Central Waters Commission (CWC) were responsible for the modernisation and upgradation of early warning systems and flood forecasting. The Bureau of Indian Standards (BIS) carried out the development of safety codes and training programmes for municipal architects and engineers, in addition to the sensitisation of local government personnel. Town planning laws were assigned for modifications for all new construction projects, in addition to complete retrofitting of prioritised structures, and to adopt model town planning laws. After the promulgation of the Disaster Management Act in 2005, the NIDM was recognised as a statutory, nodal institution. This paradigm shift was considered to be a comprehensive overhaul, symbolising 'double-loop' learning as far as federal policy making was concerned (Erramilli, 2008).

### 3.6.2 *Robustness of disaster management and response mechanism in India*

As recorded in the World Risk Index 2014, India is in the top 50% of all countries that are vulnerable to natural hazards. Further, India was severely lacking in its capacity to adapt and cope with these hazards. As a result, significant steps were taken by the national and state governments towards devising policies, plans, and legislation to deal with the risks posed by these natural hazards. A robust policy framework is provided in the Disaster Management Act of 2005 for disaster response, relief, and risk reduction. Additionally, SDMPs have been devised by many states and union territories. District management plans have been developed for 80% of the districts in the country. Several institutions such as the National Disaster Management Authority, NIDM, the Union Ministry of Home Affairs, and the state and district management authorities employ these policies into their action plans, which has been found effective in dealing with disasters (Bahadur et al., 2016).

However, it has been observed that there is further scope of strengthening the policy architecture for disaster risk management in India. With the guidelines, codes, and standards in place, response to disaster events has improved progressively over the years through incorporation of lessons learnt and solutions adapted. Nonetheless, the country's response to disasters in the past has been inhibited by several factors, including:

- Lack of early warning systems
- Lack of a national-level plan policy
- Absence of an institutional framework at the centre/state/district level
- Slow response from relief agencies
- Poor inter-sectoral coordination
- Poor community empowerment
- Lack of dedicated and trained search and rescue teams

(Srivastava, 2010).

The primary responsibility for managing disasters lies with the state governments, thereby making the SDMPs the key operational policies which guide disaster risk management actions across the country. In addition to psychosocial intervention, the disaster management approach needs administrative support and medical intervention.

### 3.6.3 *Quick response flow chart: NIDM*

The quick response mechanism is primarily dependent on the planning and preparation formulated during the L0 phase, in addition to the preparedness of the disaster team. Therefore, to ensure maximum response during the initial phase of a disaster event, it is crucial to conduct constant equipment checks and maintain a calendar of dry drills throughout the year. The quick response mechanism commences with a pre-disaster warning during the alert stage. However, in certain disasters such as flash floods, earthquakes, or accident-related disasters, a reasonable warning may not be possible, thereby reducing the feasibility of employing this mechanism (National Disaster Response Plan, 2001).

### *3.6.4    Agencies authorised to issue warnings*

Forecasting has been identified as the most effective way to indicate the onset of disasters. The information obtained through forecasting should be communicated through a warning system to the community which is prone to the disaster. However, haphazard and indiscriminate warning may lead to a lack of appropriate response in the community. Hence, it is essential to designate an officer responsible for every disaster to issue the disaster warning. The agencies authorised to issue warnings in case of any disasters have been identified in Table 3.1. Adequate and timely warning is possible for disasters such as cyclones, floods, heat and cold waves, droughts, epidemics, pest attacks, chemical and industrial disasters, landslides, and fires (National Disaster Response Plan, 2001).

At the national level, the responsibility to issue the warning lies solely with the designated authority.

### *3.6.5    National disaster response policies review: status of disaster response*

During the preparation of the Tenth Five-Year Plan (2002–2007), the development strategy for the country realised the significance of the issues related to disaster management. Consequently, a chapter titled 'Disaster Management: The Development Perspective' was included in the document, which states that

> Five Year Plan documents have, historically, not included consideration of issues relating to the management and mitigation of natural disasters. The traditional perception has been limited to the idea of "calamity relief", which is seen essentially as a non-plan item of expenditure. However, the impact of major disasters cannot be mitigated by the provision of immediate relief alone, which is the primary focus of current calamity relief efforts.

*Table 3.1* Agencies authorised to issue warning in case of disaster: NDRP, 2001

| S. No. | Disasters | Agencies |
| --- | --- | --- |
| 1. | Floods | Indian Meteorological Department |
| 2. | Earthquakes | Indian Meteorological Department |
| 3. | Adverse Climatic Conditions and Cyclones | Indian Meteorological Department |
| 4. | Landslides | Indian Meteorological Department |
| 5. | Epidemics | Public Health Department |
| 6. | Road Accidents | Police |
| 7. | Fires | Police, Fire Services |
| 8. | Chemical/Industrial Disaster | Police, Industry, Other Designated Agency |

In a study conducted by Bahadur et al. (2016), the characteristics of disaster management and India's risk policies have been analysed. This review conducted for five states revealed the following:

## i. Responsibility for preparedness, risk reduction, recovery, response, and resilience

> ➢ SDMPs were found to include a high degree of sophistication in terms of disaster response.
> ➢ However, at the national level, the roles and responsibilities related to disaster risk management were observed to need more precision and detailed definition.
> ➢ The need for disaster risk reduction to be highlighted more prominently in the SDMPs was also observed.
> ➢ A significant deficiency is the lack of focus on disaster resilience; however, some states have attempted the same and are focusing on learning and working in partnership.

## ii. Financing for disasters

> ➢ Even as equal legal importance is given to financing for disaster risk reduction and disaster response at the national level, funding for risk reduction across states is limited, despite legal and legislative mandates for the same.
> ➢ In some states, disaster risk management officials prefer to mainstream funds for disaster risk reduction within other departments; others prefer to dedicate exclusive funds towards state disaster management authorities. Currently, risk reduction is practised only through bespoke projects.
> ➢ The evidence of usage of risk transfer mechanisms and public-private partnerships was scanty (Bahadur et al., 2016).

## iii. Assessing vulnerability to disasters

> ➢ The Vulnerability Atlas of India is used in the SDMPs, which is useful to establish an understanding of the exposure of specific geographic areas to disasters, but is not quite useful to understand the socio-economic vulnerabilities.
> ➢ Comprehensive vulnerability assessments need a huge amount of data, which is already being collected, but the existing scientific data needs to be layered with the socio-economic data to conduct a composite analysis for interactions of hazard exposure with vulnerability.
> ➢ Climate change concerns are overlooked in the SDMPs, but have scope of being included and used in the form of robust climate data or models (Bahadur et al., 2016).

## iv. Mainstreaming disaster risk management

> ➢ The need for mainstreaming disaster risk management was agreed upon by the state disaster management authorities in all initiatives and responsibilities of all government departments.

> ➤ Most of the SDMPs have detailed responsibilities for all sectors and departments in terms of disaster responses, but lack significantly in outlining pathways to mainstream risk reduction.
> ➤ Capacity building was found to be useful as a significant tool for mainstreaming disaster risk management across various sectors. These mainstreaming activities require expansion in order to include all stages of the disaster management cycle (Bahadur et al., 2016).

## v.   Promoting gender and social inclusion

> ➤ While the considerations for the necessities of marginalised groups and women were found to be included in the SDMPs, these were observed to be primarily in the context of disaster response.
> ➤ Certain SDMPs were also found to include demographic data divided by disability, sex, and age; however, this data is not incorporated currently in the vulnerability analysis.
> ➤ Community participation is also recognised in the SDMPs but lacks clarity on operational implementation.
> ➤ The village-level disaster management committees take into account social inclusion concerns, which are comprised of representatives from marginalised groups (Bahadur et al., 2016).

## vi.   Alignment of SDMPs with the Sendai Framework for Disaster Risk Reduction 2015–2030

> ➤ While the SDMPs were observed to address several objectives of the Sendai Framework, the targets can be reworked to include more precision and measurement of progress.
> ➤ Data collection by state disaster management authorities is usually conducted after the occurrence of a disaster. However, consistent and systematic collection of data based on pre-disaster conditions and observations can prove to be useful for the measurement of the state's ability to anticipate, predict, adapt to, and absorb the shocks and stresses from the disaster occurrences (Bahadur et al., 2016).

In summary, the report prepared by Bahadur et al. (2016) states that in addition to their current emphasis on disaster relief and response, the SDMPs also need to focus on all stages of the disaster management cycle. Various issues regarding financing for risk reduction activities and lack of clarity regarding roles and responsibilities need to be addressed in this regard.

## 3.7   The need to place resilience over response

Disaster response mechanism and policies in the Indian subcontinent towards natural hazards and EWEs have improved significantly over the years. However, similar progress has not been observed and incorporated towards resilience and risk reduction. While the country receives sizeable investments for disaster relief, recovery, and resilience, the infrastructure has not improved proportionately so as to be able to absorb the effects of a natural hazard. The haste to recover and reconstruct the lost structures, especially critical infrastructure, is predominant and often overlooks the need and implementation of inherent resilience in these structures as well as the communities. As a consequence, recurrent hazards result in similar patterns of damage and destruction, thereby causing even higher losses and damages.

It has also been observed and recorded globally that higher investments and efforts towards the front of a natural hazard/EWE in terms of resilience and preparedness have saved major losses, aided in reconstruction, and most importantly, reduced the loss of life. This is fundamentally based on the concept of gaining more from resilience than reconstruction. Heavier investments towards the front of an EWE can make infrastructure and communities resilient in the face of these extreme weather occurrences, thereby significantly reducing the need for rescue, recovery, relief, and reconstruction.

Achieving inherent resilience in infrastructure may incur high costs during conception and execution, yet it has been found to save lives, property, infrastructure, and financing at later stages that is usually disbursed towards rescue, relief, and reconstruction operations after the disaster strikes.

## 3.8   Summary

A detailed review of the impacts of EWEs on critical infrastructure, exemplified through cases of EWEs over the past decade, highlights the losses incurred in instances where the structure and community were not resilient. It can also be observed that in the case of Cyclone Fani, 2019, Odisha, the fatalities were noticeably low, which is due to the fact that the state government invested efficiently in resilience, risk reduction, and 'build-back-better' methodology after the previous cyclones wreaked havoc on CI every year. Investments from international organisations were directed towards appropriate application, and it was ensured that the funds and finances were input with minimal risk of failure.

Additionally, the response to EWEs and climate change in the Indian context is well-informed and detailed. However, along with the implementation of disaster management reforms and response mechanisms, the focus, again, needs to be directed towards achieving and placing resilience over response. Ensuring resilience may appear to be a heavy investment ahead of EWEs but has proven to significantly reduce the need for rescue and relief operations, as can be observed in case examples.

## References

Abo, J. (2008, September-December). Hospital and health facility emergency preparedness for safer communities and sustainable development. In *Safer Health Facilities from DRR Initiatives* (p. 4).

Aubie, V. G., Murdock, T., Sobie, S., & Hohenschau, D. (2018). *Lower Mainland Facilities Management: Moving towards Climate Resilient Health Facilities for Vancouver Coastal Health*. Vancouver: Vancouver Coastal Health.

Bahadur, A., Lovell, E., & Pichon, F. (2016). *Strengthening Disaster Risk Management in India: A Review of Five State Disaster Management Plans*. London: Climate Development Knowledge Network.

Erramilli, B. P. (2008). *Disaster Management in India: Analysis of Factors Impacting Capacity Building*. Atlanta: Georgia State University.

Loosemore, M., Carthey, J., Chandra, V., & Chand, A. M. (2011). Climate change risks and opportunities in hospital adaptation. *International Journal of Disaster Resilience in the Built Environment*, 210–221.

National Disaster Response Plan. (2001). *National Disaster Response Plan. Department of Agriculture and Cooperation*. New Delhi: National Centre for Disaster Management.

Poitras, A. (2020). *Climate Data Canada*. Retrieved from https://climatedata.ca/case-study/the-effects-of-climate-change-on-hospitals/

Pryor, L. (2017). *The Impacts of Climate Change on Health*. London: Institute & Faculty of Actuaries.

Raikkonen, M., Maki, K., Murtonen, M., Forssen, K., Tagg, A., Petiet, P., . . . McCord, M. (2016). A holistic approach for assessing impact of extreme weather on critical infrastructure. *International Journal of Safety and Security Engineering*, 171–180.

Smith, K., Woodward, A., Campbell-Lendrum, D., Chadee, D., Honda, Y., Liu, Q., . . . Sauerborn, R. (2014). Human health: Impacts, adaptation, and co-benefits. In C. Field, V. Barros, D. Dokken, K. Mach, M. Mastrandrea, T. Bilir, . . . L. White (eds.), *Climate Change 2014: Impacts, Adaptation, and Vulnerability. Part A: Global and Sectoral Aspects. Contribution of Working Group II to the Fifth Assessment Report of the Intergovernmental Panel on Climate Change* (pp. 709–754). Cambridge; New York: IPCC.

Srivastava, K. (2010). Disaster: Challenges and perspectives. *Industrial Psychiatry Journal*, 1–4.

Tagg, A., Räikkönen, M., Mäki, K., & Collell, M. R. (2016). Impact of extreme weather on critical infrastructure: the EU-INTACT risk framework. In *FLOODrisk 2016–3rd European Conference on Flood Risk Management*. Lyon: E3S Web of Conferences 7, 07007.

World Health Organisation. (2012). *Atlas of Health and Climate*. Geneva: WHO Press.

World Health Organization. (2009). *Vision 2030: The Resilience of Water Supply and Sanitation in the Face of Climate Change. Summary and Policy Implications*. Geneva: World Health Organization.

# 4 Public health systems and the impact of extreme weather events

## 4.1 Overview

The healthcare infrastructure and medical services are subject to threats of varying degrees depending on the location and topography of the site. Lack of appropriate resilience and risk reduction measures can considerably affect the accessibility of medical services at times of emergencies and extreme weather occurrences. Mapping of the health infrastructure to identify the lack of medical service availability and access is critical to allocate suitable resources for service provision as well as resilient planning and design. Figure 4.1 depicts the existing infrastructure and the consequences of a lack of rational resource provision to incorporate mitigation and resilience measures.

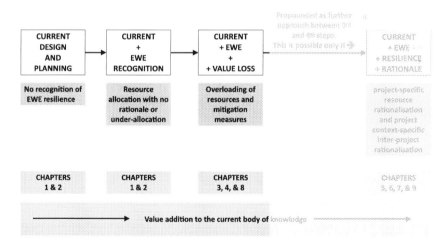

*Figure 4.1* Process of incorporating resilience: losses to healthcare due to lacking resilience.

## 4.2 Structure of the chapter

This chapter presents an overview of the Indian public health system which defines the provision of healthcare infrastructure in the country. The objective is

DOI: 10.1201/9781003393108-4

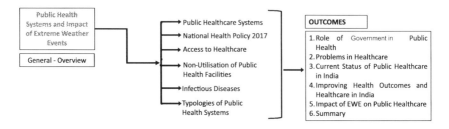

*Figure 4.2* Structure and overview of Chapter 4.

to understand the complexity and appraise the vulnerability that still exists as far as the risk of EWEs is concerned. Figure 4.2 explains the structure and outcome of this chapter.

## 4.3   Public healthcare systems

Reducing the population's exposure to diseases is the primary objective of public health services. This may be achieved through vector control, food safety regulations, monitoring of water and waste disposal systems, building citizen demand to ensure better outcomes from public health, and health education that can help improve personal health behaviour. The outcomes of public health services have intangible benefits, which further manifest and facilitate poverty reduction and economic growth (Gupta, 2006).

Poor public health conditions have been recorded to take a toll on the economy in multiple ways, including continued expenditure on combatting diseases which could have been eradicated, reduced attraction for investors and tourists, and reduced labour productivity. Communicable diseases can prove to be more dangerous for economically weaker sections of society.

A widely acceptable approach to improve public health is to adopt prevention over cure. Public health provisions in India focus significantly on public programmes and policies that furnish personal prophylactic interventions and curative care; however, public health activities have been neglected. As a result, the health indicators of India are much weaker in comparison to other Asian countries as well as globally (Gupta, 2006).

## 4.4   National Health Policy 2017

The primary aim of the National Health Policy (NHP) 2017 is to

inform, clarify, strengthen and prioritize the role of the Government in shaping health systems in all its dimensions – investments in health, organization of healthcare services, prevention of diseases and promotion of good health through cross sectoral actions, access to technologies, developing human resources, encouraging medical pluralism, building knowledge base, developing better financial protection strategies, strengthening regulation and health assurance.

Building on the changing context of public healthcare in the country, the NHP 2017 can be encapsulated in four aspects:

a) The development and progress of a robust healthcare industry
b) Changes in health priorities

   • A decline has been recorded in maternal and child mortality
   • A surge has been observed on account of infectious and non-communicable diseases

c) Enhanced fiscal capacity enabling economic growth
d) One of the major contributors to poverty has been observed to be increasing incidences of hefty expenditures due to healthcare costs

(National Health Policy, 2017)

The vision of the policy is to attain the highest possible level of health and well-being for all through:

• Universal access to high-quality healthcare services
• Not leading to financial hardship
• Promotive and preventive orientation towards healthcare in all developmental policies

It is envisioned that this can be achieved through improvement in quality, increase in access, and reduction in costs of healthcare service delivery.

Recognising the importance of the SDGs, the policy also includes goals to be achieved in a stipulated time period, which are aligned to the national efforts in progress, as well as the global strategic directions (National Health Policy, 2017).

## 4.5    Mapping of the healthcare sector in India

Healthcare mapping can aid the assessment of the existing conditions and availability of healthcare facilities and services in the country. It can also help in mapping out the various segments in order to identify potential opportunities for development and improvement in healthcare services and facilities. In addition, healthcare mapping can help pursue opportunities in certain areas of lifestyle diseases, public health, elderly and geriatric care, infectious diseases, frugal engineering, and medical education (Swecare and Swedish Trade Council, India, 2012).

A substantial dearth of healthcare service providers and infrastructure has been observed in the last decade, as has been highlighted through the mismatch between the increasing population, addition of hospital beds, and surge in ailment reports. Consequentially, Indian healthcare services and facilities require extensive improvement on major infrastructural parameters.

### 4.5.1   *Health infrastructure in India*

---

**Box 4.1   Monitoring progress of health indicators**

Health information systems and strong country data influence the progress monitoring of health indicators. The SDG data is not available comprehensively in many parts of the world. The process of strengthening the capacity of the country for information and data requires collaboration across non-governmental and governmental institutions, including national statistics offices, ministries of finance and health, local and regional governments, offices of the registrar general, academia, and think tanks.

The COVID-19 pandemic offers a key lesson on the need of investment in data and health information systems as a part of the country's overall public health capacity, before the occurrence of a disaster. Monitoring of progress with reliable, real-time, and actionable data is important in order to emerge stronger from this crisis. A fundamental requirement for improvement of the population health outcomes and meeting the SDG health targets is the strengthening of health data systems.

– Dr Tedros Adhanom Ghebreyesus, Director-General,
World Health Organization (World Health Organisation, 2020)

---

The apex body responsible for implementation of national health and family welfare programs in the country is the Ministry of Health and Family Welfare (MoHFW). The state health department is the nodal agency for the execution of healthcare services at the state level. The principal secretary (health and family welfare of the state) governs the department.

The National Rural Health Mission (NRHM), an umbrella programme focusing on enhancement of health services and infrastructure in rural areas, was launched for the period of 2005–2012 and relaunched for the period of 2013–2020. Seeking to provide affordable, equitable, and high-quality health services to the rural populace and vulnerable groups, the thrust of the mission is to establish a community-owned, fully functional, and decentralised healthcare delivery system. The programme is envisioned to have inter-sectoral convergence at all levels in order to ensure synchronised action on an extensive range of determinants of health, such as sanitation, water, nutrition, education, gender equality, and social equality. The programme is expected to focus on its outcomes measured against the Indian Public Health Standards for all healthcare facilities through institutional integration within the fragmented health sector. The Empowered Action Group (EAG) states, in addition to Himachal Pradesh, Jammu and Kashmir, and the northeastern states, have been given special focus under the NRHM (National Health Mission Department of Health & Family Welfare, 2020a).

A similar programme devised for inclusion of urban areas, the National Urban Health Mission (NUHM), was launched by the Government of India on May 1, 2013. The vision of this programme is to meet the healthcare needs of the urban population, with more attention to the urban poor. This is envisaged to be achieved by making essential primary healthcare services available to the urban poor and reduce their out-of-pocket expenses for treatment. This requires targeting the people living in slum areas, strengthening the existing healthcare delivery system, and converging various schemes relating to wide-ranging determinants of health, like sanitation, drinking water, school education, etc. The agencies responsible for implementation of the program are the Ministries of Urban Development, Human Resource Development, Housing & Urban Poverty Alleviation, and Women & Child Development (National Health Mission Department of Health & Family Welfare, 2020b).

Additionally, a number of disease-specific national programmes have been operative across the country. These include the Revised National Tuberculosis Control Program, National Vector-Borne Disease Control Program, National AIDS Control Program, and Reproductive and Child Healthcare Program.

The National Medical Council is now the statutory regulatory body for medical education in the country, after repealing the MCI Act. The nodal authority for controlling medical devices in India is the Central Drugs Standard Control Organisation (Drug Controller General of India, also known as DCGI) (Swecare and Swedish Trade Council, India, 2012).

### 4.5.2 *Access to healthcare in India*

It is crucial to ensure efficient and easy access to health services in order to meet the healthcare needs of the citizens, as well as ascertain their optimum utilisation. Healthcare services should be financially and physically accessible, acceptable, and affordable to all persons equally. While expansion of access to healthcare is a priority for the Indian government, in order to safeguard the fundamental human rights of the citizens, the government has been struggling to achieve the same in sufficient capacity for the past two decades.

The healthcare system of the country comprises a mix of private and public healthcare service providers. Regardless of the momentous public health infrastructure in the country, along with vertical health programmes, India has been recorded to have the largest private healthcare system globally, with 72% of health expenditure being incurred in the private sector (Kumar & Singh, 2016).

The 12th Five-Year Plan carries forward the initiatives devised in the 11th Five-Year Plan. This includes expansion of the reach of healthcare services and facilities towards the long-term objective of establishing a system of universal access to healthcare across the country. This initiative secures assured access to healthcare services for every individual, which is envisaged to be free for a majority of the population. While the list of assured services is limited due to budgetary constraints, the goal should be to enhance and widen the coverage with time.

Access to healthcare among weaker sections of the society has been observed to be highly disproportionate, especially among regions with variations in caste and class. It was found that access to healthcare was usually dependent on travel cost, travel time, road conditions, and convenience of mode of transport. Hence, inadequate availability of public transport in rural areas was found to be a significant reason for low accessibility of healthcare (Kumar & Singh, 2016).

Kumar & Singh (2016) conducted a study amongst the EAG states of India, i.e., Chhattisgarh, Bihar, Odisha, Jharkhand, Rajasthan, Madhya Pradesh, Uttar Pradesh, and Uttarakhand, to analyse and evaluate the accessibility to healthcare in private and public sectors. The dataset of the 71st round of the National Sample Survey (NSS) was used, which indicates the degree of access to healthcare for people in both urban and rural areas. The authors identified five reasons associated with the inability of individuals to avail public sources of healthcare: required specific services not available, service available but quality not satisfactory, quality satisfactory but facility too far, quality satisfactory but involves long waiting time, and financial constraints. To analyse the other socio-economic factors, they used logistic regression using STATA version 12.0 (Stata Corp LP, College Station, TX, USA) and SPSS 20.

The following results were recorded through the survey:

a) **Factors impeding access to public sources of healthcare** – The biggest challenge for inpatients of these states was the poor quality of healthcare services, in addition to long waiting times, absence of required services in their area, and remote location of healthcare facilities.

b) **Factors influencing accessibility to healthcare** – While the accessibility was observed to be primarily dependent on the availability of health services, it was also found that inpatients from urban areas and the top of the wealth quantile had a lower preference to avail services from public healthcare facilities, as compared to inpatients from rural households and the lower wealth quantile, respectively (Kumar & Singh, 2016).

It can therefore be observed that the failure of the public health system to expand commensurate with a growing population and its health requirements opens doors for several private practitioners to expand their medical business in the EAG states.

The low accessibility of public healthcare facilities in the EAG states indicates that the government needs to take necessary steps to increase the accessibility of public-sector health facilities. In addition, improvement in the quality of public-sector healthcare services needs to be accomplished by strengthening infrastructure, reducing waiting time, enhancing the physical reach of inpatients, providing good governance, and developing feasible partnerships with the private sector (Kumar & Singh, 2016).

### 4.5.3  *Role of government in public health*

As stated in the Constitutional Provisions of India, the concurrent list of subjects between the state and central governments includes issues such as prevention of inter-state spread of contagious or infectious diseases. However, issues of dispensaries, hospitals, public health services, etc., fall under the jurisdiction of state governments. While the role of delivery of services and the role of prevention among the two jurisdictions are distinctly segregated, the overlaps tend to generate fuzzy responsibilities, especially in systems that are multi-functional, such as healthcare services and EWEs (Lakshminarayanan, 2011).

The new agenda for public health in India includes the demographic transition (increasing elderly population), epidemiological transition (rising burden of chronic non-communicable diseases), and environmental changes. The already overstretched health systems are also under immense pressure due to HIV/AIDS, other communicable diseases, and maternal and child mortality.

Public health involves disease control and prevention at the population level, through informed choice and organised efforts of the individuals, society, organisations, and private and public communities. The government plays a crucial role in addressing these challenges and achieving health equity. A key role in guiding the public health system of the country lies with the MoHFW (Lakshminarayanan, 2011).

### 4.5.4  *Challenges in healthcare in India*

---

**Box 4.2   Improvements in India's healthcare system**

The amount of improvement and change over the past decade in India's healthcare system has been noteworthy. The Swachh Bharat Mission has enhanced its emphasis on sanitation and water, which has led to a substantial impact in the reduction in the spread of communicable diseases. Under the National Nutrition Mission & Poshan Abhiyaan and the National Food Security Act, an increase in the entitlement of food has helped in addressing the issue of malnutrition. The use of technology has helped improve efficiency of the health management systems, through platforms such as ANMOL (ANM online) to better extend new-born and maternal care services, eVIN (electronic Vaccine Intelligence Network) to track and improve coverage of immunisation, and use of artificial intelligence to improve diagnostics and treatment. The government has committed to enhancing public health expenditure to 2.5% of GDP by 2025 (NITI Aayog, 2019b).

---

With the increasing burden of emerging and re-emerging diseases and the effects of existing communicable and non-communicable diseases, the health systems of the country are struggling to provide timely and affordable services. However, inequalities in healthcare service provision have been observed to occur due to inadequate financial resources for the health sector and inefficient utilisation of the available resources. Social stratification according to education, income, gender, occupation, race, and ethnicity caused by economic, social, and political mechanisms, in turn causes health inequalities. One of the glaring failures of public health has been observed to be the lack of adequate progress on these underlying social determinants.

## 4.6    Adverse living conditions holding back health

Due to a high proportion of deaths due to communicable diseases, especially among the youth, life expectancy is low in the country. While the infant mortality rate has reduced significantly, it is still high compared to other developing countries. These young deaths chiefly include conditions that are preventable, such as respiratory infections like pneumonia, pre-term birth complications, and diarrheal diseases. These types of diseases together account for 21% of potential years of life lost due to ill health (Institute for Health Metrics and Evaluation (IHME), 2013).

The high number of young deaths are compounded by poor nutrition among mothers due to lack of accessibility, availability, and affordability. As compared to other South Asian countries, India has a higher proportion of nutrient deficiencies and low-birth-weight children. By impeding physical and mental development during foetal stages, infancy, and youth, malnutrition can cause poor health later in life and lead to a reduced quality of life. Stunted health can lead to incomplete education, reduced productivity, and lower income as adults (Spence & Lewis, 2009).

Additionally, lack of safe public health services such as clean water, sanitation services, communicable disease control, maternal and child services, etc., leads to increased spread of epidemics and diseases in both rural and urban areas.

### 4.6.1    *Limited access to healthcare and quality of care*

The healthcare system of India aspires to provide affordable and comprehensive healthcare services to all citizens as devised in strategies and policies, but struggles to implement the same in practice.

Public health facilities in India are funded by the federal and state governments and run by state governments. The quality of these facilities varies significantly between urban and rural areas and across different states. Some examples of the better-performing facilities include those in states such as Kerala and Tamil Nadu, where health facilities are reliably open (usually for 24 hours a day), are staffed by trained professionals, and are well-stocked with critical supplies and medicines. These have been found to play a role in proactively delivering essential services and being the first points of care. Another example of efficient performance is the world-class public-sector tertiary hospitals that provide specialised or sophisticated healthcare facilities. Such institutions, like the All India Institute of Medical Sciences (AIIMS), are often looked upon as a model for Organization for Economic Cooperation and Development (OECD) countries for innovation in delivering healthcare at low costs (Joumard & Kumar, 2015).

Other than a handful of well-performing facilities, the public sector has been observed to fall short in its objective of meeting the basic healthcare needs of the population. Most of the public healthcare facilities are often located far away, lack medical and equipment supplies, lack trained personnel, and are not reliably open. Private healthcare facilities have grown rapidly amidst the shortfall and absence of public facilities and lacklustre performance in order to meet the increased demands and expectations of the citizens. However, the quality, expertise, and availability of supplies in these private healthcare facilities are unregulated due to an absence of financing or regulation from the governments (Sachan, 2013).

### 4.6.2    *Absence of manpower in healthcare*

Public healthcare facilities located in rural, tribal, and remote areas are the most affected by the lack of manpower. Some of the major causes of low staffing or absence of trained manpower are remoteness of the locations, difficulty in accessibility, lack of incentives, absence of basic facilities, infrastructural inadequacy, poor training, and lack of motivation among the staff.

For an individual who has to travel a fair distance to reach a public healthcare facility, the high probability of a lack of qualified/trained staff can act as a significant deterrent to make the effort, as compared to availing the services of a traditional healer or a local non-registered practitioner. Lack of people who are also qualified/trained has been observed to substantially affect the health status of citizens living in rural, tribal, and remote areas (Mohamed Saalim, 2020).

### 4.6.3    *Affordability or the cost of healthcare*

The catastrophic cost of availing healthcare services is a major cause of impoverishment in India, considering that almost 75% of the expenditure for healthcare comes from the pockets of households. The cost of availing healthcare services from the public sector is low or nil, but is usually perceived to be unreliable, inefficient, or indifferent. Private healthcare, on the other hand, lacks regulation and leads to consequent variations in cost and quality of services. However, public healthcare is generally not considered the first choice for many individuals, unless private healthcare is not affordable (Kasthuri, 2018).

The problem of affordability in healthcare needs to be addressed through local and national initiatives that focus on scaling up the financing and expenditure on public health. Enhancing healthcare infrastructure availability, accessibility, and reliability in remote, rural, and marginal areas can help improve the condition of public health (Kasthuri, 2018).

### 4.6.4    *Current status of public healthcare in India*

Healthcare delivery in India has improved greatly in the past two decades, primarily evident in the improvement in the key health indicators, such as increase of average life expectancy at birth and decline in infant and maternal mortality rates (Swecare and Swedish Trade Council, India, 2012).

Notable accomplishments in this time period also include the elimination of polio, yaws, guinea worm disease, and neonatal and maternal tetanus. Further, the total fertility rate (TFR) has reduced sharply from 3.4 in 1992–1993 to 2.2 in 2015–2016. India also achieved the Millennium Development Goals in respect of the maternal mortality ratio (MMR level of 130 against a target of 139) and almost succeeded in meeting the under-five child mortality target (U5 MR level of 43 against a target of 42) (NITI Aayog, 2019a).

Provision of affordable healthcare services to the billion-plus population of the country is one of the major pathways of growth for public-sector healthcare. Further, the private sector is attracting growth in investments to cater to the surge in demand of high-quality healthcare services for the rising middle class of the country.

### 4.6.5   *EWEs and the position of disadvantage in the healthcare system in India*

As noted in the section of experts' opinions, one of the interviewees mentioned in great detail the negligence of the healthcare infrastructure in the rural, district, and suburban regions of the country. Many towns, villages, and districts have crude infrastructure in terms of the availability, equipped/educated staff, and medical practitioners. Further, even as the designs and codes are present on paper and code provisions, it has been observed that these are not followed during the design and construction processes. In some cases, it has even been found that these facilities do not exist as mentioned in the records.

The facilities that exist are usually inadequately designed and constructed, without employing applicable norms and resilience strategies. These structures are extremely vulnerable to natural hazards and EWEs.

In the urban context, while the condition of healthcare is found to be better than rural, the designs are frequently uninformed, non-resilient, and lacking functionalities to accommodate EWEs and therefore are vulnerable to destruction and losses in case an EWE or other natural hazard strikes.

The public healthcare system in India is significantly disadvantaged not only in terms of infrastructure and availability but also equipped/educated staff, medical practitioners, doctors, paramedics, and emergency services.

## 4.7   Infectious diseases

One of the leading causes of mortality in India, infectious/communicable diseases, typically affect people in rural settings more as compared to urban populations. With the demographic, health, and epidemiological transition in India, the emphasis is shifting from communicable to non-communicable diseases, whereby factors such as increased life expectancy, changing lifestyles, etc., determine the prevalence of the diseases.

Nevertheless, infectious diseases are still widespread and contribute to almost 34% of mortality in the country. While rural areas report almost 41% of total deaths due to infectious diseases, the proportion of deaths in these areas due to lifestyle diseases and non-communicable diseases is much less (around 40%) as compared to urban areas (Swecare and Swedish Trade Council, India, 2012).

With varying emphasis across private and public healthcare facilities, infection control is at a nascent stage in India. Private-sector health facilities have a relatively higher emphasis on controlling cases related to hospital-acquired infections. Among non-communicable diseases, water-borne diseases are prevalent in the country, which can be observed through more than 10 million cases of diarrhoea detected annually. Respiratory illnesses due to increased tobacco consumption and rising pollution levels are also common.

The MoHFW has initiated several national programmes to combat the prevalence of various diseases. However, many communicable diseases are interlinked as well, one such being TB-HIV co-infection. To address this disease, the National TB-HIV framework has been devised jointly by the National AIDS Control Programme (NACP) and the Revised National Tuberculosis Control Programme (RNTCP), wherein the policy of TB/HIV collaboration has been articulated (Swecare and Swedish Trade Council, India, 2012).

### 4.7.1 Upsurge in infectious diseases because of climate change

With increase in global temperatures and rapidly depleting natural resources, an upward trend has been observed in the spread of infectious diseases due to the increased density of number of persons per sq. km. and enhanced surface and atmospheric heat. Further, EWEs typically lead to debris, filth, and decreased distancing, accompanied by water logging or backflow of drainage, thereby increasing the transmission of such infectious diseases in the affected areas.

EWEs can also disrupt the functional and operational efficiency of infrastructural interdependencies, such as difficulty in access to medical services and healthcare facilities due to obstructions or damage to transport, communication, or power infrastructure. Due to similar reasons, medical help may or may not be able to reach affected areas, thereby worsening the condition of the victims and affected persons and leading to increased chances of spread of diseases to other people in the affected communities.

## 4.8    Healthcare delivery systems in India

The Bhore Committee Report (1946), a report on the Health Survey and Development Committee, has been a landmark move for India, from which the current health systems and policies have evolved (Ma & Sood, 2008).

The report recommended a three-tiered healthcare system for the provision of curative and preventive healthcare in urban and rural areas. This system placed health workers on government payrolls, as well as regulated the need for private practitioners. The current healthcare systems have been founded on these principles. This approach ensured that individual socio-economic conditions did not affect access of citizens to primary healthcare. However, the lack of capacity of public healthcare systems to provide access to quality healthcare to the general public led to a simultaneous evolution of private health systems, followed by a gradual and constant expansion of private healthcare services (Peters et al., 2003).

The first National Health Policy of India (NHP) was formulated in 1983, and its primary focus was on providing primary healthcare to all citizens by the year 2000. A network of primary healthcare services was set up in terms of priority, using simple technologies and health volunteers. Therefore, an integrated network of specialty facilities and well-functioning referral systems was established. Building on NHP 1983, NHP 2002 was improved with the objective of providing healthcare services to the public through decentralisation, increased public expenditure on healthcare, and increased association with the private sector. Additionally, it highlighted the need to strengthen the decision-making processes at the decentralised state level. The use of non-allopathic forms of medicine, such as Unani, Ayurveda, and Siddha, was also encouraged (MoHFW, 2002).

### 4.8.1   *Public healthcare infrastructure: modes of delivery*

The areas of operations and governance of healthcare systems in the country have been divided between the state and union governments. The Union Ministry of Health and Family Welfare is responsible for the control and prevention of major communicable diseases, implementation of various health and family welfare programmes on a national scale, setting guidelines and standards, and promotion of indigenous and traditional systems of medicines. The areas of sanitation, hospitals, public health, etc., come under the purview of the state government. The state government is also responsible for controlling and preventing the spread of epidemics and seasonal disease outbreaks, which is supported by the Union Ministry through technical assistance. The areas that have wider ramifications on a national level are jointly governed by the state and union governments. These include medical education, population control, family welfare, quality control in manufacturing of drugs, prevention of adulteration in food, etc. (Chokshi et al., 2016).

While the country has a mixed healthcare system, including private and public healthcare service providers, most of the private healthcare providers are concentrated in the urban regions, inclined towards providing secondary and tertiary healthcare services. However, rural areas predominantly have public healthcare facilities, developed as a three-tier system, based on the population norms. These norms have been described as follows (MoHFW, 2012):

### a)  Sub-centres

A sub-centre (SC) is established using the following norms:

- One establishment in a plain area with a population of 5000 people
- One establishment in a tribal/difficult to reach/hilly area with a population of 3000 people

The SC is the most peripheral and first point of contact between the community and the primary healthcare system. Each SC is required to be staffed by at least one female health worker/auxiliary nurse midwife (ANM), and one male health worker.

In addition to provision of services, including family welfare, maternal and child health, immunisation, nutrition, diarrhoea control, and programmes to control communicable diseases, SCs are also designated the tasks relating to interpersonal communication to facilitate behavioural change in communities (Chokshi et al., 2016).

## b) Primary health centres

A primary health centre (PHC) is established using the following norms:

- One establishment in a plain area with a population of 30000 people
- One establishment in a tribal/difficult to reach/hilly area with a population of 20,000 people

The PHC is the first point of contact between the community and the medical officer. It has four to six beds for in-patients and acts as a referral unit for five to six SCs. PHCs were envisaged to provide integrated preventive and curative healthcare services to the rural populace. The focus is on the promotive and preventive attributes of healthcare.

The PHCs are established and maintained by the state governments under the Minimum Needs Program (MNP)/Basic Minimum Services (BMS) programme. Each PHC is required to be staffed by a medical officer and supported by 14 paramedics and other staff. In addition, under NRHM, two additional staff nurses are to be provided on a contract basis (Chokshi et al., 2016).

## c) Community health centres

A community health centre (CHC) is established using the following norms:

- One establishment in a plain area with a population of 120,000 people
- One establishment in a tribal/difficult to reach/hilly area with a population of 80,000 people

CHCs are established and maintained by the state governments under the MNP/ BMS programme. Each CHC is required to be staffed by four medical specialists, i.e., physician, surgeon, paediatrician, and gynaecologist/obstetrician, and is supported by 21 paramedics and other staff. The facility is also required to include 30 beds, an x-ray room, operating theatre, labour room, and laboratory facilities. A CHC acts as a referral centre for PHCs within the block (Chokshi et al., 2016).

## d) First referral units

An existing facility (CHC/sub-divisional hospital/district hospital) can be declared a fully operational first referral unit (FRU) only if it is equipped to impart round-the-clock services for new-born care and emergency obstetric services, in addition to all other emergencies that a hospital should provide.

A healthcare facility can be declared an FRU using three critical determinants:

- (i) Care for small and sick new-borns
- (ii) Twenty-four-hour-available blood storage facility
- (iii) Emergency obstetric care including surgical procedures/caesarean sections (Chokshi et al., 2016).

## 4.9     Impact of EWEs on the healthcare infrastructure

---

**Box 4.3    Efficiency of healthcare infrastructure after disruption due to disasters**

A community's recovery after a major disaster event depends to a significant extent on the ability of health facilities to function without interruption and to provide the extra care to large number of patients affected in a disaster. Hospitals are often identified as cornerstones of response to disaster, but many hospitals are not adequately prepared to respond effectively.

– Loy Rego, Editor-in-Chief, *Asian Disaster Management News* (2008)

---

The increasing effects of climate change and anthropogenic activities on weather patterns, with the intensified likelihood of the occurrence of natural disasters and EWEs, have significantly affected human health and the demand for a healthcare infrastructure. Due to natural disasters/EWEs, the injured and affected victims project increased demands on the healthcare infrastructure, with the added pressure of seeking refuge during these events (Carthey et al., 2008).

While the role of healthcare facilities has been acknowledged in both research and practice, in terms of their response and medical services to relieve the impacts of both natural and man-made disasters, this role is not considered sufficient in the development of disaster management strategies. These disasters range from the impact of pandemics such H1N1, SARS, COVID-19, etc., to the devastation and endangerment to life caused by natural disasters/EWEs such as floods, droughts, hurricanes, fires, etc.

The first type of disaster, i.e., a pandemic, is usually managed by a health system response, with a focus on frontline healthcare service delivery and clinical issues. For natural disasters/EWEs, the responsibility typically lies with emergency services organisations for mobilisation of resources in order to provide immediate relief, including removal of sources of danger/risk of death or injury. In both situations, the healthcare infrastructure is assumed to be available for continuous delivery of healthcare services and with sufficient coping capacity to handle a surge in demand (Carthey et al., 2008).

The need for continuous delivery of healthcare services assumes that these healthcare facilities are resilient to the impacts of disasters/EWEs and are not isolated or damaged due to failure of the surrounding infrastructure (such as power, roads, and communication). However, the disasters have a substantial likelihood of causing disruption to these facilities, thereby compromising the delivery of healthcare services to the affected communities. The nature of disasters can considerably affect the need for and demand of healthcare services. A major reason for failures and disruptions in healthcare facilities and services is the inadequate attention paid to disaster prevention and mitigation planning by healthcare planners, designers, and administrators. Without efficient planning, a disaster can unexpectedly over-whelm the operational and functional capacity and safety of a healthcare facility (Carthey et al., 2008).

Health facilities can get affected in terms of their functioning and operations, and this has a direct impact on health equipment, patients, access to patient docu-mentation, structure of the building, and food/medicine supplies. Some of the most typical impacts identified by the Disease Control Priorities Project were failure in energy resources of the facility, loss of health equipment, lack of staff, issues in accessing hospital buildings, and difficulty in accessing patients' documents and medical records (Nia & Kulatunga, 2017).

### 4.9.1 Risks to the healthcare system due to climate change and EWEs: impacts on human health and health facilities

The study conducted by Carthey et al. (2008), which aims to assess the adaptive capacity of hospital facilities to cope with EWEs, used inputs from focus groups with key stakeholders who would be involved in EWE response. The authors recorded their responses through the risk and opportunity management method-ology (ROMS).

Firstly, the study found that adaptation to EWEs was often hindered by the lack of understanding and perception of the likely nature and amount of the impacts of such incidents on the facility and its functions. Prior to endeavours at adaptation, the quantification of impacts of climate change and consequent EWEs is crucial to reinforce the understanding of the gravity and immediacy of the problems. Other researchers also observed similar obstacles regarding the lack of reliable data to assess the risks of disaster/EWE incidents in the healthcare sector that are neces-sary to establish disaster management strategies (Carthey et al., 2008).

Secondly, responding to the threats posed by EWEs needs an evidence-based approach in order to buttress the adaptation strategies. The authors state that the need to include these adaptive strategies in the current processes of planning and developing healthcare establishments is not considered, i.e., the tendering pro-cesses and design documentation do not incorporate this requirement yet. A major reason for this is the anticipated decrease in the likelihood of proposing innovative strategies in order to accommodate for adaptive planning while tendering. This may lead to rendering the bid as non-conforming. Additionally, lack of experi-ence and evidence from previously attempted projects that demonstrate the transla-tion of adaptation strategies into healthcare facility design and requirements, along with their effectiveness and associated costs, impede the adoption of this approach (Carthey et al., 2008).

Thirdly, a lack of certainty was observed about the impact of climate change on the communities. Even as a sense of urgency is being acknowledged, this has not been translated into policies and adaptation strategies yet. For the healthcare infra-structure to cope with the impacts of climate change and EWEs, a change in the attitude of stakeholders towards awareness, adaptation, and ensuring behavioural change must emerge as important factors. Further, the funding received for intro-ducing and incorporating adaptive strategies in healthcare services needs to be augmented. Due to the difference in priorities that govern the delivery of these projects, the issues of adaptation and mitigation are not ranked sufficiently in order to be acted upon (Carthey et al., 2008).

Countries such as the UK, United States, and Australia consider adaptation strate-gies under the domain of emergency planning and disaster management in order to manage outbreaks of communicable diseases or terrorist attacks. Further, impacts of climate change, including the increase in occurrence of EWEs, place additional loads on the structure of the facility. These climate/EWE loads are often overlooked as compared to the focus placed on the impacts on human life and health. For instance, the 2008 update of the 2001/2002 Department of Health/Health Protection Agency Report into the Health Effects of Climate Change in the UK includes little informa-tion about the potential structural failures and their effect on healthcare service avail-ability and delivery in the event of occurrence of a disaster/EWE.

Hence, it can be observed that the generic disaster management strategies devel-oped by health services or emergency management organisations do not identify definitive adaptation strategies for the healthcare infrastructure. Consequently, lit-tle attempt has been made to address the issues faced by the health infrastructure that would support the safeguarding of its critical service functions. More recently, some of the practical guidelines have emerged in the United States that direct the development of healthcare facilities in The Joint Commission and in response to events such as Hurricane Katrina. The need for surge capacity and redundancy in both existing and new health infrastructures is being widely accepted to cope with the increase in demands due to emergency situations and extreme weather occurrences. However, the amount of additional requirements or locations of these healthcare facilities and surge resources has not been robustly investigated or iden-tified in the United States and UK (Traub et al., 2007).

## 4.10   Summary

Public healthcare systems and their existing status highlight the position of disad-vantage in terms of the negligence faced by the health infrastructure in peri-urban and rural areas. Lack of implementation of bylaws and code provisions also indi-cates the lack of resilience or recovery mechanisms in these structures and commu-nities. This implies the risk of failure on the part of healthcare facilities, which are expected to continue their functioning and operations and provide medical, shelter, and nutrition assistance in the aftermath of any EWEs. Further, such structures add to the vulnerability of the existing patients, as well as injured and traumatised persons in the case of EWEs.

In addition, the healthcare infrastructure in both rural and urban contexts is une-venly mapped and distributed, apart from their lack of structural and non-resilient construction and functioning, both of which add to the vulnerability of structures. Further, these structures are not proportionate to the populations that they are expected to cater to and may end up with a sudden overload in case of extreme weather occurrences.

With an insight into the health statistics of the country and the spread of infectious diseases, it becomes evident that the healthcare facilities need to ensure resilience and quick recovery to be able to curb the outbreak of infectious and water-borne diseases during and after an EWE.

It can therefore be said that the public healthcare system in India is significantly disadvantaged not only in terms of the infrastructure and availability but also the equipped/educated staff and medical practitioners, doctors, paramedics, and emergency services.

## References

Carthey, J., Chandra, V., & Loosemore, M. (2008). Assessing the adaptive capacity of hospital facilities to cope with climate-related extreme weather events: A risk management approach. In A. Dainty (ed.) *Procs 24th Annual ARCOM Conference* (pp. 1145–1154). Cardiff: Association of Researchers in Construction Management.

Chokshi, M., Patil, B., Khanna, R., Neogi, S., Sharma, J., Paul, V., & Zodpey, S. (2016). Health systems in India. *Journal of Perinatology*, 9–12.

Gupta, M. D. (2006). *Public Health in India: An Overview*. Washington, DC: World Bank.

Institute for Health Metrics and Evaulation (IHME). (2013). *Global Burden of Disease 2010*. Retrieved from www.healthmetricsandevaluation.org/gbd

Joumard, I., & Kumar, A. (2015). *Improving Health Outcomes and Health Care in India*. Paris: Organisation for Economic Co-operation and Development.

Kasthuri, A. (2018). Challenges to healthcare in India – the Five A's. *Indian Journal of Community Medicine*, 141–143.

Kumar, V., & Singh, P. (2016). Access to healthcare among the Empowered Action Group (EAG) states of India: Current status and impeding factors. *The National Medical Journal of India*, 267–273.

Lakshminarayanan, S. (2011). Role of government in public health: Current scenario in India and future scope. *Journal of Family and Community Medicine*, 26–30.

Ma, S., & Sood, N. (2008). *Comparison of the Health Systems in China and India*. Santa Monica, CA: Rand Corporation.

Mohamed Saalim, P. K. (2020, February). *Public Healthcare Infrastructure in Tribal India: A Critical Review*. Bengalluru: The Institute for Social and Economic Change.

MoHFW. (2002). *National Health Policy*. New Delhi: Ministry of Health and Family Welfare, Government of India.

MoHFW. (2012). *Indian Public Health Standards: Revised Guidelines*. New Delhi: Ministry of Health and Family Welfare, Government of India.

National Health Mission Department of Health & Family Welfare. (2020a, November 01). National Rural Health Mission. *National Health Mission*. Retrieved from https://nhm.gov.in/index1.php?lang=1&level=1&sublinkid=969&lid=49

National Health Mission Department of Health & Family Welfare. (2020b, November 01). National Urban Health Mission. *National Health Mission*. Retrieved from https://nhm.gov.in/index1.php?lang=1&level=1&sublinkid=970&lid=137

National Health Policy. (2017). *National Health Policy*. New Delhi: Ministry of Health and Family Welfare.

Nia, S. P., & Kulatunga, U. (2017). Safety and security of hospitals during natural disasters: Challenges of disaster managers. *International Journal of Safety and Security Engineering*, 234–246.

NITI Aayog. (2019a). *Health System for a New India: Building Blocks*. New Delhi: NITI Aayog.

NITI Aayog. (2019b). *SDG India: Index and Dashboard 2019–20*. New Delhi: NITI Aayog.

Peters, D., Rao, K., & Fryatt, R. (2003). Lumping and splitting: The health policy agenda in India. *Health Policy Plan*, 249–260.

Sachan, D. (2013). Tackling corruption in Indian Medicine. *The Lancet*, 23–24.

Spence, M., & Lewis, M. (2009). *Health and Growth*. Washington, DC: World Bank Publishing.

Swecare and Swedish Trade Council, India. (2012). *Report on Mapping of Healthcare Sector in India*. Delhi: Swecare and Swedish Trade Council, India.

Traub, M., Bradt, D., & Joseph, A. (2007). The Surge Capacity for People in Emergencies (SCOPE) study in Australasian hospitals. *The Medical Journal of Australia*, 394–398.

World Health Organisation. (2020). *World Health Statistics 2020: Monitoring Health for the SDGs*. Geneva: World Health Organisation.

# 5 The case for resilience in healthcare facilities

## 5.1 Overview

Resilience and risk reduction approaches are often advocated to be incorporated into the planning, design, construction, and operations of the critical infrastructure. However, as observed in the previous chapters, resource allocation to integrate resilience and risk reduction can become an exercise in futility if these resources are not allocated rationally. Such allocation without raison d'être can lead to disruption in services and damages to the structure and equipment, as depicted in Figure 5.1. This chapter elaborates on the disruption to healthcare facilities due to EWEs and highlights the importance of providing continuity of services.

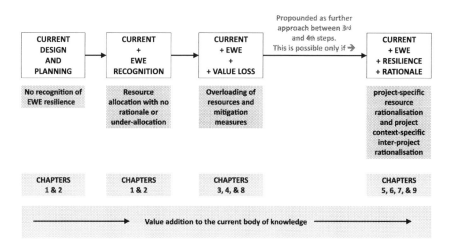

*Figure 5.1* Process of incorporating resilience: curtailing disruption through rational resource allocation.

## 5.2 Structure of the chapter

This chapter introduces the disruption caused to the healthcare infrastructure due to uncertainties and continues to establish the need for resilience and redundancy

DOI: 10.1201/9781003393108-5

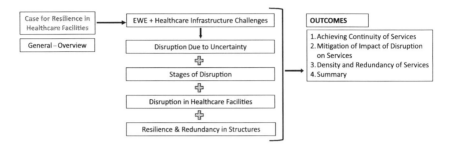

*Figure 5.2* Structure and overview of Chapter 5.

in these structures. The objective of incorporating resilience and redundancy is to ensure continuity of services in the healthcare facility in case an EWE strikes (both during and after the EWE). Figure 5.2 explains the structure and overview of this chapter.

## 5.3    Disruption due to uncertainty of events

Extreme weather events can overwhelm healthcare facilities for many days after their occurrence and retreat. A surge in the demand for medical needs and supplies is usually found to be the reason for the increase, especially for patients who lack the resources or finances to cope with the outcomes. Since uncertainty is characteristic of EWEs, healthcare facilities that are not prepared for such sudden surges in demand for emergency medical care jeopardise the safety and health of incoming as well as existing patients in the emergency and in-patient departments. Many hospitals are already functioning at maximum or near-maximum capacity. Healthcare facilities that are not equipped to handle shocks due to EWEs or natural disasters may need to be evacuated and transfer the evacuated patients to other functioning facilities (Joy, 2017).

In addition to the patients suffering from mental or physical trauma, the medical and technical staff could be subject to stress due to the increased workload. It is important to identify the signs of physical or mental distress amongst healthcare providers and alleviate the pressure and anxiety. While these signs are typically overlooked in day-to-day functioning, it is all the more crucial to deal with them in the aftermath of a disaster scenario (Joy, 2017).

### 5.3.1    *Disruption in healthcare facilities*

Challenges to the continuity in operations and functioning of the healthcare infrastructure can be broadly categorised into two types: (a) supply disruptions, which include loss or attenuation of resources, infrastructure, or staff necessary for the facility to continue functioning and deliver care; and (b) demand disruptions, which include an upsurge in patients, anticipated or actual, exceeding the capacity of the facility. EWEs, which are uncertain and often unprecedented, have negatively affected healthcare delivery in all settings (Guenther & Balbus, 2014).

## 5.4    Stages of disruption

### 5.4.1    *The first rescue stage: disruption of the initial emergency response*

In the immediate aftermath of a natural disaster/EWE, the affected community has often been found to initiate immediate rescue efforts. Medical response measures typically begin within the first few hours, and the most critically injured and accessible patients receive emergency healthcare service within the first 24 hours. However, in extreme events, the critical infrastructure can get considerably disrupted, leading to a delay in an appropriate, comprehensive, and organised medical response (March, 2002).

In developing countries, the critical infrastructure may or may not be fully developed or resilient to natural disasters/EWEs, thereby causing power failures, water supply shortages, inaccessible transport routes, and structural damage to healthcare facilities. Further, damage to emergency vehicles such as ambulances and fire trucks may cause a delay in rescue operations, especially for victims who are critically injured and may require care at the scene or en route to the medical facility (March, 2002).

Damage to medical storage facilities and supply depots providing essentials such as intravenous (IV) lines, dressings, medications, etc., can lead to a disruption or delay in the delivery of emergency medical needs. Loss of medical personnel may also exacerbate the lack of adequate medical care. Off-duty personnel are often called upon in the event of a natural disaster/extreme weather occurrence (March, 2002).

Resilient and safe emergency care systems ensure that disaster protocols and procedures learned during training are followed, in addition to the efficient functioning of trauma and emergency departments. Further, large tertiary hospitals play a pivotal role in the provision of not only medical and emergency care but also as a central point of organisation for the community. In case of developed countries where healthcare facilities may or may not be resilient or efficient, emergency medical care tasks may get assigned to healthcare workers who are not particularly trained in emergency medical services. In such circumstances, the response to the disaster may be diffuse, with no central point of organisation for the community (March, 2002).

### 5.4.2    *The second rescue stage: disruption of the infrastructure critical to*
### *public health and welfare*

In the aftermath of the disaster, it is important to ensure shelter for victims and survivors, in addition to providing appropriate and timely emergency medical care. While rescue operations continue, recovery and reconstruction operations begin in the next 48 hours after the occurrence of the disaster. Depending on the resilience and structural stability of the houses, some collapse entirely, some have severe damage and may need reconstruction, and others may be slightly damaged and can be used again after the effects of the disaster have passed (March, 2002).

Damage to fuel lines and power grids can lead to a shortage of electricity for several days or weeks, thereby causing individuals to lose the ability to cool or heat their homes and adequately refrigerate food, causing food spoilage, further leading to food shortages and potential large-scale malnutrition. The risk of fire and carbon dioxide poisoning also increases due to the increased usage of gas or kerosene heaters and candles on account of power outages. In such conditions, the general safety of the community may also be jeopardised (March, 2002).

Clean water may get contaminated during disasters due to the following reasons: water treatment plants cease to function due to a power shortage, leading to unsanitary water supply; water supply mains and pipelines may get damaged, causing contamination; water filtrations systems may get overwhelmed; and water basins may become impure due to infiltration of flood waters containing toxins and debris. The consequential water crisis can lead to a lack of hygiene, illness, and dehydration (March, 2002).

Firefighting activities may also be hindered due to damage to water mains or pump failure. The transportation network may get damaged or disrupted during and after disasters, impeding emergency vehicle response and delivery of essential services and supplies. Damage or obstruction of tunnels, bridges, key mountain passes, or long jungle roads connecting island or remote communities to the mainland can cause large populations to become stranded and isolated from external aid (March, 2002).

Disruption of communication networks due to damaged infrastructure can cause disruption in the integrated response and relay of information to and from field command posts to an emergency operations centre. Specific sites within the area affected by a disaster need to request resupply to ensure swift recovery. To ensure the effectiveness and efficiency of response and revitalisation efforts, it is necessary to ensure that the communication network and infrastructure is restored and is stable and comprehensive.

The location of emergency operations centres and their proximity to disaster-affected sites play a significant role in time-sensitive rescue and response actions. Typically, these are located near supply stockpiles or government offices. The primary function of the emergency operations centre is to arrange efficient and accurate distribution of rescue supplies to the affected areas so as to save the maximum number of lives possible and minimise subsequent damage. Loss of communication facilities can cause a delay in the call for emergency aid, thereby setting back emergency medical care by several hours. Furthermore, lack of contact with authorities or isolation of communities and individuals can lead to severe psychological impacts on victims who find themselves without reassurance or direction from authorities (March, 2002).

### 5.4.3   *The recovery stage: short-term and long-term public health concerns*

A few days after rescue efforts commence, recovery and reconstruction processes are also set in motion. At this stage, public health concerns, restoration of communities, and rehabilitation of individuals and their occupations are focused upon. Major procedures include control of endemic disease outbreaks, establishment of suitable hygiene protocols, and re-establishment of routine health activities (March, 2002).

One of the chief priorities of the local health officials is to recommence the regular health practices in the affected regions. This involves resuming regular operations of local healthcare centres, clinics, and hospitals; public health programmes; and disease monitoring systems. In addition to control and prevention of water-borne and vector-borne diseases and endemic outbreaks, any existing disease control programmes are also re-commenced. Along with government-devised programmes and recovery procedures, external aid can be utilised for the resumption of common medical practices (March, 2002).

It is also important to encourage victims to maintain their personal hygiene conditions and ensure consumption of clean water and food in their homes or temporary shelters. This can be done through imparting education and awareness of maintaining cleanliness and sanitary living conditions, free of disease vectors such as insects and rodents. Some of the common diseases that are observed in temporary shelters include tuberculosis, influenza, malaria, typhoid, measles, scabies, whooping cough, and other skin infections.

Disruption of distribution networks for food supplies or destruction of food stocks due to the disaster can increase the risk of large-scale malnutrition. The nutritional status of the community before the disaster influences their risk of malnutrition post-disaster. Communities that were experiencing famines or food shortages pre-disaster are almost certain to be subjected to nutritional problems post-disaster. The nutritional status of the community also affects its functionality and the ability of the individuals to recover from or resist diseases. It has been observed that providing timely food supplies to malnourished victims leads to a higher rate of survival, especially among children (March, 2002).

In terms of healthcare, victims with pre-existing medical conditions, individuals with regular healthcare needs such as dialysis, the very old, and the very young are at a greater risk of illness or death as compared to others. Their conditions may get exacerbated by the development of co-morbid conditions, lack of medical aid, or lack of timely access to medical facilities due to a disruption in transportation networks. These individuals with specific needs must be ensured safe and regular check-ups and medical care. Additionally, collection and transportation of the deceased must also be conducted in a timely manner to safeguard the community's health and well-being (March, 2002).

## 5.5    Impact of disruption on the health of victims

EWEs and disasters have a considerable impact on public health, environmental health, and functioning of the healthcare systems. Administration of medical countermeasures through critical workforce and public health responders may also get disrupted. Critical workforce groups are targeted depending upon the severity of the threat; medical countermeasure supply; risk of severe illness; and associated disruption to the economy, society, and security (Centers for Disease Control and Prevention (CDC), 2018).

It has also been observed that some victims may develop secondary medical conditions during the recovery period in the aftermath of a disaster. A significant cause for this has been found to be psychological attributes, anxiety, and stress due to the trauma of witnessing a disaster and subsequent losses. While the stress might be felt immediately by victims upon the occurrence of a disaster, psychological impacts may surface after a few days or weeks. Many patients have been found to be suffering from post-traumatic stress disorder (PTSD) or general anxiety disorder (GAD).

In the case of combustible disasters such as forest fires and volcanic eruptions, pollutants are ejected into the air on a large scale, thereby increasing instances and severity of respiratory conditions like asthma and allergies for a few days or weeks after the disaster (March, 2002).

## 5.6    Resilience in structures

It is vital for healthcare centres and hospitals to remain safe and operational for community well-being and health during and after natural disasters, in addition to providing emergency services, regular medical services, and shelter. Hence, these structures need to be resilient to disasters/EWEs in terms of design, planning, construction, and management.

It has been observed in various studies that the resilience of social and physical systems is defined by four major properties: robustness, redundancy, rapidity, and resourcefulness (Bruneau & Reinhorn, 2007). Redundancy can be understood as the ability to efficiently mobilise available resources. Robustness refers to the inherent strength or resistance of a system to endure stress without losing functionality. Resourcefulness is the diversity of options; rapidity indicates the speed with which disruptions can be overcome in an appropriate time and to avoid future losses. These four characteristics of a resilient system determine its adaptive capacity.

This dynamic aspect of resilience reflects the need for systems to be able to learn, innovate, and be flexible in adapting to continuous changes in the environment. In the context of a healthcare facility, resourcefulness can be understood as the availability of back-up utility services, medical supplies, water supplies, power generators, and back-up systems of communication that are critical to maintain the continuity of healthcare service delivery during and after the occurrence of an EWE. The physical strength of the building materials imparts robustness to the elements of the structure. Rapidity can be understood as the ability of the healthcare infrastructure to be rebuilt quickly and to return to 'normal' or 'new normal' or 'improved' system functions quickly. This can be provided by implementing flexible designs or pre-fabricated or demountable materials that can be bolted back together after the occurrence of an EWE. An engineering resilience perspective is adopted for the research of resilience in the infrastructure, which emphasises the robustness of the building and the recovery time for the structure to return to normal delivery of services (Chand & Loosemore, 2013).

From an alternative perspective of ecological stability and adaptability, the resilience of a hospital building/infrastructure can be understood as the magnitude of an EWE that can be absorbed by the building without affecting the delivery and quality of medical services and facilities provided to the community within its catchment area. Higher resilience in healthcare buildings/infrastructure can help them resist and adapt to a higher magnitude and impact of an EWE. Hence, from both ecological and engineering perspectives, a resilient healthcare facility can absorb, adapt, and withstand the severity and impact of EWEs in order to ensure undisrupted medical services during and after the EWE occurrence. In addition, it can reorganise and bounce back to normal or a new state of permanent, higher-quality healthcare service delivery (Chand & Loosemore, 2013).

## 5.7  Redundancy in structures

Overlap and duplication have been pointed out in various studies to serve as a repository of heightened responsiveness and needed variety, which offer a crucial safeguard against system component failure. From this perspective, redundancy can be regarded as the excess capacity of a system that offers options to manoeuvre in the face of deficiency or uncertainty. Options such as these are expected to make the systems more effective in the sense that when one component of the system fails, the entire system does not fail. Reliability, then, implies effectiveness. That is, systems are effective to the extent that they are able to maintain dependable and predictable performance in the face of environmental uncertainty and individual component failures (Streeter, 1991).

In case of a healthcare facility, redundancy is the system property that allows for alternatives or different options to be made available in order to ensure continuity of services. These options could be in the form of usage of outpatient centres; community buildings; and other health facilities such as healthcare centres, alternative travel routes for movement of patients, electricity supply via backup generators, and alternatives for medical supplies and equipment (Chand & Loosemore, 2013).

Structural, non-structural, and functional preparedness can also be useful to maintain the redundancy of the healthcare facility. The structural preparedness characteristics include foundations, columns, beams, slabs, load-bearing walls, braces, and trusses that enhance the overall safety of the structure. The non-structural preparedness characteristics include electrical, mechanical, and water supply systems, also referred to as critical engineering infrastructures, which ensure a continuous supply of electricity, fresh air, water, etc., to keep the functions and operations of the healthcare facility running. Functional preparedness characteristics include storage and reserves of hospital facilities in communication, emergency, and transportation. These characteristics include:

- *Communication facility reserves*: emergency medical information system; communication devices or tools useful in case of emergency

- *Emergency reserves*: in-house power generators; medicine and medical equipment for emergencies; triage tags; folded beds; tents for emergency medical service dispensing; food; water
- *Transportation reserves*: cars for the disaster medical assistance team; road accessibility; heliport space

(Samsuddin et al., 2018).

## 5.8   Objective: continuity of services

The primary objective of achieving and maintaining resilience, redundancy, and robustness in a healthcare facility is to ensure its safety and continuity of service and functions during and after an EWE occurrence. In addition to emergency services and treatment of disaster victims and injured persons, the healthcare facility is also expected to continue the provision of treatment to existing in-patients. Further, continuity of prevention and promotion programmes also needs to be ensured, such as haemodialysis and prenatal care, which increases pressure on the organisation (Nia & Kulatunga, 2017).

Hence, ensuring continuity of services, emergency as well as elective, along with the functionality of the building, availability of equipment and medical supplies, and backup of services requires planning, preparedness, and risk mitigation programmes to manage and resist the impacts of potential hazards and EWEs that the healthcare facility may be exposed to. However, prevention-related activities also need to be incorporated into these plans in order to fortify the impact of the committee's hospital disaster risk management system (Nia & Kulatunga, 2017).

Formalising these considerations in the planning, design, and construction of healthcare facilities is critical in order to ascertain enhanced safety, security, and preservation of critical areas such as the intensive care units, operation theatres, emergency departments, medicine and food storage areas, diagnostic facilities, pharmacies, and services for booking and registration. Consequently, the structural and architectural design and planning of a hospital need to address safety specifications in relation to natural physical phenomena as well as economic, social, and human needs (Nia & Kulatunga, 2017).

### 5.8.1   *Density of healthcare services*

While services at a healthcare facility are running at an optimum during regular days, the services are required at a higher efficiency and frequency when an EWE strikes. With the overload of patients and affected persons during and after an EWE, the healthcare infrastructure must be able to adapt to provide sufficient rooms, space, and medical care to the affected. In addition to the structural and provisional safety of the healthcare facility, the density of the services in the facility must be enhanced, since it is critical to ensure delivery of medical care to all, without interruption and paucity.

### 5.8.2 Redundancy of healthcare services

EWEs may or may not cause damage to the healthcare facility in terms of loss of structure, manpower, or equipment. However, the facility must ensure it has redundancy, i.e., include extra components which would function in the case of failure of primary or functioning components. This also applies to medical and paramedical services, with redundancy in the case of staff and medical practitioners, who can act as extra support or function as primary staff in the case of the unavailability of regular or resident staff.

### 5.8.3 Mitigation of the impact of disruption on healthcare services

The impact and disruption due to the destructive effects of EWEs vary with the vulnerabilities of different social and economic groups in society. Risk, in such cases, can be defined as a community's vulnerability combined with the nature and impact of the impending hazard/EWE. To safeguard against the inherent risk and impact of the hazard/EWE, the vulnerability of the community needs to be reduced. Accordingly, a health disaster management programme needs to be established and adequately practised in order to efficiently prepare for a natural catastrophic event (Pan American Health Organization, 2000).

To establish the effectiveness of such disaster management and mitigation programmes, aspects of professional training, public education, and multi-discipline collaboration must be included. Disaster responses have been found to be successful when the disaster management and mitigation programmes include educating the public on their communities' vulnerabilities and risk mitigation measures, in addition to promoting EWE/disaster awareness and personal disaster safety. On a larger scale, specialised training of professionals involved in the management and conduction of disaster management and response programmes must ensure specialised training for specific and relevant skills, especially for doctors, nurses, paramedics, engineers, military personnel, and police officers. Catastrophe training for healthcare professionals is essential to enable them to efficiently modify daily triage protocols in order to manage and adjust to the sudden surge of victims and injured persons (Purcell, 1998).

Additionally, training and equipment handling for engineers helps enable them to assess the structural stability of various houses and buildings quickly. Specialised training for police and military personnel for the management of expanded levels of authority in relation to civil rights during times of crisis can help prepare them for the management and controlling of crowds and enforcing civil order before, during, and after the occurrence of an EWE/disaster. Disaster management and mitigation plans must also include efficient search and rescue resources, as well as organising and handling any mass evacuations (March, 2002).

## 5.9 Summary

EWEs have been observed to disrupt not only daily lives and critical infrastructure but also the operation and functioning of the healthcare infrastructure owing to the impact on the structure of the facility as well as the population/community. With an overwhelming effect on healthcare facilities due to increased patient load, increased workload, and a surge in medical needs and medical practitioners, hospitals that are not prepared for sudden upsurges critically affect existing patients and staff members in addition to increased need of resources.

Further, structural losses, healthcare overload, and disruption in the community due to loss of lives, loss of housing, and disruption of routine life also cause anxiety and stress disorders in the affected population apart from the outbreak of diseases.

The focus, again, shifts to the need for resilience in healthcare facilities and communities to minimise such losses and trauma. Resilience in infrastructure as well as healthcare services is important to ensure the density, frequency, and availability of medical staff in the case of an EWE. Redundancy in structure and medical services ensures that the impact of disruption is contained and the services are continued, even during and after the EWE. Provision of healthcare services, shelter, and nutritional supplies ensures reduced impact on communities and reduced risk of outbreaks and mental health problems.

## References

Bruneau, M., & Reinhorn, A. M. (2007). Exploring the concept of seismic resilience for acute care facilities. *Earthquake Spectra*, 41–62.

Centers for Disease Control and Prevention (CDC). (2018). *Public Health Emergency Preparedness and Response Capabilities*. Atlanta: U.S. Department of Health and Human Services.

Chand, A. M., & Loosemore, M. (2013). Reconceptualising hospital facility resilience to extreme weather events using a Panarchy model. In *Proceedings 29th Annual Association of Researchers in Construction Management Conference, ARCOM 2013*. Reading: ARCOM.

Guenther, R., & Balbus, J. (2014). *Primary Protection: Enhancing Health Care Resilience for a Changing Climate*. Washington, DC: U.S. Department of Health and Human Services.

Joy, K. (2017, September 11). Industry DX. *M Health Lab*. Retrieved from https://medicine. umich.edu/sites/default/files/content/downloads/The%20Effect%20of%20Natural%20 Disasters%20on%20Hospital%20Care%20%26%20Healthcare%20Staff.pdf

March, G. (2002). *Natural Disasters and the Impacts on Health*. Ontario: The University of Western Ontario.

Nia, S. P., & Kulatunga, U. (2017). Safety and security of hospitals during natural disasters: Challenges of disaster managers. *International Journal of Safety and Security Engineering*, 234–246.

Pan American Health Organization. (2000). *Natural Disasters – Protecting the Public Health's*. Washington, DC: PAHO.

Purcell, M. (1998). *Emergency Preparedness and Response Issues: Queen's University Ice Storm '98 Study*. Ontario: Queen's University.

Samsuddin, N. M., Takim, R., Nawawi, A. H., & Alwee, S. N. (2018). Disaster preparedness attributes and hospital's resilience in Malaysia. In *7th International Conference on Building Resilience; Using Scientific Knowledge to Inform Policy and Practice in Disaster Risk Reduction, ICBR2017* (pp. 371–378). Bangkok: ICBR.

Streeter, C. L. (1991). Redundancy in social systems: Implications for warning and evacuation planning. *International Journal of Mass Emergencies and Disasters*, 167–182.

# 6 The theory of resilience and risk in healthcare facilities

## 6.1 Overview

Incorporating resilience measures in new as well as existing buildings can substantially reduce the losses and damages to the structure and the functioning of the critical infrastructure. This chapter investigates the domains of resilience, risk analysis, and their components to underscore the significance of introducing resilience based on rational resource allocation. Figure 6.1 demonstrates the usefulness of introducing the rationale into resilient planning and design and its importance in reducing losses.

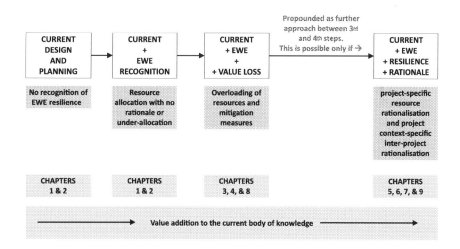

*Figure 6.1* Process of incorporating resilience: instituting the approach of risk reduction and resilience.

## 6.2 Structure of the chapter

This chapter reviews the various definitions and theories that explain the concept of resilience. Resilience, however, works in cohesion with redundancy in structures, especially in the case of EWEs, which are sporadic and often unpredictable.

DOI: 10.1201/9781003393108-6

*Figure 6.2* Structure and overview of Chapter 6.

In the times of global climatic change, many EWEs are observed to be striking the country; to be specific, events that have not been observed in the past decades in those locations. Instances of the same can be recognised as Cyclone Nisarga that hit the state of Maharashtra in June 2020, 11 years after 2009, and flash floods due to extreme precipitation in Hyderabad in 2020. Such events are erratic and unforesee-able and may get ignored during the design of structures. It has also been observed that there is a scarcity of redundancy in structures in the country, specifically in healthcare infrastructure. Thus, this chapter sheds light on resilience in healthcare structures, associated risks, and the loss potential in the structure due to EWEs and climate change. Figure 6.2 explains the structure and outcome of this chapter.

## 6.3   Resilience, reduction, and safety

While resilience is applicable as a concept as well as a function in critical infrastruc-ture, reduction is used in the context of risk reduction and loss potential reduction. Safety for the infrastructure includes not only structural safety but also economic and social safety for the users of the critical infrastructure.

### 6.3.1   *Defining resilience*

After the adoption of the Hyogo Framework for Action 2005–2015: Building the Resilience of Nations and Communities to Disasters, the concept of disaster resil-ience has gained wider popularity and interest. With the adoption of the Hyogo Framework, the main goal of disaster planning has shifted from reducing vulner-ability to reducing risk as well as building community resilience (Mayunga, 2007).

Derived from the Latin word 'resiliere', which means 'to jump back', the term resilience was used for an ecosystem to mean "the measure of the ability of an ecosystem to absorb changes and still persist" (Holling, 1973). The theory of resil-ience was aligned with the notion of stability, which Holling (1973) defined as "the ability of a system to return to its equilibrium after a temporary disturbance". This implies that the more quickly a system returns to its equilibrium, the more stable it is. With the conclusion of realising stability and resilience as the two important properties of an ecological system, it was also inferred by the author that certain systems can be very resilient and yet fluctuate greatly, thereby pointing to their low stability. The definition of the concept of resilience was redefined by Holling as "a buffer capacity or the ability of a system to absorb perturbation, or the magnitude of the disturbance that can be absorbed before a system changes its structure by changing the variables" (Holling et al., 1995).

As described by Foster (2006), a social system with high resilience also needs to be able to reconfigure itself without a major decline in the critical functions in relation to the economic prosperity and primary productivity of the community.

While various authors define resilience in terms of ecological aspects, self-reorganising capacities of systems, long-term recovery processes, sustainability, and vulnerability, Mayunga (2007) defines community disaster resilience as

> the capacity or ability of a community to anticipate, prepare for, respond to, and recover quickly from impacts of disaster. This means that it is not only the measure of how quickly the community can recover from the disaster impacts, but also the ability to learn, cope with or adapt to hazards. Thus, resilient communities should be organized in such a way that the effects of a disaster are minimal and the recovery process is quick.

Even as the understanding of resilience has been established by multiple authors using different parameters of measurement and assessment, the existing and incorporated degrees of resilience vary significantly over time for communities, groups, and individuals.

### 6.3.2   *Need for resilience*

With a long multi-disciplinary history, resilience has its origins in the 19th-century study of materials and has since been used in psychology (from the 1940s), ecology (from the 1970s), social sciences (from the 1990s), development aid (starting with DFID's 1999 sustainable livelihoods perspective), and, in the last decade, economics and the study of organisations.

It has been established in various literature sources that disaster resilience closely works with disaster risk management (DRM) and disaster risk reduction (DRR). Lessons and tools central to risk management, risk reduction, prevention, preparedness, recovery, response, and mitigation have been found to be critical for addressing challenges faced due to the hazards. However, resilience combines learnings, knowledge, and practices from other domains such as climate change adaptation, state building, poverty reduction, and conflict resolution with tools and approaches from DRM and DRR (Combaz, 2014).

The UN World Conference on Disaster Reduction (UNISDR) adopted the Hyogo Framework for Action 2005–2015: Building the Resilience of Nations and Communities, which acknowledged the severity and exposure of threats from natural disasters and EWEs in addition to the deficiencies of existing international response to these severities. The framework epitomised the connection between risk mitigation and resilience, calling for national and international governments and stakeholders to invest in disaster resilience. It also advocated the integration of climate change adaptation, DRR, sustainable development, poverty reduction, and good governance into a single resilience framework. The framework emphasised mitigation, prevention, vulnerability reduction, and preparedness in addition to faster recovery and response activities (Combaz, 2014).

The growing recognition of the severity of impact and the vulnerability of communities and infrastructure, along with the observed inadequacy of international efforts to reduce vulnerability and risks, has highlighted the need for resilience through the increasing consensus that:

i.    Disasters and EWEs cause setbacks in the development of societies and economies
ii.   Exposure to EWEs and natural hazards is increasing
iii.  Severity and frequency of weather- and climate change–related hazards is increasing
iv.   Disaster resilience has always been found to be underfunded
v.    Traditional development and humanitarian approaches to achieve reduced risks have been observed to be inadequate, given the exponential increase in frequency, intensity, exposure and vulnerability of communities and infrastructure
(Combaz, 2014)

### 6.3.3   *Resilience versus redundancy*

Resilience is characterised by four main properties: redundancy, resourcefulness, robustness, and rapidity (Bruneau & Reinhorn, 2007). While redundancy essentially aims at enabling the infrastructure to mobilise extra resources in case the resources are affected in the case of an EWE, resilience is the overall capacity of the community as well as the infrastructure to absorb shocks in case of EWE and recover quickly. Resilience can be seen as an umbrella term that encompasses attributes of absorbent community and infrastructure, and redundancy ensures resilience as well as reliable backup.

### 6.3.4   *Domain of disaster resilience and reconstruction*

In her paper, Owner-Driven Housing Reconstruction as a Means of Enhancing Disaster Resilience of At-Risk Communities in India, Vahanvati (2018) has identified the following five areas of influence that shaped ideas and frameworks for disaster resilience and reconstruction:

i.    *Technological and built-environment studies*:
      The underlying theory of these studies is to reduce the use of temporary or makeshift shelters and understand and focus on appropriate technology for housing using indigenous materials, construction techniques, skills, and labour. Simultaneously, there is a need to recognise and apply the spatial characteristics of settlements to acknowledge and establish the significance of social infrastructure and amenities (Vahanvati, 2018).

ii.  *Economic and development studies:*
     These studies suggest the disparity of the impact of disasters and EWEs on different social and economic groups. Since disasters affect the economically weaker sections of the society more severely, the process of reconstruction and resilience needs to address human capabilities development, affordability issues of the low-income groups, and livelihood security, which can help restore the local economy (Vahanvati, 2018).
iii. *Human geography, sociology, and political studies:*
     This area of study proposes active participation of communities and political leaders on both national and state levels to encourage safe and resilient construction (Vahanvati, 2018).
iv.  *Socio-ecological systems (SES) studies:*
     The fundamental outlook of this area of study is to acknowledge the importance of the ecosystem and environment for the survival and well-being of humans and the built environment.

(Vahanvati, 2018)

### 6.3.5   Defining risk reduction

---

**Box 6.1   India's efforts in DRR**

India has been proactive and leading in global efforts on Disaster Risk Reduction. A signatory to the "Delhi Declaration on Emergency Preparedness 2019", and Sendai Framework for Disaster Risk Reduction, the country is also a permanent chair of the CDRI.

(Mohanty, 2020)

---

DRR has been defined by Arya & Gupta (2010) as "the technical, social or economic actions or measures used to reduce direct, indirect and intangible disaster losses". DRR encompasses the two aspects of a disaster reduction strategy: mitigation and preparedness.

Mitigation aims at reducing the risk as well as the severity of the impacts of a disaster/EWE or a threatening disaster situation. Preparedness is the state of readiness of a group of people, community, organisations, or infrastructure to manage a disaster/EWE and its effects.

Mainstreaming risk reduction can be understood as a process that fully incorporates DRR into relief and development policy and practice. This implies that DRR is enhanced and expanded to become a part of the regular process and practice and is fully institutionalised within an organisation's development agenda (Trobe & Davis, 2005).

*i   Current DRR governance frameworks*

According to the United Nations Office for Disaster Risk Reduction (UNDRR), "disaster risk reduction is the concept and practice of reducing disaster risks through methodical efforts to analyse and diminish the pivotal factors of disasters that interrupt the development pathways" (UNDRR, 2019). A successor to the Hyogo Framework (2005–2015), the Sendai Framework for Disaster Risk Reduction (2015–2030) is a voluntary, non-binding agreement that brought together 185 countries to act on climate risks through DRR (Yokomatsu & Hochrainer-Stigler, 2020).

In addition to being an active member of the international and national treaties of significance in 2019, India is also a signatory to the Delhi Declaration on Emergency Preparedness in the South-East Asia Region. The national DRR framework, aligned with the Sendai Framework, entails precise and detailed risk assessment processes and applications, but does not detail climate-proof developmental pathways and mainstreaming of localised risk assessments (Mohanty, 2020).

Policies and frameworks for DRR in the Indian context were not drafted until August 1999. The importance of disaster management was recognised by the Government of India after the occurrence of the devastating Gujarat earthquake in 2001. Disaster management was declared a national priority hereafter, and a high-powered committee (HPC) and national committee were set up to mainstream disaster management and establish the blueprint for disaster management plans in India (National Disaster Management Authority, 2020).

With a mandate of fiscal provisions in the 12th Five-Year Plan, a chapter was included on disaster management for the first time. The Disaster Management Act was ratified by the Government of India on December 23, 2005, establishing the National Disaster Management Authority (NDMA) at the national level, which was headed by the prime minister. At the sub-national level, State Disaster Management Authorities (SDMAs) were established and were headed by the chief ministers of their respective states. The primary goal of these governance arrangements was to reduce risks and build resilience (Mohanty, 2020).

*ii   Mainstreaming DRR into the health sector*

Mainstreaming DRR into the health sector involves the development or strengthening (or extending the existing capacity) of a systematic strategy for risk mitigation measures, intended for curative and promotive healthcare services in the health sector at all levels (planning, implementation, monitoring, and evaluation stages). The risks can arise from potential disease epidemics and hospital/pre-hospital–based management of non-epidemic medical conditions after disasters. It can also be understood as "development of a robust public and clinical health care service provision institutional mechanism to reduce the mortality and morbidity risks induced by any disaster" (NIDM & UNDP, 2012).

### 6.3.6   Defining safety

In the context of disasters and EWEs, safe healthcare facilities refer to the safety of all health centres and hospitals, irrespective of their location, size, type, ownership, specialities, or facilities available, in the face of a disaster. These healthcare facilities are expected to continue functioning during and after the occurrence of a disaster or EWE (NIDM & UNDP, 2012).

Hence, the objectives of a safe healthcare facility comprise the following:

a. The building needs to withstand structural damage or collapse to avoid any physical/economic losses or loss of life
b. Continues to function after the disaster to serve the disaster-affected critical mass
c. Organisation, management, and staff are prepared for any catastrophe, along with a well-drafted and analysed hospital network plan and hospital disaster management plan

(NIDM & UNDP, 2012)

Hospital safety entails the optimum functioning and operations of the facility at all times as well as during and after a disaster. Further, it also ensures no or minimal injury to the occupants due to damage to structural and non-structural elements of the healthcare facility during and after a disaster (NIDM & UNDP, 2012).

## 6.4    Risk during EWEs/hazards

Risk is a function of a hazard/EWE, the exposure of people and assets, and the conditions of vulnerability of the exposed assets or population. According to UNISDR (2012), the significant extreme weather risk drivers include:

- Growth of urban populations and increase in density, causing additional pressure on land and services
- Increase in settlements in coastal lowlands, unstable slopes, and other hazard-prone areas
- Weakness in local governance and inadequate participation of local stakeholders in planning and urban management
- Lack of efficient water resource management, solid waste management, and drainage systems that lead to landslides, floods, and health emergencies
- Decline of ecosystems due to anthropogenic activities such as wetland reclamation, road construction, pollution, and unsustainable resource extraction, which jeopardise the ability to provide essential services like flood protection and regulation
- Danger of collapse of older structures due to unsafe building stocks and decaying infrastructure
- Effect of patterns of extreme temperatures and precipitation due to climate change, depending on localised conditions, having an impact on intensity, frequency, and location of climate-related disasters (Guenther & Balbus, 2014)

### 6.4.1    Risk assessment

The term risk assessment refers to the total process of risk appraisal and analysis, which includes social evaluation as well as determination of levels of risks due to natural disasters/EWEs. Risk determination encompasses both identification of risks and estimation of the likelihood and magnitude of their occurrence. Risk evaluation considers a measure of both risk acceptance (acceptable degree of societal risk) and risk aversion (methods of avoiding risk) as alternatives to risks that are imposed involuntarily.

Risk identification and risk estimation are important aspects of risk assessment and involve scientific and technical determinations. These often involve considerable uncertainty, and the interpretation of the impact of uncertainties relies less on scientific consideration than on technical and social value judgements (Rowe, 1980).

### 6.4.2    Risk identification

Identification of disaster risks and their sources, along with their areas of impact, changes in circumstances, causes, and potential consequences of such events, is crucial in order to generate a thorough list of risks that helps enhance, create, accelerate, degrade, or delay the fulfilment of objectives associated with risk mitigation (ISO 31000, 2009).

Risk identification should take into account investigation of the knock-on effects of specific consequences, including cumulative and cascading effects. It should also incorporate a wider range of consequences, even if the cause or source of risk may not be evident. In addition to anticipating or predicting the risks and indicating what might happen, it must also consider the plausible scenarios showing what consequences may transpire.

Changes in levels of risks can be identified in three circumstances: (a) when a new risk is created, (b) when the magnitude of an existing risk changes, and (c) when perception of an existing risk changes. All three circumstances may occur simultaneously (ISO 31000, 2009).

The risk identification tools and techniques can be useful for healthcare organisations that are seeking to identify and analyse the risks posed to their infrastructure and operations due to natural/man-made disasters and EWEs.

A major challenge in risk identification concerns the source of catastrophes. These large, disruptive events – natural hazards to be specific – generally result from local and regional changes in energy balance patterns, which result in storms, cyclones, floods, earthquakes, droughts, famines, and other occurrences. In many cases, technological approaches to mitigate the impact of natural events have reduced the number of events occurring but have increased the magnitude of the consequences of those that do occur (Rowe, 1980).

### 6.4.3    Risk estimation

The process of risk estimation has five steps:

i.   Identifying the cause of risk
ii.  Measuring its effects
iii. Determining the risk exposure

iv.  Defining the consequences of exposure
v.  Valuing the consequences of exposure

(ISO 31000, 2009)

The first step of risk estimation entails the identification of causative events, or the events that generate a probability of incidence of risks. Each causative event may result in numerous possible outcomes. The second step determines these outcomes and their relative probability. In the third step, the exposure pathways are defined, i.e., the means by which risks are transmitted. The fourth step involves definition of the possible consequences due to exposure to risks and determination of the probability of occurrence of the consequences (of each risk). The final step considers the value placed on risk consequences by affected individuals (Rowe, 1980).

### 6.4.4  *Risk probability*

The probability of risk occurrence and the value placed on risk consequences by affected individuals determine the public's response to risks. Hence, the process of risk estimation requires two basic determinations: a consequence probability determination and a consequence value determination (Rowe, 1980).

### 6.4.5  *Risk quantification*

Risk is a forward-looking concept, which denotes an eventuality of an occurrence. Hence, risk quantification or risk assessment involves identification of the occurrence of possible events, quantification of their likelihood of occurrence, and appraisal of the potential consequences, should they occur. Assessment of risks only on the basis of past events does not furnish thorough evidence on the current state of the risks, for various reasons:

• Records of past events may span a limited time period, during which the infrequent but severe hazards may not have occurred
• No two events are exactly the same; hence, assessment of risks based only on past incidents may not reflect the anticipation of risks/consequences in their entirety
• Records of past events may not include comprehensive spatial and temporal information of the occurrence and its consequences, especially the severity of impacts on a local level

(Mauro, 2014)

An approach that not only builds on past event records but also considers the events and their potential consequences in the future allows better coverage of the impact and risks posed by possible future events. Such an approach presents an improved estimation of the probability of occurrence of these events and the associated losses. This probabilistic risk assessment can prove to be useful for decision-makers who need detailed information about the potential events and consequent losses, as well as the frequency and likelihood of their occurrence. While the scale of the risk and intensity of the occurrence determines specific application of risk management strategies, probabilistic risk assessment can generally be used for:

- Estimating vulnerability and exposure, using probabilistic information on hazard intensities, and designing risk reduction interventions
- Budgeting and financing for disaster risk reduction
- Cost-benefit analysis and comparison of the cost of specific interventions with the reduction in losses when these interventions are implemented (Mauro, 2014)

### 6.4.6   *Risk analysis*

Risk analysis entails the development of in-depth understanding of the risks. The analysis furnishes inputs for risk evaluation, decision-making for treatment of risks, and selection of the most appropriate risk reduction methods or risk treatment strategies. The sources and causes of risks are identified, along with their positive and negative consequences, and the likelihood of occurrence of the risks and consequences is determined.

Risk analysis can be conducted with varying degrees of detail, depending on the risks, the intent of the analysis, and the data and resources available. The analysis can be quantitative, semi-quantitative, qualitative, or a combination of some or all of these, depending on the circumstances (ISO 31000, 2009).

### 6.4.7   *Risk management framework*

The success of DRM is influenced by the effectiveness of the risk management framework, which provides the arrangements and foundations that will implement the framework at all levels in an organisation/healthcare facility. The risk management framework is useful in the effective management of disaster risks through application of the process of risk management at different levels within specific contexts of the organisation/healthcare facility. It ensures that the data about the risks obtained from the DRM process is adequately organised and recorded and is used as a basis for accountability and decision-making at all relevant levels of the organisation/healthcare facility (ISO 31000, 2009).

The DRM process should be developed to fit suitably and become an integral part of the organisational processes. DRM, in particular, must be embedded into the organisation's/healthcare facility's change management process, business and strategic planning and review, and policy development (ISO 31000, 2009).

### i   *Resources*

Allocation of suitable resources by the organisation for DRM should also take into account the following:

- People, skills, competence, and experience
- The tools, methods, and processes of the organisation that can be used for managing disaster risk

- Documented procedures and processes
- Information and knowledge management systems
- Training programmes

(ISO 31000, 2009)

*ii   Establishing internal communication and reporting mechanisms*

In order to encourage and support accountability and ownership of disaster risks, the organisation/healthcare facility should establish internal communication and reporting mechanisms. These mechanisms will help ensure communication and transparency of the key components, modifications, effectiveness, availability of information, and processes for consultation with internal stakeholders (ISO 31000, 2009).

*iii   Establishing external communication and reporting mechanisms*

Communication with external stakeholders should be included in the risk management plan, which ensures effective exchange of information; compliance with regulatory, legal, and governance requirements; feedback and reporting; and communication with stakeholders in case of contingency or crisis (ISO 31000, 2009).

*iv   Implementing the framework for managing risk*

Implementation of the DRM framework for the organisation/healthcare facility should include the following:

- Compliance with regulatory and legal requirements
- Definition of a suitable strategy and timing for implementation of the framework
- Ensuring that decision-making, including the development of objectives, is aligned with the outcomes of risk management processes
- Application of the risk management process and policies to the organisational processes
- Training sessions
- Consultation and communication with stakeholders to ensure that the framework remains relevant

(ISO 31000, 2009)

### 6.4.8   Risk evaluation

The intent of risk evaluation is to support decision-making about the risks that need attention and priority for treatment implementation, based on the outcomes of risk analysis. Evaluation of risk involves a comparison of the level of risks identified in the analysis process with the risk criteria established when the context was taken into account. The need for treatment is determined based on this comparison.

Decisions about disaster risks need to consider wider contexts of the risks and tolerance of the risks borne by other stakeholders. These decisions must be made in accordance with regulatory, legal, and other requirements. Additionally, the decisions are affected by the risk attitude of the organisation/healthcare facility and the risk criteria that have been established (ISO 31000, 2009).

### 6.4.9    Acceptable risks

A risk is said to be acceptable when those affected by the consequences are not, or are no longer, apprehensive about it. Further, experts and regulators must have a positive response on the low potential impact of the risks. Under this, two variables exist:

i.  How much risk is acceptable for an entirely new undertaking
ii. Which alternative should be selected to reduce risk to a residual level

Acceptable levels of risk are both visible measures of residual risk and targets to be achieved. For public officials who are responsible for public safety and who need to balance tax levels against other sources seeking to use the funding, the presence of specific levels of acceptable risks can pose significant challenges (Rowe, 1980).

## 6.5    Resilience in relation to critical infrastructure

---

**Box 6.2    Benefits and opportunities from resilient infrastructure**

Depending on the processes implemented, resilient infrastructure can generate a variety of benefits.

- *Increased reliability of service provision* – Reliability in the infrastructure yields benefits ex post by reducing the severity and frequency of disruption. It also decreases the need for users to invest in backup measures ex ante.
- *Increased asset life, reduced repair, and maintenance costs* – Preparedness for impacts of climate change and EWEs can help avoid the need for expensive retrofitting and reduce the risk of the structure/asset becoming obsolete prematurely.
- *Increased efficiency of service provision* – Taking into consideration the impacts of climate change and EWEs and applying remedial or risk reduction measures can help reduce the unit costs of providing services, as compared to typical approaches.
- *Co-benefits* – Certain processes to achieve resilience in infrastructure, particularly using natural infrastructure, can help furnish equivalent services to traditional approaches, along with other co-benefits such as climate change mitigation, biodiversity conservation, and amenity value.

(OECD, 2018)

---

Critical infrastructure (CI) represents a complex and intricate system designed to facilitate the permanent availability of essential services to ensure smooth functioning of the society. The requirement of high reliability and availability of services, especially in highly urbanised regions (concentrated utilisation) makes these systems unique. At the same time, this system is composed of extensive subsystems of infrastructure networks, which are inherently decentralised and extend over vast areas. Individual CI subsystems are therefore constantly exposed to the effects of various threats that lead to the occurrence of disruptive events. Hence, it is crucial to improve the awareness and understanding of the interdependencies and linkages between CI systems and individual subsystems, as well as interdependencies between the society and subsystems, so as to develop a basis for the systems of resilience and protection of CI and its elements.

While the debate over the need for ensuring protection of CI has been deliberated upon for a long time, resilience in CI was originally defined in detail in the document Critical Infrastructure Resilience Final Report and Recommendations. In 1998, the Presidential Decision Directive PDD-631 was issued. However, resilience began receiving more comprehensive attention only after the Presidential Decision Direction PDD-21 was published (Rehak et al., 2018).

### 6.5.1   *The concept of resilience in critical infrastructure systems*

The integration and subsequent reinforcement of resilience in any CI requires explicitly defined initial conditions, in addition to the conditions of functionality and operations. The principal initial condition typically entails the setting up of the management process for introduction and incorporation of resilience in CI elements, including the framework for strengthening resilience. Conversely, well-defined perception and specification of factors that determine CI resilience are crucial as a part of the fundamental functional condition. The principles of the Plan-Do-Check-Act (PDCA) cycle are typically adapted to develop the management process for protection of the CI elements (Rehak et al., 2018).

---

**Box 6.3   Designing climate-resilient infrastructure**

Infrastructure that is climate resilient has the potential to increase asset life, safeguard asset returns, and enhance the reliability of service provision. Integrating climate resilience typically entails a package of:

- **Structural measures** (such as increasing the height of bridges to account for a rise in sea levels or use of natural infrastructure such as improving or protecting natural drainage systems)
- **Management measures** (such as inclusion of adaptive management to account for future uncertainties or changing maintenance schedules)

Adaptive, flexible approaches used in infrastructure development can be used to reduce the costs of incorporating climate resilience, given the uncertainties about the future.

(OECD, 2018)

---

Strengthening resilience has been observed to minimise the vulnerability of subsystems, which in turn reduces the intensity, occurrence, and propagation of failures and their impacts on CI systems and society. In addition to the principal initial conditions and fundamental functional conditions, the resilience of CI can be identified as a cyclic process which involves enhancement of prevention, absorption, recovery, and adaptation (Rehak et al., 2018).

Absorption comes into play when a subsystem is damaged or interrupted due to a disruptive event. Robustness determines the absorption of the CI system. Robustness can be understood as the capability of a CI element to absorb the effects of disruption caused by any event, without any variability in service.

The recovery phase commences after the weakening of the effects of the event that caused disruption. Recoverability is characteristic of this phase, which can be understood as the capacity of a subsystem to recuperate its operations and functions back to the required and/or original level of performance. The duration of the recovery phase is determined by the time period needed to fulfil the individual recovery processes and the resources available for the same.

The final phase of the CI resilience cycle, i.e., adaptation, indicates the ability of a CI facility/organisation to learn from the disruptive events that occurred previously. This involves adapting an operative subsystem to become flexible in terms of the potential recurrence of the event. Hence, it represents the long-term and dynamic capability of a facility/organisation to adapt to fluctuating conditions. The key purpose of ensuring adaptation is to strengthen the resilience of the organisation and its functions through risk management, innovative processes, and education/development processes (Rehak et al., 2018).

### *6.5.2   Factors determining the resilience of critical infrastructure*

Resilience of CI can be defined as a condition shaped by three types of factors (Rehak et al., 2018):

i.   *Factors determining resilience*
     This includes variables and components of organisational and technical resilience.
ii.  *Factors limiting resilience*
     This includes statutory regulation of the level of availability of financial resources or operations of the infrastructure.
iii. *Factors affecting resilience*
     This includes resilience-strengthening instruments or threats to resilience.

The resilience of elements in a CI system is determined by two fundamental fields – organisation management and physical and technological protection of elements. The area of organisation management, also known as organisational resilience, is ascertained by the level of internal processes of the organisation. The principal intent is to create optimum conditions to help CI elements adapt to disruptive events. Technical resilience is ascertained by the robustness and recoverability of system elements. This can be improved with respect to a specific element or a group of similar elements. For instance, the recoverability and robustness in the electricity sector can be secured by different methods depending on the systems used, i.e., systems employed for distribution and transmission or systems for production of electricity (Rehak et al., 2018).

### 6.5.3    Factors determining robustness

Robustness can be defined as the ability of an attribute of a building to absorb the impacts of a disruptive event. The effects of the event may be absorbed via the security attributes of the building (i.e., security robustness) and/or the structural attributes and technologies used (i.e., structural robustness).

The following variables determine the robustness of the structure:

- Redundancy
- Crisis preparedness
- Responsiveness
- Detection ability
- Physical resistance

When the level of robustness reaches 100%, the concerned attribute is said to become resistant to the impacts of the given disruptive event. This indicates that the attribute is fully capable of resisting the impacts of the event without distinct negative impact on the service provision (Rehak et al., 2018).

### 6.5.4    Factors determining recoverability

In the context of CI, recoverability can be defined as reparability, in which the repair or replacement is executed only for the destroyed or damaged components of an element. The following variables help determine recoverability:

- *Financial resources*: ensuring rapid recovery of the element through ascertaining financial reserves
- *Material resources:* ensuring availability of components necessary for repair or replacement
- *Recovery processes:* processes to enable rapid recovery of the element and its performance
- *Human resources:* ensuring availability of human resources with the necessary qualifications (Rehak et al., 2018)

### 6.5.5    Factors determining adaptability

Adaptability can be defined as the capability of the CI organisation to ascertain preparedness of the various attributes of the building against the recurring effects of a disruptive event. It denotes the dynamic or long-term ability of an organisation to adapt to changing conditions. The important processes that improve the adaptability of CI elements to disruptive events are innovation processes, risk management, and development/education processes.

The innovation processes of the organisation significantly contribute to the strengthening of the CI elements' resilience at the prevention stage. Development and education processes formulate and reinforce the organisational resilience of the CI elements, thereby boosting the ability of the organisation to adapt to the impacts of disruptive events (Rehak et al., 2019).

### 6.5.6   *Observations*

Strengthening of resilience relies on the continual improvement of the level of factors that govern it. Hence, the fields of organisational resilience as well as technical resilience require appropriate attention. At the same time, the other types of factors influencing resilience, i.e., factors affecting resilience and factors hindering resilience, are equally important.

While these principles are generally acceptable across different sectors of CI, effective implementation of the evaluation system requires this concurrence to manifest at deeper levels as well. For instance, at the level of individual resilience factors, the manifestation varies considerably in different CI sectors.

## 6.6   The concept of resilience in healthcare

---

**Box 6.4   Planning to improve the resilience of healthcare facilities**

A significant share of resilience is comprised of the planning and briefing processes of an organisation/healthcare facility. This is due to the information that is provided through these processes about the potential opportunities and risks. Additionally, it helps with understanding the needs of the stakeholders. Hence, healthcare logisticians need to uphold the level of consciousness regarding critical supplies and evaluate the capacity for prolonged sustainment, if needed in the future.

The purpose of maintaining a supply chain is to ensure that the end users are being served efficiently through a process that cannot be put at risk in the incidence of a disaster. Thus, planning ahead and comprehending the role of the supply chain manager can significantly contribute to the establishment of resilience. On the other hand, efficiency of planning ahead can be achieved only if a considerable amount of information is available. Amongst this information, a major dataset that can provide decent and timely information about the risks is the data from early warning systems (Vactor, 2011).

---

The emphasis of resilience in health facilities has been historically centred on acute care hospitals. Due to the compromised health of in-patients and the complexity of evacuation and transport, hospitals are designed and constructed to 'shelter in place' during and after critical events, including extreme weather (Guenther & Balbus, 2014).

### 6.6.1 The need for resilience in healthcare systems in the face of climate change

The unpredictable, complex, and multi-faceted ways in which climate change affects the healthcare infrastructure and systems make it crucial to incorporate resilience into healthcare sector. Health systems that are vulnerable may not be able to withstand the threats posed by the manifestations of climate change. Therefore, it is important to ensure that all new investments in the healthcare sector include resilience as a substantial component in order to ascertain the following:

- Rising population pressures
- Responding to climate change manifestations, such as increased precipitation, higher temperatures, and stronger storms
- Outbreaks of communicable diseases
- Local environmental degradation

(World Bank Group, 2017)

The role of the health community in societal resilience and broader adaptation policy is momentous and must be recognised. Hence, reframing climate change as a health issue and positioning health as a cross-cutting theme for adaptation strategies can enhance the efficiency of resilience measures and investments. Additionally, the need for advocating for increased awareness and understanding of the relationship between health and climate change must be acknowledged while integrating evidence into both policy and practice (World Bank Group, 2017).

### 6.6.2 Features of a resilient health system

Natural hazards encompass geological, hydrological, and meteorological extreme events that tend to disrupt the regular functioning of society. While resilience and safety measures for structures in earthquake-prone areas already exist in great detail, other events have also been defined by various Indian Standard (IS) codes. However, for an integrated resilience system, community and ecological perspectives need to be taken into account for other hazards as well, in addition to the technical perspective.

Kruk et al. (2015) propose five elements for a resilient health system:

- **Aware**: updated information about potential threats and health system assets, vulnerabilities, and strengths
- **Diverse**: ability to respond to a range of threats
- **Self-regulating**: ability to control threats before they overwhelm the system
- **Integrated**: convening the key factors needed to support the system, both within the health sector (including communities and private and public actors) and beyond it (for example, education, transportation, media)
- **Adaptive**: flexibility to transform in the face of challenges so as to improve performance

(World Health Organisation, 2008)

World Health Organisation (2015) explains the building blocks of healthcare systems that promote resilience to climate change impacts. The same has been depicted in Figure 6.3.

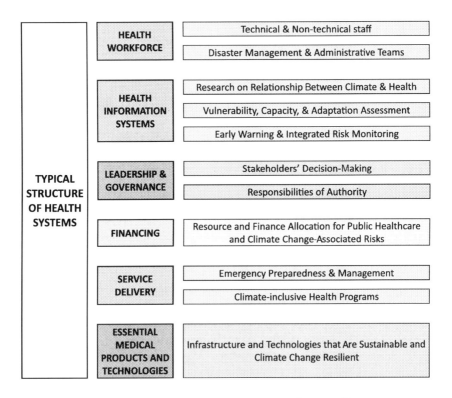

*Figure 6.3* Building blocks of health systems that promote climate resilience.

*Source:* Adapted from World Health Organisation, 2015.

### 6.6.3 *Climate-smart healthcare*

The key risks due to climate change as identified by the IPCC include land-slides and flood impacts due to extreme precipitation, wildfire impacts, impacts on water availability, and heat-related mortality. These impacts substantially affect health in communities where the risks materialise. As first responders, healthcare facilities need to be resilient to such risks and consequent impacts and continue to function during and after the occurrence of such events to provide emergency medical care to affected communities. With these health systems and infrastructure exploring options for low-carbon healthcare, a major overlap has been found between climate change resilience interventions and the sustainability measures (World Bank Group, 2017). The possible intersection of achieving sustainability and resilience in healthcare infrastructure has been depicted in Figure 6.4.

Climate-smart healthcare aligns with low-carbon development strategies, as well as health transformation and strengthening strategies. It emphasises the need for transformation to achieve an integrated approach across primary, secondary, and tertiary care, with technical and financial focus placed on primary care. Additionally, it improves health by mitigating the environmental impacts of healthcare.

It has been observed that the highest quality of appropriate healthcare is provided to the public when the healthcare institutions are located close to local communities and compares their progress with similar health centres in their region and across the globe. Climate-smart healthcare derives from this observation and involves matching the workforce skills to tasks and locations (World Bank Group, 2017).

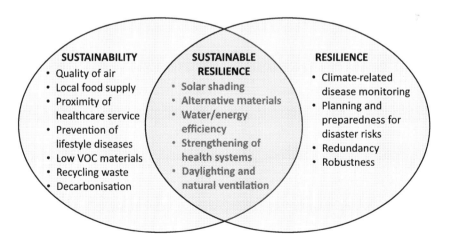

*Figure 6.4* Intersection of sustainable healthcare and resilience.

*Source:* Adapted from Health Care without Harm/World Bank

### 6.6.4   *Indicators for healthcare resilience*

A literature review conducted by Paterson et al. (2014) identifies indicators of climate change resilience in a healthcare facility. These were further used to develop the assessment checklist in the study. The listing of indicators is adapted in Table 6.1.

*Table 6.1* Climate change resilience indicators for healthcare facilities

| Category | Indicators |
| --- | --- |
| **General Resilience Indicators** | |
| | i. Cost-effectiveness of adaptation to climate change |
| | ii. Quantification of costs and benefits of implementing risk management measures |
| | iii. Opportunities to increase awareness about climate change |
| | iv. Knowledge capacity augmentation |
| | v. Ensuring adequate leadership |
| | vi. Allocating roles and responsibilities to staff to enhance resilience |
| | vii. Partnerships and mutual support for building adaptive capacity |
| **Emergency Management and Strengthening Healthcare Services** | |
| General | i. Assessment of effectiveness of existing resilience measures |
| | ii. Assessment of health risks to patients, visitors, and staff due to climate-related hazards |
| | iii. Developing plans for managing staff shortage in case of emergency |
| | iv. Securing access to critical backup resources and supplies (such as treatment supplies, medical equipment, and alternative energy supplies) |
| | v. Availability of expansion of emergency facilities to respond to surge capacity in the face of climate-related emergencies or disasters |
| | vi. Allocating resources for preventing and mitigating climate change impacts |
| | vii. Adopting an incidence management system |
| | viii. Ensuring availability of communication and coordination mechanisms with external agencies in case of emergency |
| | ix. Developing systems for monitoring of diseases, injuries, and health outcomes of patients affected due to climate-related hazards |
| Extreme Weather | i. Establishing mutual assistance/aid agreements with other institutions in case of climate/EWE-related emergency |
| | ii. Ensuring consistency of emergency plans with community disaster management plans |
| | iii. Updating emergency plans regularly based on new information on vulnerabilities, risks posed, and ways of improvement |
| | iv. Providing psychological first aid for patients, visitors, and staff to address mental health impacts in case of emergencies/disasters |
| | v. Developing systems to act upon climate and extreme weather warnings/advisories to manage health risks |

*Source*: Adapted from Paterson et al., 2014

## 6.7    Loss potential

The loss potential of a healthcare facility can be explained as the number of losses – tangible, intangible, market, value losses, etc. – that a hospital may incur when an EWE strikes. These losses may be structural, staff losses, fatalities, development losses, or financial losses. Loss potential can be calculated for structures that are already built to get an overall figure of the possible losses in the face of an EWE, which can further help the administration to minimise the losses and make necessary arrangements. Loss potential can also be calculated for structures that are in the design, planning, or construction stages, which can help the administration to incorporate the necessary elements in the structure to avoid losses to the maximum extent possible. The book entails calculation methods for potential value losses when a healthcare facility is subject to disruption due to EWEs. These calculations and formulae can be used in upcoming healthcare structures to ensure minimal value losses by incorporating appropriate measures in planning, design, and construction phases. The cost model also helps existing structures to salvage and save as much as possible in vulnerable cases. However, this model does not include a resilience cost calculation model for healthcare facilities. Nevertheless, the book recognises the vital premise of resilience and incorporates the same throughout.

## 6.8    Summary

A detailed review of the definitions of resilience brings to the surface the major themes under the umbrella term. Resilience focuses not only on safety and structural integrity but also draws attention to absorbing the disruption and recovering normalcy as quickly as possible. Ensuring resilience in structures and communities also ensures reduced losses, faster recovery, and lower impacts. Further, resilience holds five attributes – robustness, rapidity, resourcefulness, redundancy, and adaptability – which enhances the recoverability and absorption of disruption in a healthcare facility as well as a community.

This chapter also brings to light the risks encountered by CI during EWE. The processes for risk analysis and risk assessment bring together a robust risk management framework that can be implemented ahead of an EWE. However, risk management and risk estimation entail the need for resilience, especially in the case of critical healthcare infrastructure. Features of resilient healthcare infrastructure are highlighted in the chapter, along with the indicators for achieving resilience in medical facilities.

An overall review of risk assessment and risk evaluation, along with the existing levels of resilience in a healthcare facility, helps arrive at a loss potential for the facility, which helps identify and evaluate the losses that the structure might face, given the structural stability and service redundancy in case an EWE strikes.

## References

Arya, A. S., & Gupta, T. N. (2010). *Mainstreaming Disaster Risk Reduction in Housing Sector*. New Delhi: National Institute Of Disaster Management.

Bruneau, M., & Reinhorn, A. M. (2007). Exploring the concept of seismic resilience for acute care facilities. *Earthquake Spectra*, 41–62.

Combaz, E. (2014). *Disaster Resilience: Topic Guide*. Birmingham: GSDRC, University of Birmingham.

Foster, K. A. (2006, November). *A Case Study Approach to Understanding Regional Resilience: A Working Paper for Building Resilience Network*. New York: Institute of Urban Regional Development, University of California.

Guenther, R., & Balbus, J. (2014). *Primary Protection: Enhancing Health Care Resilience for a Changing Climate*. Washington, DC: U.S. Department of Health and Human Services.

Holling, C. (1973). Resilience and stability of ecological systems. *Annual Review of Ecology and Systematics*, 4, 2–23.

Holling, C., Schindler, D., Walker, B., & Roughgarden, J. (1995). Biodiversity in the functioning of ecosystems: An ecological synthesis. *Biodiversity Loss: Economic and Ecological Issues*, 44–83.

ISO 31000. (2009). *Risk Management – Principles and Guidelines*. Geneva: ISO Copyright Office.

Kruk, M. E., Myers, M., Varpilah, S. T., & Dahn, B. T. (2015). What is a resilient health system? Lessons from Ebola. *Lancet*, 385(9980), 1910–1912.

Mauro, M. D. (2014). Quantifying risk before disasters occur: Hazard information for probabilistic risk assessment. *World Meteorological Organisation*. Retrieved from https://public.wmo.int/en/resources/bulletin/quantifying-risk-disasters-occur-hazard-information-probabilistic-risk-assessment

Mayunga, J. S. (2007). *Understanding and Applying the Concept of Community Disaster Resilience: A Capital-based Approach*. Austin, TX: Texas A&M University.

Mohanty, A. (2020). *Preparing India for Extreme Climate Events*. New Delhi: Council on Energy, Environment and Water (CEEW).

National Disaster Management Authority. (2020). Evolution of NDMA. *NDMA*. Retrieved from https://ndma.gov.in/about-us/introduction#:~:text=The%20Government%20of%20India%20(GOI,Management%20plans%20and%20suggesting%20effective

NIDM & UNDP. (2012). *Mainstreaming Disaster Risk Reduction into Health: Strategies, Methodologies & Tools*. New Delhi: National Institute of Disaster Management.

OECD. (2018). *Climate-resilient Infrastructure: Policy Perspectives*. Paris: Organisation for Economic Co-operation and Development.

Paterson, J., Berry, P., Ebi, K., & Varangu, L. (2014). Health care facilities resilient to climate change impacts. *International Journal of Environmental Research and Public Health*, 13097–13116.

Rehak, D., Senovsky, P., Hromada, M., & Lovecek, T. (2019). Complex approach to assessing resilience of critical infrastructure elements. *International Journal of Critical Infrastructure Protection*, 125–138.

Rehak, D., Senovsky, P., & Slivkova, S. (2018). Resilience of critical infrastructure elements and its main factors. *Systems*.

Rowe, W. (1980). Assessing the risk of fires systematically. In *Fire Risk Assessment* (pp. 3–15). Hilton Head: ASTM Special Technical Publication.

Trobe, S. L., & Davis, I. (2005). *Mainstreaming Disaster Risk Reduction: A Tool for Development Organisations*. Middlesex: Tearfund.

UNDRR. (2019). *Global Assessment Report on Disaster Risk Reduction*. Geneva: UNDRR.

UNISDR. (2012). *Annual Report 2012*. Geneva: United Nations Office for Disaster Risk Reduction (UNISDR).

Vactor, J. D. (2011). Cognizant healthcare logistics management: Ensuring resilience during crisis. *International Journal of Disaster Resilience in the Built Environment*, 2(3), 245–255.

Vahanvati, M. (2018). *Owner-driven Housing Reconstruction as a Means of Enhancing Disaster Resilience of at-Risk Communities in India*. Melbourne: RMIT University.

World Bank Group. (2017). *Climate-Smart Healthcare: Low-Carbon and Resilience Strategies for the Health Sector*. Washington, DC: World Bank Group.

World Health Organisation. (2008). *61st World Health Assembly: Climate and Health*. Geneva: WHO.

World Health Organisation. (2015). *Operational Framework for Building Climate Resilient Health Systems*. Geneva: World Health Organisation.

Yokomatsu, M., & Hochrainer-Stigler, S. (2020). *Disaster Risk Reduction and Resilience*. Singapore: Springer.

# 7 The economics of resilience

## 7.1 Overview

Disruption in the structure and functioning of critical infrastructure can lead to momentous value losses. These losses have been elaborated in this chapter. Figure 7.1 shows how these losses can be reduced through project-specific resource rationalisation and project context–specific inter-project rationalisation allocated to incorporate resilience and risk reduction measures.

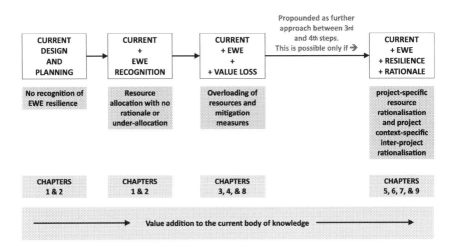

*Figure 7.1* Process of incorporating resilience: through project-specific resource allocation and rational financing.

## 7.2 Structure of the chapter

This chapter gains ground from Chapters 4 and 5 to recognise the losses caused due to disruption in healthcare facilities and the need to incorporate resilience and

DOI: 10.1201/9781003393108-7

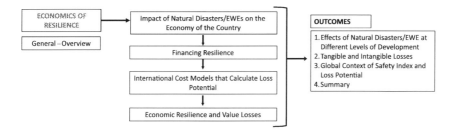

*Figure 7.2* Structure and overview of Chapter 7.

risk reduction in the design and planning processes. These losses are categorised as direct and indirect, tangible and intangible, and the value losses are identified. International models that analyse and calculate the loss potential are observed and reviewed to gather and apply implications on the cost model proposed in Chapter 8. Figure 7.2 explains the structure and outcome of this chapter.

## 7.3 Impact of natural disasters/EWEs on the economy of the country

Natural disasters and EWEs cast a momentous impact on the resources of the nation in several ways. While most of the observed and recorded impacts are negative and generate losses, certain studies argue for the undetected advantages for the country on a broader scale.

According to Raddatz (2007), disaster shocks and climate-related disasters such as floods, droughts, windstorms, extreme temperatures, etc., can affect the per-capita GDP of a country greatly (in the short run). Climate-related disasters have been recorded to cause an average real per-capita income loss of 2%, whereas humanitarian disasters such as famines or epidemics cause an average real per-capita income loss of 4% in the short run (Raddatz, 2007).

In contrast, Skidmore & Toya (2002) argue that the GDP does not constitute the damage to capital and durable goods in the short run. Rather, the GDP may get augmented owing to the development of new capital in the immediate timeline. The authors also established a positive correlation between natural disasters and growth in the long term. Using a panel dataset in 89 countries, the authors analysed the effects of disaster occurrences on the per-capita growth rates/GDP. It was observed that climatic disasters had a positive and significant effect on the growth rates. The research postulates that the positive effect on growth can be attributed to capital stock accumulation, human capital accumulation, or improvements in technological capacity (Skidmore & Toya, 2002).

In the long term, growth rates may get affected owing to replacement of outdated/older technologies by more productive/newer technologies. Even as the capital and infrastructure get damaged, the return to human capital compared to investment capital increases after the disaster. As newer and more productive technologies are introduced and adopted, the total factor productivity also increases. The research, therefore, highlights the important macro-economic channels through which countries may grow after the occurrence of a catastrophe (Skidmore & Toya, 2002).

On the contrary, the benefits of investment in technologically advanced capital have been observed to offset this, owing to the short-run productivity losses in the aftermath of a disaster. Installation and incorporation of new technology along with training of workers require extra time. This leads to immediate replacement of capital with older and outdated technology. It has been argued that this tendency may cause long-run productivity to remain unchanged in comparison to the pre-disaster levels (Hallegatte & Dumas, 2009).

This trend of continual replacement of damaged capital with similar capital as existent before the disaster increases the risk of stagnation of the community and infrastructure safety and development. While the capital is replaced quickly in order to resume previous productivity levels, low-income countries suffering from frequent disasters may get trapped in a labyrinth of poverty. This can occur due to suppressed possibilities of increase in productivity in the future as a result of outdated and low-productivity capital and infrastructure (Kellenberg & Mobarak, 2011).

Natural disasters also significantly impact labour markets. A study conducted by Sarmiento (2007) analyses a panel dataset on floods across the United States. The results depicted that after a flood, the workers escape from the affected region, thereby leading to a decrease in the aggregate local employment by 3.4% on average (Sarmiento, 2007). However, according to Belasen & Polachek (2009), income levels increase after a disaster.

### 7.3.1   *Effects of natural disasters/extreme weather events at different levels of development*

The most significant impacts of natural disasters and EWEs are observed on human capital, labour, physical capital, short- and long-run GDP, and real estate markets. As disasters and EWEs affect the trajectory of development considerably, similarly the state of development of a country has a bearing on the impact of a natural disaster/EWE. This trend can be understood with the help of developmental changes accompanying economic development. A country can focus on its weaker characteristics only after achieving an acceptable and functional level of development. The improvement of weaker characteristics may include creation of better insurance markets, reduction in corruption, development of more stringent building standards, and establishment of advanced emergency response and warning systems. It can therefore be inferred that less developed countries are more likely to be severely affected by natural disasters/EWEs as compared to more developed countries owing to their higher levels of development and improvement (Kellenberg & Mobarak, 2011).

---

**Box 7.1    Economic impacts of EWE on healthcare**

Damage to healthcare facilities due to natural disasters and EWEs causes considerable economic losses and disruption in functioning and operations of the health facility. Losses may be direct, such as damage to structures, life support installations, expensive medical equipment, medical supplies, and hospital furniture. Indirect losses may include loss of life, injuries, loss of income, unforeseen expenses such as temporary field hospitals, or increased risk of outbreaks. Further, since the healthcare facilities are huge and involve substantial economic investments, the effects of disasters on the health-care infrastructure are amplified. Recovery in the health sector may require immediate large outlays, which may not be available promptly, especially in low-resourced areas (Geroy & Pesigan, 2011).

---

The rise in vulnerability of communities and infrastructure to EWEs can be largely attributed to the citizens and governing bodies. Individuals with low levels of income may be more inclined to participate in income-generating activities that involve considerable environmental risks. An example of such activities is the cutting of mangrove forests for shrimp farming developments. Such practices are bound to increase the vulnerability, exposure, and risk of the individuals as well as communities to a natural disaster/EWE. However, higher levels of development and involvement of high-income groups may offer extra protection and mitigation that the increase in income allows. Hence, a risk-return trade-off between higher income and advantages of higher levels of development and the disaster-associated risks can explain the non-linear correlation between disaster damages and level of development (Kellenberg & Mobarak, 2007).

Schumacher & Strobl (2008) point out that the adaptation expenditure associated with increased risk of cyclones, floods, or earthquakes is higher only in the cases of considerable risk aversion, availability of necessary amount of wealth, or in case of low costs of development. This phenomenon can be observed in flood dams in the Netherlands and hydraulic-balanced skyscrapers in Japan, where significant marginal benefits are obtained. Additionally, countries that are poor or developing and are at a high risk have a greater tendency to spend a substantial percentage of their GDP on adaptation, since a higher percentage of their capital is prone to being destroyed upon the occurrence of a natural disaster/EWE. Incentives to invest in adaptation are reduced due to an increase in the marginal value of wealth (Schumacher & Strobl, 2008).

Countries that are at low risk of being affected by natural disasters/EWEs, especially those that are developing and less prosperous, typically have small marginal benefits for capital adaptation expenditure. In such countries, less finances are allocated towards adaptation to natural hazards. Consequentially, these countries with a low probability and exposure to a natural disaster/EWE suffer greater destruction when a natural disaster/EWE strikes, as compared to countries that have high risk and exposure. With the growth in economy and wealth of low-risk-exposure countries, higher economic losses can be expected in the event of a disaster until the peak of the curve, when the wealth will be used for adaptation expenditure, leading to reduction in losses (Kellenberg & Mobarak, 2011).

The migration of populations to urban regions overwhelms the capacity of the cities and their infrastructure to provide necessary public services. This leads to inadequate housing, supply shortages, and congestion, thereby resulting in a rise in the number of people exposed to natural hazards/EWEs and intensified risks of losses. Further, the increase in requirement for newer infrastructure development leads to degradation of the natural environment and a higher risk of damage (Kellenberg & Mobarak, 2011).

## 7.4   Financing resilience

While it has been widely observed that disaster resilience is underfunded, evidence for the same entailing the costs and cost-effectiveness of resilience interventions is limited, but increasing. Typically, multi-year funding for disaster resilience is encouraged, especially for prolonged crises. A desk-based study commissioned by the DFID that examines the value for money and cost-benefit of multi-year humanitarian funding found that gains in economy, effectiveness, and efficiency were generated with the funding throughout the disaster management cycle, but evidence for the same was limited and the advantages were dependent upon the type of crisis (Combaz, 2014).

It is challenging to allocate scarce resources, and resilience programming essentially involves trade-offs among various sectors and groups. 'Building Back Better' involves higher costs, comprehensive technical solutions, and stricter building standards. These may be out of reach for the communities that need help the most. Resilience in vulnerable communities can be developed through small-scale livelihood diversification by way of expansion into larger industrial and agricultural projects (Combaz, 2014).

Numerous studies have observed that building disaster resilience before the occurrence of a disaster can prove to be more cost-effective and consume less finances as compared to post-disaster humanitarian response. For instance, in Bangladesh, modest funds were expended on weather forecasting, shelters, evacuation plans, and warning systems, which were found to be effective in mitigating loss of life in the event of cyclones. The Global Facility for Disaster Reduction and Recovery (GFDRR) encourages funding expenditure on well-maintained and functioning critical infrastructure and early warning systems that continue to serve during and after the occurrence of disasters in addition to physical protection through environmental buffers. It also states that the cost-effectiveness of prevention can be enhanced through government-led initiatives such as:

- Easy access of information and analysis related to disasters provided to the public
- Reflection of hazard risks in property values

- Security of property in safer locations for the poor
- Adequate availability and quality of infrastructure and services
- Assessment of each mode of financial coping mechanism (in terms of remittances, borrowing, dedicated funds, insurance, drawbacks, aid, prevention, uncertainties, and cost-effectiveness)

(Combaz, 2014)

However, evidence regarding the effectiveness of disaster resilience has the potential to be strengthened further in terms of assessment of costs and benefits of long-term resilience and hefty investments such as road networks and education. Efficiency of resilience measures also involves assessment in terms of local participation and buy-in (Combaz, 2014).

## 7.5   International cost models that calculate loss potential

Approved by 168 countries in 2005, the Hyogo Framework for Action (HFA) provides a blueprint for building countries that are resilient to disasters. The HFA requires all new hospitals to be developed on standards that ensure their stability and functioning during and after disasters.

With support from the WHO/PAHO and assessment of past and present projects, the safety of hospitals has been established as a requisite. The safety can be improved in the case of disasters or emergencies with the help of available tools and knowledge. The Hospital Safety Index, a tool developed by Bittner, is a new method of evaluation to facilitate this goal (Bittner, 2008).

In a case presented by Patricia Bittner (2008) in her paper, 'The Hospital Safety Index', the author has highlighted the significance of pre-determining hospital safety. The study discusses the case of Juarez Hospital in Mexico, where 561 doctors, patients, and nurses lost their lives due to the collapse of an entire wing of a 12-storey tower. Even though the hospital staff was well-prepared to respond in the event of mass casualties, the structural vulnerability obliterated lives as well as infrastructure.

### 7.5.1   Hospital Safety Index

The Hospital Safety Index is an evaluation tool used to assist hospital administrators or directors to determine the likelihood of their healthcare facility to continue functioning in emergency situations. It is an easy-to-apply tool that provides a snapshot in time of a hospital's level of safety. In order to monitor safety levels continuously, the index can and should be applied various times over an extended period. This offers a new outlook on the safety of the healthcare facility as a feature that can be enhanced gradually, instead of being perceived or tested as an absolute state of 'all-or-nothing' or 'yes-or-no'. The index is designed as a cost-effective first step for vulnerability analyses and does not intend to replace the detailed studies (Bittner, 2008).

The determination of the Hospital Safety Index of a healthcare facility can be initiated with the application of the Safe Hospitals Checklist. This standardised checklist entails examining the level of safety of 145 items or aspects that affect the safety of a healthcare facility. The items in the checklist are divided into four categories: structural safety, non-structural safety, geographical location of the hospital related to natural hazards, and items that have an impact on the functional capacity of the hospitals – concerns such as whether the healthcare facility/hospital has an emergency plan, a disaster committee, or if maintenance is conducted regularly.

A team of evaluators with advance training implements the Safe Hospitals Checklist. The profile of the team members usually consists of experienced professionals, such as hospital staff (directors, doctors, maintenance staff, paramedical staff, etc.), in addition to external specialists such as engineers or architects. The evaluation team may work together or in small teams to appraise the items included in the checklist. Individual components of the facility are graded or scored based on standardised rating – high, medium, and low. Objective evaluation of various components or areas of the hospital can be conducted with the help of a guide for evaluators, which provides a comprehensive description of the processes and factors involved.

After completion of the checklist, the results are discussed and harmonised. In the concluding step of the process, the Safety Index Calculator is used to determine the safety score of the healthcare facility. Using an established formula, the scores given to each component are weighed. The data obtained is input into the Safety Index Calculator, through which a numerical score is automatically generated, which assigns the healthcare facility to one of the three categories of safety – high, medium, or low. The output is generated in an easy-to-understand graphic format (Bittner, 2008).

### 7.5.2   *Interpretation of results*

Prior to the commencement of the process of determining the Hospital Safety Index, a meeting is organised between the hospital staff and the evaluation team to describe the purpose and rationale of the 'safe hospitals' program. After the completion of the checklist and data input in the scoring calculator, which yields an objective, numerical score, the results are analysed by the evaluation team and discussed with the hospital staff to help interpret the score in order to determine the subsequent steps to be taken by the health facility to improve their safety (Bittner, 2008).

While the Hospital Safety Index does not generate a detailed analysis, it assists the hospital administrators to derive a sound overview of the status of the healthcare facility in terms of safety. This can help them decide the measures to invest in so as to ensure maximised safety and returns. Elements that have been assessed can be divided into three categories – Category C (safety score 0–0.35; the healthcare facility requires urgent measures immediately, since the current safety levels are not satisfactory to ensure patient and staff protection during and after the occurrence of a disaster); Category B (safety score 0.36–0.65; the healthcare facility requires necessary measures at some point, since the current safety levels may put the staff and patients at risk potentially during and after the occurrence of a disaster); and Category A (0.66–1; the healthcare facility may require preventative measures at some point, since the current safety levels may potentially cause certain acceptable damages, which eventually reduce the overall safety level of the facility). It has been observed that the safety can be improved significantly through low-cost improvements (relative to the overall cost of the facility), making it possible for some facilities to move up from Category C to Category B, or better.

It is critical that the decision-makers and administrators of the healthcare facility perceive the safety score in a positive light – which is why the tool is called 'Safety Index' instead of 'Vulnerability Index'. The final score obtained must be perceived as a starting point and not as a failing grade. The score is useful for assessing how a healthcare facility is expected to perform and respond to major emergencies or natural disasters (Bittner, 2008).

### 7.5.3  *The global context of safety index and loss potential*

The model proposed by Bittner provides evidence that hospital/critical infrastructure safety has been a subject of concern for a long time, and significant work has been done in the realm of hospital safety and vulnerability. While this framework/tool looks at the safety index and indicates how unsafe a hospital structure could be in the event of a hazard, the framework proposed in this book quantifies the potential consequences of a hazard. The cost model looks at the loss potential of the structure, i.e., what elements may be lost and which ones would cause the maximum damage in case of an EWE. This helps hospital management devise plans to safeguard their most valuable assets and make arrangements in advance in case of an EWE to minimise their damages.

However, these two frameworks are expected to work better in conjunction, where the existing structure's safety index and loss potential are used in unison, and list the categories where a hospital is lacking and which ones can be improved.

## 7.6  Defining economic resilience

Rose (2009) defines economic resilience under two sub-heads:

### a)  Static economic resilience

Static economic resilience can be defined as the ability of a system to uphold its growth and production, even after facing a shock. It is related to the underlying economic problem of efficient allocation of resources, which is aggravated in the event of a disaster. This attribute is understood as static, since it can be sustained with the need for repair or reconstruction activities that affect the current and future path of the economic activities. Additionally, static economic resilience is primarily a demand-side phenomenon, which involves consumers rather than suppliers. In contrast, the supply-side phenomenon typically involves repair and reconstruction.

---

**Box 7.2   Diversification away from disaster risk**

A well-established strategy of risk aversion, as well as a generic response to uncertainties and risks in the market economies, is diversification of economic structures. One of the ways to achieve this is through livelihood diversification, which typically involves engaging in multiple sources of income and is central to coping strategies of the poor. However, disaster mitigation programmes often overlook the long-term implications of the economic structure. Diversification for disaster reduction can take many shapes, and methods can be devised at different levels of aggregation (Haen & Hemrich, 2006).

---

b) **Dynamic economic resilience**

This can be understood as the swiftness with which the system recovers from a shock to achieve a stable or desirable state. This also includes the concept of mathematical or system stability, as it indicates the system's ability to bounce back. This form of resilience is relatively more complex, since it entails a long-term investment problem related with reconstruction and repair – processes that are uniquely applicable to a post-disaster scenario. This type of economic resilience is usually defined contextually – the level of functioning of the system can be compared to the level that would have existed if the ability to bounce back had been absent, i.e., a worst-case scenario or a reference point needs to be established first.

(Rose, 2009)

Resilience relating to the economy is applicable at three levels:

- Micro-economic (individual household or business)
- Meso-economic (individual market or industry)
- Macro-economic (combination of all economic entities)

The macro and meso levels usually overlap with a focus on community resilience and denote a more holistic scenario. Nevertheless, micro-economic foundations for macro-economic analysis have been valued significantly by economists for various reasons. Firstly, individual building blocks of consumer and producer behaviour constitute the micro-economy, which underpins the macro-economic considerations stemming from group interactions. Secondly, behavioural concerns addressed at the most elemental level are managed better. These points are also applicable for community resilience (Rose & Krausmann, 2013).

## 7.7   Defining value losses

The consequences of structural failures caused by natural disasters and EWEs are typically observed in multiple forms, for instance, severe structural damage, fatalities, injuries, damage to contents of the building, environmental damage, and loss of functionality. Various terms are used by experts in the discipline of disaster cost estimation, which may or may not be consistent. However, the terminology can be defined as follows:

i.  In general terms, the impacts of a disaster include both:

    a.  **Market-based effects** – These include decrease in sales and income and damage to property
    b.  **Non–market-based effects** – These include psychological impacts and environmental consequences (National Research Council, 1999)

ii. Negative economic impacts are represented by the losses incurred during and after the disaster. These include:

    a.  **Direct losses** – Losses that occur due to physical damage to structures and natural resources
    b.  **Indirect losses** – Losses that occur as a consequence of the physical damage, such as temporary unemployment or interruption in business

While economic losses to the hospital and administration are in the shape of cash flow, finances, and funds, value losses can be defined as the loss of value of a service, which can be higher than the economic losses. Value losses could be to the patient, who not only loses services of the hospital rendered dysfunctional in case of an EWE but also the costs he or she bears to move to and access another hospital. Value losses to staff include their income as well as the extra earnings in the case of increased number of hours of service in the case of an EWE. Value losses to the administration would include not only machinery, equipment, and structural losses but also the anticipated commerce for the number of days that the hospital is rendered dysfunctional, alongside their operating data and outstanding liabilities (National Research Council, 1999).

## 7.8   Defining tangible and intangible losses due to EWEs

Tangible losses can be defined as the consequences of structural failures in the case of natural disasters/EWEs, which leads to loss of property and employment. Tangible losses can be estimated based on the visible and calculable entities, such as structural/civil architectural losses, equipment losses, inventory losses, machinery losses, land losses, employment losses, vehicle losses, operating data, and reserve funds.

Intangible or non-market losses can be understood as the losses from natural disasters/EWEs that may not necessarily be quantified in monetary terms. These include impact on public health, damage to cultural heritage, and impact on the environment. These intangible losses are usually not included or evaluated in cost assessments of natural hazards/EWEs, resulting in incomplete and biased cost assessments. Such cost assessments are not useful for optimising fund allocation, nor can the design measures for damage mitigation be ensured. Hence, the intangible impacts and their cost implications must be included in order to derive an integrated risk assessment and management framework/plan (Markantonis & Schwarze, 2012).

Intangible losses usually vary depending on the type of natural disaster/EWE or severity of the event. These can be included in monetary form for a cost-benefit analysis framework, or in non-monetary form for a multi-criteria analysis framework.

Intangible losses can be calculated for the following elements in case of health-care infrastructure: loss of lives, cultural characteristics, environmental characteristics, loss of communication, losses to patients, losses to staff, loss to society due to absence of staff, losses to administration in terms of anticipated earnings, and loss of efficiency (Markantonis & Schwarze, 2012).

## 7.9   Summary

As has been discussed in the previous chapters, resilience invites heavy investments ahead of an EWE. The idea is to make the structure and the communities absorbent and recoverable in case an EWE strikes. However, financing towards resilience accompanies robust implementation mechanisms and investment strategies to ensure the right direction of funds.

The cost model proposed in this study arrives at an assessment of loss, including tangible and intangible losses, which are therefore intended to be financed to reduce the losses to a minimal benchmark. Further, these losses help arrive at the condition of a healthcare facility in terms of its performance in case an EWE strikes, thereby helping in the preparedness and recovery mechanisms, including financial, administrative, and structural recovery.

## References

Belasen, A., & Polachek, S. (2009). How disasters affect local labor markets: The effects of hurricanes in Florida. *The Journal of Human Resources*, 251–276.

Bittner, P. (2008, September-December). The hospital safety index. *Asian Disaster Management News*, 7–8.

Combaz, E. (2014). *Disaster Resilience: Topic Guide*. Birmingham: GSDRC, University of Birmingham.

Geroy, L. S., & Pesigan, A. M. (2011). Disaster risk reduction for health facilities in the Western Pacific Region. *International Journal of Disaster Resilience in the Built Environment*, 268–277.

Haen, H. D., & Hemrich, G. (2006). *The Economics of Natural Disasters – Implications and Challenges for Food Security*. Brisbane: 26th Conference of the International Association of Agricultural Economists.

Hallegatte, S., & Dumas, P. (2009). Can natural disasters have positive consequences? Investigating the role of embodied technical change. *Ecological Economics*, 777–786.

Kellenberg, D., & Mobarak, A. M. (2007). Does rising income increase or decrease damage risk from natural disasters? *Journal of Urban Economics*, 788–802.

Kellenberg, D., & Mobarak, A. M. (2011). The economics of natural disasters. *Annual Review of Resource Economics*, 297–312.

Markantonis, V., & Schwarze, R. (2012). Review article: Valuating the intangible effects of natural hazards: Review and analysis of the costing methods. *Natural Hazards and Earth System Sciences*, 12, 1633–1640.

National Research Council. (1999). The impacts of natural disasters: A framework for loss estimation. *The National Academies Press*. Retrieved from www.nap.edu/read/6425/chapter/3

Raddatz, C. (2007). Are external shocks responsible for the instability of output in low-income countries? *Journal of Development Economics*, 155–187.

Rose, A. Z. (2009). *Economic Resilience to Disasters*. Los Angeles, CA: Published Articles & Papers.

Rose, A. Z., & Krausmann, E. (2013). An economic framework for the development of a resilience index for business recovery. *International Journal of Disaster Risk Reduction*, 73–83.

Sarmiento, C. (2007). The impact of flood hazards on local employment. *Applied Economics Letters*, 1123–1126.

Schumacher, I., & Strobl, E. (2008). Economic development and losses due to natural disasters: the role of risk. *Working Papers* HAL-00356286. https://ideas.repec.org/p/hal/wpaper/hal-00356286.html

Skidmore, M., & Toya, H. (2002). Do natural disasters promote long-run growth? *Economic Inquiry*, 664–687.

# 8 Cost model for calculating tangible and intangible value losses

## 8.1 Overview

This chapter includes the fundamentals of disaster resilience in terms of the healthcare infrastructure and proposes a methodology for the quantitative evaluation of the losses incurred in the event of a natural disaster/EWE. A unified terminology framework is proposed to conduct a potential value loss evaluation of healthcare facilities that are subject to EWEs like cyclones and floods. The evaluation of potential losses is based on non-dimensional analytical functions that describe the variations of functionality which consider indirect and direct losses. The loss estimation approach is presented in the form of simple equations for an existing healthcare facility and a hospital network.

Considerable research exists on the assessment of indirect and direct losses caused due to various hazards and the associated estimation and mitigation of these losses using policies, scenarios, or specific actions. However, the idea of resilience is not limited to only reduction of monetary losses; it also entails a much more comprehensive framework of adaptation. It is, therefore, imperative to understand and employ the concept of resilience in more quantitative applications and assessments, in order to develop a better understanding of the factors that contribute to resilience. This can also help in a systematic assessment of the potential benefits and influence of various research activities.

With increasing emphasis on resilience and its implementation in design and construction activities, the risks to society are reduced, which opens up more opportunities for improving the safety and quality of life. However, development of a value-driven healthcare system requires reliable, accurate, and valid formulations of both cost and benefit variables of the value equation. A part of health economics is economic evaluation, which is a tool for the comparison of costs and consequences of various interventions.

The literature advocates the application of both qualitative and quantitative methodologies. However, Rivera (2021) explored the possibility of integrating a geographic information system (GIS) with qualitative and quantitative methodologies to map resilience. Russo (2021) underlined the process of applying a mixed-methods approach to achieve efficient results in disaster risk management. Though

DOI: 10.1201/9781003393108-8

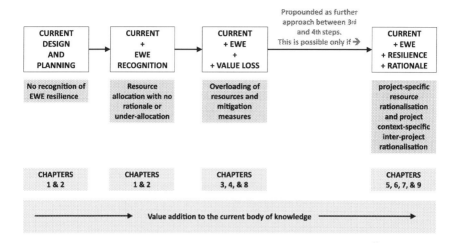

*Figure 8.1* Process of incorporating resilience: value loss quantification in the case of an EWE occurrence.

the actual implementation of a mixed-methods approach has many challenges, the best way for applying them to real case studies depends upon the heterogeneity and inter-disciplinarity of the disaster and emergency management fields. The process of applying the mixed-methods approach has been attempted by various researchers. Rivera (2021), Norman (2022) demonstrated how these approaches truly apply and can be utilised in disaster research using real catastrophe studies. Taking insights on similar lines, Chapter 8 presents the methodology that considers both quantitative and qualitative approaches to quantify the impact of disaster risks on case projects. Figure 8.1 depicts that the assessment of value losses is an important step to develop the risk reduction and resilience approach.

### 8.1.1 Loss estimation approach

Economic and social loss estimation and assessment are an integral part of relief management, reconstruction, and resilience programmes. Additionally, this assists the government at all levels to make informed decisions to support safe and sustainable development of communities. Loss estimation also forms an integral part of risk assessment and management. Processes of assessing and estimating losses facilitate decision-makers to develop their methodologies and decisions in order to mitigate the effects of disasters and EWEs in the future (Emergency Management Australia, 2002).

The government body Emergency Management Australia puts forth in detail the loss assessment or loss estimation process. The following diagram in Figure 8.2 has been adapted from the guidelines.

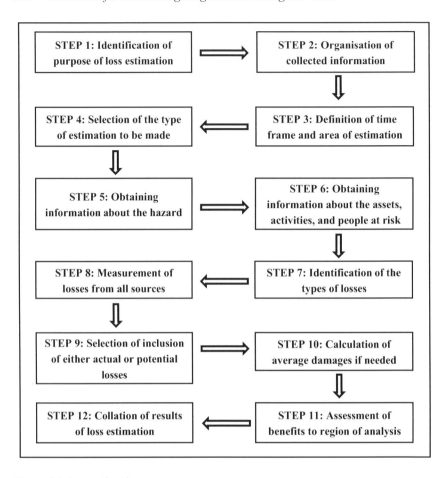

*Figure 8.2* Loss estimation process.

*Source:* Adapted from Emergency Management Australia

### 8.1.2   *Quantification of dimensions of resilience*

Disaster resilience, as commonly understood, is the ability of individuals as well as the communities, states, and organisations to absorb and bounce back from hazards, stresses, and shocks sustainably, without compromising the long-term prospects for development.

The Department for International Development (DFID) framework outlines the core elements of disaster resilience as follows:

i.   **Context**: The group for which resilience needs to be built, such as a social group, community, institution, organisation, or environmental context
ii.  **Disturbance**: The shocks, stresses, or hazards that the group is intended to be made resilient to

iii. **Capacity to respond**: The ability or capacity of a system or a group to process the shock, stress, or hazard; depends upon the adaptive capacity, sensitivity, and exposure

iv. **Reaction**: The responses of the group can be varied, including bounce back better, bounce back, recover but worse than before, and collapse (Combaz, 2014)

### 8.1.2.1    *Analysing and measuring disaster resilience*

Among the various frameworks that have developed guidelines to measure disaster resilience, the most widely cited example is the Hyogo Framework of Action that defines in detail the characteristics of a resilience framework and recommends a range of indicators to measure each of the characteristics (see Table 8.1).

### 8.1.2.2    *Quantifying disaster resilience*

In addition to the challenge of deficient standards and metrics for appraising resilience, studies suggest a lack of consensus on how to measure resilience.

*Table 8.1* Hyogo Framework of Action

| S. No. | Thematic Area | Components/Indicators of Resilience |
|---|---|---|
| 1. | Governance | • Partnerships<br>• Responsibility allocation<br>• Integration with emergency recovery and response<br>• Integration with development policies and planning<br>• Planning, policy, priorities, and political commitment<br>• Regulatory and legal systems<br>• Community participation and accountability<br>• Institutional capacities, mechanisms, and structures |
| 2. | Risk Assessment | • Data for risks/hazards and their assessment<br>• Technical and scientific capacities and innovation<br>• Vulnerability/capacity and impact assessment |
| 3. | Knowledge and Education | • Education and training<br>• Research and learning<br>• Motivation, attitudes, and cultures<br>• Information sharing and management<br>• Public awareness, skills, and knowledge |
| 4. | Risk Management and Vulnerability Reduction | • Financial instruments<br>• Health and well-being<br>• Sustainable livelihoods<br>• Planning regimes<br>• Technical and structural measures for physical protection<br>• Natural and environmental resource management |
| 5. | Disaster Preparedness and Response | • Early warning systems<br>• Emergency recovery and response<br>• Contingency planning and preparedness<br>• Voluntarism, participation, and accountability<br>• Emergency infrastructure and resources<br>• Organisational coordination and capacities |

*Source:* Twigg, 2009

Nevertheless, various frameworks define the components being measured and the characteristics of these measurements. In a report called *Disaster Resilience Measurements by UNDP*, authored by Thomas Winderl (2014), the following elements of resilience are included in the measurements:

i.   **Measuring well-being before and after a disaster:**
     The Community-Based Resilience Analysis (CoBRA) tool, developed by UNDP, uses a household economy approach (HEA) that serves as a meta-indicator. For example, the total income needed to cover the costs of water, food, and food preparation is represented by the survival threshold. Similarly, the total expenditure for medium-term livelihoods, basic survival services, and standard of living is denoted by the livelihoods' protection threshold.

ii.  **Measuring vulnerability:**
     Two key variables used to measure the vulnerability are exposure (how endangered the people are to disasters) and susceptibility (how likely it is for them to be harmed).

iii. **Measuring resilience capacities to cope, adapt, and transform in case of a disaster:**
     The delineation of different components of resilience capacity can be accomplished through differentiation between adaptive, absorptive, and transformative capacities. An analytical and measurement framework is formed with the combination of these structuring elements, which is aimed to obtain clarity on the meaning of 'strengthening resilience'.

iv.  **Measuring disaster-related shocks, losses, and stress:**
     Information on the impact of disasters on humans is provided by the International Disaster Database EM-DAT. Data on losses, damages, and general impacts of disasters can be captured by the tool DesInventar that generates national disaster inventories and constructs databases.

v.   **Measuring the reaction to and recovery from disasters:**
     The reactions to disasters are typically measured through a frequently used framework known as ResilUS. It is a prototype simulation model of community resilience in the United States that emphasises loss estimation and recovery.

vi.  **Measuring programme results:**
     Programme results can be different from the general measurements of resilience in the following ways:

     a) Programme results emphasise the narrower aspects of resilience (such as a specific sector, specific type of disaster, or specific resilience capacity)
     b) The results consist of more details on the activity and the output level instead of broader measurements in order to better highlight the specifics of a programme intervention

(Winderl, 2014)

### *8.1.3    Quantification of vulnerability*

The measurement or quantification of vulnerability, as defined in the previous section, needs the determination of two factors: one, exposure, indicating how exposed the people or the communities are to disasters, and two, susceptibility, indicating how likely they are to be harmed.

Two of the most recognised software programs for quantification of vulnerability of a group are Global Focus Model (GFM) and Prevalent Vulnerability Index (PVI).

The GFM aims at vulnerabilities, hazards, and response capacity at the national level. The PVI is a part of a set of four indicators which quantify the potential impact of natural hazards (Winderl, 2014).

### *i    Global Focus Model*

This risk model developed by the UN Office for the Coordination of Humanitarian Affairs (OCHA) in 2007 analyses the natural and human-induced hazards and vulnerabilities at the national level using quantitative indicators. The model has been adopted as a corporate risk model and is updated yearly as a part of the annual work planning cycle at OCHA.

The model is designed to answer the following questions:

i)    Which communities are the most exposed to hazards that could trigger a humanitarian emergency?
ii)    What factors affect the ability of a community to survive the impact of a hazard?
iii)    What factors influence the impact of a hazard on a community or group?
iv)    Given the organisation's tools, mandates, and services, to what extent is OCHA likely to have a role in a country?

These questions are answered by GFM through data analysis in the following four areas:

• Vulnerability
• Hazards
• Demand for humanitarian coordination support
• Capacity

International standards are employed for risk calculation in these categories. These areas grant flexibility for accounting for the factors specific to the humanitarian mandate stipulated by OCHA. The sub-index on capacity is directly associated with resilience and highlights the capacity of the government and the civil society. This comprises economic health, institutional resilience, and infrastructure in equal parts (Winderl, 2014).

*ii    Prevalent Vulnerability Index*

The PVI quantifies the exposure in vulnerable areas, lack of social resilience, and socio-economic fragility, which thereby determine the predominant vulnerability conditions. These factors denote a measure of direct, indirect, and intangible impacts of hazards. The PVI is a composite indicator that denotes a comparative measure of a country's situation or pattern (Winderl, 2014).

The PVI is one of the four composite indicators employed for measuring the potential impact of natural hazards. The Inter-American Development Bank devised the four indicators of disaster risk and management of risk in 2005. The other three indicators in addition to PVI are the Disaster Deficit Index (DDI), the Local Disaster Index (LDI), and the Risk Management Index (RMI).

The PVI comprises three sets of eight high-level indicators and entails eight specific indicators of (lack of) resilience (Winderl, 2014). These are:

- Environmental Sustainability Index (ESI)
- Hospital beds per 1000 people
- Television sets per 1000 people
- Housing and infrastructure insurance as a percentage of GDP
- Governance Index
- Social expenditures on health, pensions, and education as a percentage of GDP
- Gender-related Development Index (GDI)
- Human Development Index (HDI)

### 8.1.4    Value-based or value-driven healthcare system

In healthcare, value is defined as "the measured improvement in a patient's health outcomes for the cost of achieving that improvement". The aim of value-based care transformation is to ensure a sufficiently enabled healthcare system in order to create more value for patients. Hence, value-based healthcare can be understood as a healthcare delivery model, wherein the healthcare providers are paid on the basis of the patient health outcomes. Value is 'created' only when the patient's health outcomes improve. Value-based healthcare is not based solely on costs, but focuses significantly on quality, process compliance, consistency, and better health outcomes (Teisberg et al., 2020).

Value is different from patient satisfaction, which incorporates the opinions of patients and treating them with dignity and respect. Since the main purpose of healthcare is to improve the health of patients, value implies the improvement in health outcomes of the patients. Health outcomes can be articulated in terms of capability, comfort, and calm. Value-based healthcare connects the medical practitioners with their purpose as healers, supports their professionalism, and can turn out to be a useful mechanism to counter burnout. The primary focus on achieving better health outcomes aligns the patients with their medical caregivers (Teisberg et al., 2020).

Benefits of value-based healthcare can be seen for:

- **Patients**: Lower costs and better outcomes
- **Providers**: Better care efficiencies, higher rates of patient satisfaction

- **Payers**: Reduced risks, stronger cost control
- **Suppliers**: Alignment of costs with patient outcomes
- **Society**: Better overall health, reducing expenditure on healthcare

(NEJM Catalyst, 2017)

## 8.2 Value losses quantification approach

The definition and measurement of value is a challenging task in healthcare, where the benefit or the resources employed to achieve these benefits are not straightforward. Even as considerable research has been conducted using numerous econometric approaches to determine cost and benefit correlations in healthcare, standard definitions or practices for measuring value have not been established (Institute of Medicine, 2010).

However, various studies include the assessment and quantification of indirect losses, such as the econometric analyses, modelling of losses, and rule of thumb, as identified by Stephane Hallegatte in the Policy Research Working Paper (2015) on 'The Indirect Cost of Natural Disasters and an Economic Definition of Macroeconomic Resilience for the World Bank' (Hallegatte, 2015).

## 8.3 Measuring indirect losses using econometric analyses

Econometric analyses are usually used for the quantification of output losses, such as reduction in GDP post-disaster. However, they have often been observed to arrive at contradictory conclusions. As discussed previously in Section 7.2, some studies state that natural disasters may cast an overall positive impact on the long-term economic growth owing to better reconstruction and replacement of damaged capital and infrastructure with newer and contemporary technology. On the other hand, some studies robustly describe the overall negative impact of natural disasters on economic growth (Hallegatte, 2015).

Various models have been proposed to be used for modelling indirect losses, such as the calculable general equilibrium (CGE) and the commonly used input-output (IO). These models depict the economy as an ensemble of economic sectors that interact through intermediate consumptions. However, these models present different depictions on the interactions between various sectors and their reactions to shocks (Hallegatte, 2015).

Some of the models that are based on the IO linear assumption involve the production of one unit in one sector, which needs a fixed number of inputs from other sectors, without the role of the price being considered. Models that are based on the CGE framework assume that changes in relative prices balance supply and demand in each sector.

The results obtained from these models are sensitive to various parameters and limitations in existing tools. They can prove to be useful as tools for exploring indirect consequences of disasters. However, they cannot be used for a precise estimation of the total economic cost of a disaster (Hallegatte, 2015).

The following section details the loss estimation methodology. The study of different definitions of resilience reveals the four dimensions, i.e., robustness, resourcefulness, redundancy, and rapidity. While these dimensions are crucial to ensure improvement in resilience, the true value of resilience can be identified through loss estimation. The first step of this process is the identification of damage descriptors on the basis of which loss estimation can be carried out. While these damage descriptors are varying and depend upon the type of event, most studies categorise these as tangible and intangible (monetary and non-monetary). The components of tangible and intangible damage descriptors in the context of healthcare infrastructure are presented in Figure 8.3.

The components of damage descriptors are categorised under four groups, i.e., losses due to damage to physical assets, losses related to damage to contents and inventories, human losses in the form of deaths and injuries, and losses due to interruption in business operations.

The process of loss estimation can be a source of uncertainty by itself, since it varies with the type of natural disaster/EWE, intensity of the disaster, and the level of healthcare facility (i.e., primary, secondary, or tertiary). The loss estimation procedure adopted for this study is for a tertiary healthcare facility.

To determine the quantification of losses associated with extreme events, the first step involves translation of these damage descriptors into monetary values and similar measurable/tangible units. The total losses can be divided in two types: tangible losses and intangible losses. The tangible and intangible losses can be further sub-divided into four categories as mentioned in Figure 8.3 and can be quantified using Equation 8.1.

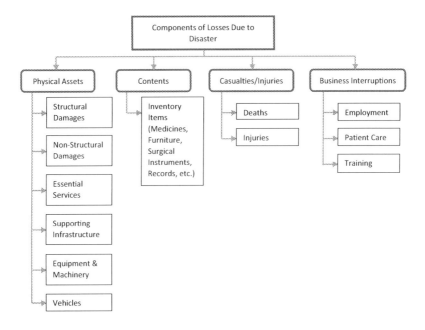

*Figure 8.3* Components of losses due to disaster.

$$L(t)_{(I,TRet)} = L_{pa} + L_{co} + L_{ci} + L_{bi} \tag{8.1}$$

Where:

$L(t)_{(I,TRe)}$ are the total losses due to the disaster subject to the ($I$) intensity of the event and ($TRet$) total recovery time to make the infrastructure functional
$L_{pa}$ are the losses due to damage to physical assets
$L_{co}$ are the losses due to damage to the contents
$L_{ci}$ are the losses in terms of deaths and injuries
$L_{bi}$ are the losses due to business interruptions

For simplicity, $L_{pa}$ is described with reference to a particular essential facility as a hospital. The losses to physical assets consist of five contributions: (1) structural losses $L_s$ (or damages to structural elements); (2) non-structural losses $L_{ns}$ (or damages to non-structural components in the building); (3) essential services losses (or losses due to damage of essential services in the building); (4) supporting infrastructure losses $L_{si}$ (or damages to external infrastructure); and (5) equipment, machinery, and vehicle losses $L_{emv}$. Hence, the total losses to physical assets can be expressed as follows:

$$L_{pa} = L_s + L_{ns} + L_{es} + L_{si} + L_{enw} \tag{8.2}$$

Structural losses depend on the number of damaged elements ($k$), recovery costs incurred to repair those damaged components $RC_{kd}$, and the age of the structure ($C_{as}$), since with an increase in the age of the structure, the probability of damage impact increases.

$$L_s = \left( \sum_{k=1}^{Ns} RC_{kd} \right) * C_{as} \tag{8.3}$$

Where:
$L_s$ are the total structural losses
$RC_{kd}$ are the repair costs for the damaged components ($k$) at damage stage ($d$)
$C_{as}$ is the coefficient of age of the structure
$N_s$ is the total number of damaged structural components

Non-structural losses include ceilings, partitions, windows, flooring, etc. The total non-structural losses are obtained using the following equation:

$$L_{ns} = \sum_{k=1}^{Nns} wei * (RC_{kd} + REC_k ) \tag{8.4}$$

Where:
$L_{ns}$ are the total non-structural losses associated with component $k$
$N_{ns}$ is the total number of damaged non-structural components in the buildings
$wei$ is an importance weightage factor associated with each non-structural component of the building
$RC_{kd}$ is the repair cost for the damaged components ($k$) at damage stage ($d$)
$REC_k$ is the replacement cost of each of the damaged components ($k$)

Essential services–related losses are associated with damages to services like piping, electricity, plumbing, drainage, etc., that disrupt the functioning of healthcare activities. These losses are time dependent, i.e., depend upon recovery time or how quickly these services can be restored. These losses are even more significant than the structural and non-structural losses, as the disruption in services may cause immediate impact on the admitted patients.

$$L_{es} = \left( \sum_{k=1}^{Nes} RC_{kd} + REC_k \right)^{1/Ret} * C_{as} \tag{8.5}$$

Where:
$L_{es}$ is the total losses due to damages in essential services
$Nes$ is the total number of damaged components
$C_{as}$ is the coefficient of the age of the structure
$RC_{kd}$ is the repair cost for the damaged components ($k$) at damage stage ($d$)
$REC_k$ is the replacement cost of the damaged components ($k$) subject to recovery time Ret to make the infrastructure functional

These losses occur due to damages in the supporting infrastructure essential for the functioning of the healthcare facility. These losses can be identified as indirect losses. They mainly consist of connectivity losses due to damages to external roads and external services, such as damages to substations, transformers, electricity poles, telecommunication linkages, external landscape, etc. Since many of these damages can cause immediate disruption in the functioning of a healthcare facility, an importance weightage factor is associated with each of these components. The equation to quantify these losses is expressed as:

$$L_{si} = I_e \left( \sum_{k=1}^{Nsi} wei * \left( RC_{kd} + REC_k \right) \right) \tag{8.6}$$

Where:
$L_{si}$ is the total losses in supporting infrastructure that depend upon the intensity of an event $I_e$
wei is importance weightage of component $k$
$RC_{kd}$ is the repair cost for the damaged component ($k$) at damage stage ($d$)
$REC_k$ is the replacement cost of the damaged component ($k$)

The next category of losses includes the damages in medical equipment, machinery, lifts, water treatment plants, vehicles, etc. These losses are expressed as:

$$L_{emv} = \sum_{k=1}^{Nemv} \left( RC_{kd} + REC_k \right)^{1/Ret} + \left( \frac{1+d_t}{1+r_t} \right) \tag{8.7}$$

Where:
$L_{emv}$ is the total losses in equipment, machinery and vehicles
$RC_{kd}$ is the repair cost for the damaged components ($k$) at damage stage ($d$)
$REC_k$ are the replacement costs of the damaged components ($k$)
$Ret$ is the recovery time to make the infrastructure functional
$r_t$ is the annual discount rate
$t$ is the time range in years between the initial investments and the occurrence of the event
$d_t$ is the annual depreciating rate

Equation 8.7 assumes that the initial value of the equipment/machinery/vehicle is affected by the discount rate, but the value also decreases with time according to the depreciating rate $d_t$.

   The contents and inventory losses consist of essential supplies like medicines, surgical aids, etc., and inventory items like furniture, records, etc. These are important for the manufacturing and retail facilities and to lifelines. These losses are also time dependent, hence the recovery time factor is considered and expressed in Equation 8.8.

$$L_{ci} = \sum_{i=n}^{Ni^n} (Ci)^{1/Ret} \tag{8.8}$$

Where:
$L_{ci}$ is the total losses in content and inventory
$Ci$ is the cost of inventory
$Ni^n$ is the total number of inventory items i.e., 1 to $n$
$Ret$ is the recovery time to make the infrastructure functional

   An important factor in loss estimation is the determination of conversion factors for intangibles (non-monetary values), such as human life and injuries. However, it is not possible to assign a monetary value to these factors. Here, the direct casualties and injury losses ($L_{di}$) are calculated based on the prevalent compensation amount paid by the government for death and injury in the event of a disaster. The product of compensation amount and number of deaths/injuries gives the total losses in monetary terms.

$$L_{di} = \sum_{p=n}^{Np^n} (D_p * \alpha) + (I_p + \beta) \qquad (8.9)$$

Where:
$L_{di}$ is the total losses due to deaths and injuries
$D_p$ is the total number of deaths
$\alpha$ is the ex gratia amount per death paid by the government as compensation
$I_p$ is the total number of injuries
$\beta$ is the ex gratia amount per injury paid by the government as compensation
$Np^n$ is the total number of deaths and injuries

Due to damages to structural and non-structural components, essential services may get disrupted, such as the functions and business operations in a healthcare facility. This results in significant revenue losses. They primarily entail employment losses, patient care losses, and losses associated with training and research. These indirect losses are time dependent. Apart from revenue losses, which are monetary, there are also social losses (non-monetary) associated with business interruptions. However, the equation expressed next is an estimation of monetary losses due to business interruptions, as the estimation of social losses is subjective and depends on various parameters such as the catchment area, demography, criticality of admitted patients, research and training facilities of a hospital, etc. Hence, the social losses estimation is considered uncertain and not included in this study.

The total business interruption losses ($L_{bi}$) can be expressed as a combination of total employment losses ($L_{em}$), the total patient care losses ($L_{pc}$), and the total training and research losses ($L_{tr}^*$):

$$L_{bi} = L_{em} + L_{pc} + L_{tr}^* \qquad (8.10)$$

Employment losses consider the number of staff unemployed because of hospital dysfunction. This is expressed in Equation 8.11 as the total number of staff unemployed in respective healthcare facilities and the total non-functioning days:

$$L_{em} = \sum_{e=n}^{Ne^n} IC_e * nf_d \qquad (8.11)$$

Where:

$L_{em}$ is the total employment losses

$Ne^n$ is the total number of employees i.e., 1 to $n$

$IC_e$ is the income losses of an employee

$nf_d$ is the number of non-functioning days

Total patient care losses are the most important, as they contribute significantly to all the previous losses determined. The patient care losses depend on the impacted facilities i.e., OPD, IPD, ICU, OT, diagnostics, etc., and the capacity of the respective facilities to serve the patients. It has been expressed as the product of the number of affected patients $Np_f$ in an impacted facility (f) and depends on the criticality of patients, number of non-functioning days $nf_d$ of a facility, and approximate treatment costs $T_c$:

$$L_{pc} = \sum_{f=1}^{Nf} \left( Np_f * I_f * nf_d * T_c \right) \qquad (8.12)$$

Where:

$L_{pc}$ is the total losses due to impacted patient care

$Nf$ is the total number of patients in all facilities

$Np_f$ is the number of affected patients in a particular hospital facility (f)

$I_f$ is the impact factor; depends upon the criticality of a patient

$nf_d$ is the number of non-functioning days

$T_c$ is the treatment cost

## 8.4    Application of the cost model

The cost model derived in this chapter incorporates the potential value losses that a healthcare facility may incur when struck by an EWE. The model takes direct inputs in the form of number of beds; quantities of equipment, machinery, and tools lost; and direct/indirect costs. However, even as the required data inputs are exhaustive and reasonably detailed, they pose a challenge in terms of retrieving sensitive information, which sometimes may not be recorded by the organisations and rescue/relief workers. The framework, therefore, would add to the detailed understanding of cost implications indicative of the potential loss of service of the healthcare infrastructure. Over a period of time, it is reasonable to expect that the databases of risks and impacts will affect the cost model in terms of providing the detailed information necessary for robust management decisions.

In the event that comprehensive data is not available, it is recommended to extrapolate data from relevant sources of information as recorded/archived by the hospitals for the occurrence and the losses incurred in similar EWEs.

Nevertheless, with the growth of the healthcare industry and increase in research in the domain, it is necessary to have detailed data available for research and development purposes.

## 8.5   Summary

This chapter defines in detail a cost model for quantification of potential value losses, tangible and intangible, for a healthcare infrastructure in the event of an extreme weather occurrence or a natural disaster. The equations have been derived from detailed reviews, informed calculation methodologies, in-depth literature studies, and experience in the field. This model provides a significant step towards achieving resilience in healthcare facilities by providing specific as well as overall losses in value when an EWE strikes. While various models have been defined that calculate the direct losses post-disaster, few exist in practice that present a comprehensive model involving the value of the infrastructure.

Even as a healthcare infrastructure suffers tangible losses, the value of the structure is significant, owing to its nature of service and criticality not just at regional but also at state and national levels. Hospitals and medical facilities serve the community beyond just medical attention, such as in the form of refuge areas and safe spaces in case of disasters. It is therefore of utmost significance that the structure be safeguarded against external factors to the maximum extent.

The cost model also highlights the need for resilience in hospitals and other medical facilities. While the model gives definitive results on the potential value losses, the natural successor activity is making the structure resilient to future EWEs. The motive of the cost model, as well as the book, is to highlight the importance of making healthcare structures resilient: structures that respond, recover, and provide aid and service during and after the natural disaster/EWE and suffer minimum losses.

## References

Combaz, E. (2014). *Disaster Resilience: Topic Guide*. Birmingham: GSDRC, University of Birmingham.

Emergency Management Australia. (2002). *Disaster Loss Assessment Guidelines*. Canberra: Emergency Management Australia.

Hallegatte, S. (2015). *The Indirect Cost of Natural Disasters and an Economic Definition of Macroeconomic Resilience*. Washington, DC: World Bank Group.

Institute of Medicine. (2010). *Value in Health Care: Accounting for Cost, Quality, Safety, Outcomes, and Innovation: Workshop Summary*. Washington, DC: The National Academies Press.

NEJM Catalyst. (2017, January 1). Innovations in care delivery. *NEJM Catalyst*. Retrieved from https://catalyst.nejm.org/doi/full/10.1056/CAT.17.0558

Norman, B. (2022). *Urban Planning for Climate Change*. New York: Taylor & Francis.

Rivera, J. D. (2021). *Disaster and Emergency Management Methods: Social Science Approaches in Application*. Routledge.

Russo, B. R. (2021). Mixed-methods research in disaster and emergency management. In J. D. Rivera (ed.), *Disaster and Emergency Management Methods* (pp. 67–84). Routledge.

Teisberg, E., Wallace, S., & O'Hara, S. (2020). Defining and implementing value-based health care: A strategic framework. *Academic Medicine*, 682–685.

Twigg, J. (2009). *Characteristics of a Disaster Resilient Community: A Guidance Note*. London: NGO Inter-Agency Group.

Winderl, T. (2014). *Disaster Resilience Measurements: Stocktaking of Ongoing Efforts in Developing Systems for Measuring Resilience*. New York: United Nations Development Programme.

# 9 Conclusion and a way forward

## 9.1 Background

The research conducted in this book is a conjunction of the dynamics between climate change and the ensuing EWEs, their impact on a healthcare infrastructure, and the preparedness and resilience of the healthcare infrastructure to minimise disruption and maintain continuity of services during and after the occurrence of an EWE. The overall objective of the study, therefore, is to develop a cost model that evaluates the tangible and intangible losses that a healthcare facility may encounter in the wake of an EWE. Further, the research recommends resilience investment strategies to minimise the losses recognised and enhance the safety and resilience.

The objective of the study is achieved in nine steps, which form nine chapters of the book. The first chapter of the book aims to identify and assess the challenges posed to the built environment due to climate change and EWE. With inputs from the SDGs, challenges and implications of achieving those, and vulnerability of the healthcare infrastructure to EWEs and climate change, the challenges in infrastructure development and its resilience are identified. Through a literature study, the nexus of climate change and EWE, and the paradox of development versus environment, is established.

After detecting and ascertaining the challenges in the development of an infrastructure due to an EWE, the impact of an EWE on critical infrastructure is characterised in Chapter 2. Global and Indian responses to climate change and the impact of EWEs on the healthcare infrastructure are identified through the literature and expert opinions. The chapter concludes with the need to place resilience over response and a review of the national disaster response policies. The need for capacity building and supplementing knowledge of infrastructure and community is highlighted through this chapter.

The third chapter sets a discourse to identify and evaluate the impact of EWEs on critical infrastructure and how the communities and countries respond to such events. A detailed premise of impact on critical infrastructure through case examples of the EWEs in the past decade is illustrated. The chapter also streamlines the focus of the study towards impacts of climate change and EWEs on human health and the healthcare infrastructure.

DOI: 10.1201/9781003393108-9

The fourth chapter outlines an overview of the public health systems in India, including their functioning, access, and preparedness. This leads to a detailed review of the role of government in public health, along with the problems and current status of public healthcare availability and accessibility in the country. The chapter closes in on the impact of EWEs on public healthcare facilities and how these facilities and health outcomes can be improved.

Carrying forward from the fourth chapter, the fifth chapter identifies the disruption caused in healthcare facilities due to EWEs and their uncertainty of occurrence. The aim of the chapter is to analyse the enforcement of resilience in the healthcare infrastructure, which helps achieve continuity of services and minimises disruption. For this, the resilience and redundancy in structures are studied in detail, concluding with mitigating the impact of disruption on services.

To understand the evaluation methodology of the risks in healthcare infrastructure due to EWEs, the sixth chapter identifies the risks during hazards/EWEs and describes the processes of risk assessment, risk probability, risk quantification, risk analysis, and risk evaluation, which are useful in formulating a risk management framework. The chapter also includes the features and indicators of a resilient health system and studies resilience in relation to critical and health infrastructure. This chapter concludes with the concept of loss potential through the literature, observations, and derivations.

Progressing from the identification of loss potential, the seventh chapter aims to assess the economics of achieving resilience in the healthcare infrastructure. The chapter commences with the impact of EWEs on the economy of the country and their effects on different levels of development. Strategies and methods to finance resilience are identified, along with international cost models that calculate loss potential and safety index of healthcare facilities. Losses, tangible and intangible, are studied, along with direct and indirect value losses. Establishing the global context of a safety index and loss potential, the chapter concludes with techniques to achieve economic resilience and financial strategies.

The eighth chapter aims to derive a cost model for the calculation of tangible and intangible value losses for a healthcare facility. Using the equations and formulae derived for evaluation of these losses, a cost model is proposed. Therefore, the outcome of the chapter entails a set of equations that form a calculative framework to evaluate the potential value losses in a healthcare structure in the face of an EWE.

This final chapter of the book highlights the significance of resilience in healthcare structures in the wake of an EWE. The cost of destruction caused to a healthcare facility/critical infrastructure can be used as the loss potential. This amount may or may not reduce. However, the impact of an EWE on services can be reduced, thereby influencing the ability of the healthcare infrastructure to make medical care and availability of aid more effective.

The following matrix in Table 9.1 summarises the outcomes of the study vis-a-vis the overall objectives outlined for the book.

*Table 9.1* Overall objective and outcome of the study and steps to achieve the objectives

| Objective | Methodology | Outcome |
|---|---|---|
| **Overall Objective** – to develop a cost model to evaluate the tangible and intangible value losses that a healthcare facility may encounter in the occurrence of an EWE and recommended resilience investment strategies for such an infrastructure. | | |
| **To identify and assess challenges posed to the built environment due to climate change and EWEs** | • Need for capacity building/ supplementing knowledge<br>• Anthropogenic effects<br>• Sustainable development<br>• Status of response to disasters/EWE | • Challenges for achieving SDGs<br>• Implications of unfinished agenda of SDGs<br>• Resilience and challenges in infrastructure development |
| **To analyse the impact of EWEs on critical infrastructure** | • Nexus of climate change and EWE<br>• EWE and CI – concepts and challenges<br>• Impact of EWE on CI | • How climate change is intensifying disasters in India<br>• Impact of climate change on health infrastructure<br>• Need to place resilience over response<br>• Responses to climate change |
| **To assess public health systems and impact of EWEs** | • Functioning and typologies of public healthcare systems<br>• Access to healthcare<br>• Non-utilisation<br>• Infectious diseases | • Role of government in public health<br>• Problems and current status of public healthcare<br>• Improving health outcomes and healthcare<br>• Impact of EWEs on public healthcare |
| **To analyse the enforcement of resilience in the healthcare infrastructure** | • EWE + healthcare infrastructure challenges<br>• Disruption due to uncertainty<br>• Stages of disruption<br>• Resilience and redundancy in structures | • Disruption in healthcare facilities<br>• Achieving continuity of services<br>• Mitigation of impact of disruption on services |
| **To evaluate the risks in the healthcare infrastructure** | • Resilience, reduction, and safety<br>• Risk during EWEs/hazards<br>• Resilience in relation to critical and healthcare infrastructures | • Risk assessment, identification, probability, quantification, and analysis<br>• Risk management framework and risk evaluation<br>• Features and indicators of a resilient health system<br>• Loss potential |

(*Continued*)

*Table 9.1* (Continued)

| Objective | Methodology | Outcome |
|---|---|---|
| **To assess the economics of resilience in the healthcare infrastructure** | • Impact of natural disasters/ EWEs on the economy of the country<br>• Financing resilience<br>• International cost models that calculate loss potential<br>• Economic resilience and value losses | • Effects of natural disasters/ EWEs at different stages of development<br>• Tangible and intangible losses<br>• Global context of safety index and loss potential |
| **To derive a cost model for calculation of tangible and intangible value losses** | • Evaluation of tangible and intangible value losses through equations and formulae<br>• Dependency on number of beds | • Cost model for tangible and intangible losses<br>• Resilience investment strategies<br>• As the availability of data enhances, assumptions can be amplified (using data analytics)<br>• Risk resilience calculation |

## 9.2   Project evaluation and realisation process

The promulgation of resilience in the research culminates in a methodology that identifies the crucial elements and processes where resilience practices can be incorporated in critical and healthcare infrastructures. The conventional process of project inception, evaluation, and realisation is established, as illustrated in Figure 9.1, to characterise the key activities for project development. Against each activity, the prospective measures of incorporating resilience are introduced in Table 9.2. The underlying intent is to ensure assimilation of resilience practices using a strategic approach to minimise the losses in infrastructure in the event of an extreme weather occurrence.

## 9.3   Tasks ahead

The tasks ahead are related to defining risks in EWEs and the resilience that is to be implemented for risk mitigation.

With climate change wreaking havoc on the weather alongside the frequency and occurrence of extreme events, communities as well as critical infrastructures are exposed to potential losses, structurally, functionally, and socially. These potential losses, due to the vulnerability of such communities and infrastructure, can be interpreted as risks. The critical infrastructures, subject to uncertainties and risks, are potential sites of maximum losses in terms of structural as well as societal effects. Among critical infrastructure, healthcare facilities are the most integral to the functioning and recovery of the community during and after an EWE. While all critical infrastructure is essential to the smooth functioning of society, the heaviest accountabilities lie on the healthcare infrastructure.

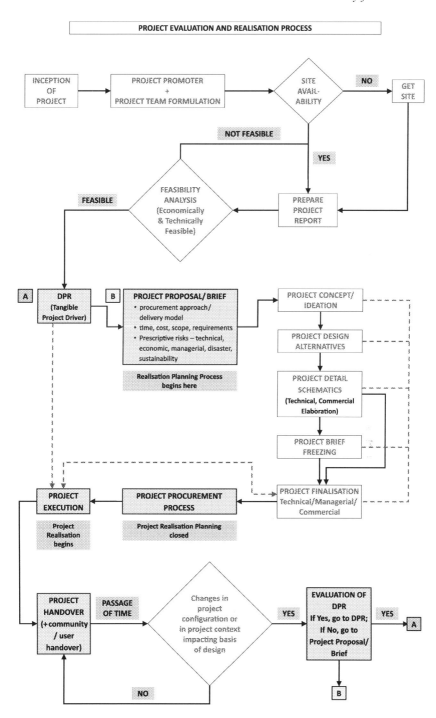

*Figure 9.1* Conventional process of project realisation and evaluation.

*Table 9.2* Incorporating resilience strategies in conventional project development processes

| S. No. | Project Stages | Proposed Resilience Strategies |
| --- | --- | --- |
| 1. | **Inception of Project** | • EWE and disaster awareness<br>• Establishing safety as a priority<br>• Articulating sustainability and environmental consciousness |
| 2. | **Project Team Formulation** | • Inclusion of EWE and disaster research and implementation team<br>• Creation of disaster management team<br>• In-house institution of disaster manager for the project/building/infrastructure<br>• Induction of project professionals having experience and/or specialisation in disaster risk reduction and resilience<br>• Assigning consultancy for:<br>  a) Environmentally conscious considerations<br>  b) Sustainability conscious considerations |
| 3. | **Site Availability/ Site Selection** | • Geography/topography of site<br>• Location/vicinity to neighbouring communities<br>• Awareness of potential hazards to which the site is exposed<br>• Reconnaissance of site in alignment with Vulnerability Atlas of India<br>• Seismic micro-zonation<br>• Disasters that the site has previously been subject to<br>• Reconnaissance of site with respect to:<br>  o Vulnerabilities<br>  o Risks<br>  o Potential hazards<br>  o Previous incidences<br>  o Climate change impacts<br>• Contextual influences on site<br>  o Availability of similar facilities in the vicinity to ensure coordination with others for backup in case of disruption to the current service<br>  o Road and air accessibility of site in case a disaster occurs |
| 4. | **Project Report** | • Vulnerability indicators and indices<br>• Risk indicators and indices<br>• Potential risks on site<br>• Risk assessment and analysis<br>• Risk and vulnerability mitigation measures<br>• Sustainable development strategies<br>• Environmentally sensitive strategies<br>• Resilience incorporation measures in design, planning, and structure<br>• Alternative materials and techniques<br>• Low-carbon footprint<br>• Local skill and labour<br>• Indigenous techniques and practices<br>• Locally sourced materials<br>• Community involvement programmes<br>• Social and cultural resilience programmes |

*(Continued)*

*Table 9.2* (Continued)

| S. No. | Project Stages | Proposed Resilience Strategies |
|---|---|---|
| 5. | **Feasibility Analysis** | • Environmental feasibility<br>• Geographical feasibility<br>• EWE and disaster risk vulnerability<br>• Proximity to emergency/healthcare facility<br>• Minimised vulnerabilities and risks<br>• Cultural and social acceptability<br>• Social and cultural disruption analysis<br>• Disruption to occupations and livelihoods |
| 6. | **Project Proposal/ Brief** | • Requirements for resilience and DRR<br>• Environmental impact and conservation<br>• Contextual influence and suitability<br>• Role delineation of disaster management and research teams<br>• Disaster and EWE awareness and preparedness strategies<br>• Contractual provisions for incorporating resilience<br>• Green rating and sustainability benchmarking<br>• Relief and recovery mechanisms in aftermath of disaster and EWE occurrence |
| 7. | **Project Concept/ Ideation** | • Resilient designing and conceptualisation for:<br>  o Architectural design<br>  o Structural design<br>  o Services<br>  o Functionality<br>  o Operations<br>  o Organisational strategies<br>• Planning for:<br>  o Contextual accessibility<br>  o Resilient site development<br>  o Safe parking provision<br>  o Congregational spaces for emergency<br>  o Evacuation routes |
| 8. | **Project Design Alternatives** | • Alternative DRR techniques and strategies<br>• Rationalisation of redundancy and robustness<br>• Analysis of resilience strategy effectiveness<br>• Impact analysis on project performance and cost<br>• Acceptance of stakeholders<br>• Verification of statutory compliances |
| 9. | **Project Detail Schematics** | • Verification of designs and details with disaster management team and consultants<br>• Evaluation of technical schematics and updating of basis of design |
| 10. | **Project Procurement Process** | • Contractors with experience in sustainable and resilient designs<br>• Project report on resilient methods to be deployed<br>• Resilience-specific financing<br>• Preparedness and awareness strategies and orientation of participating teams and stakeholders |

(*Continued*)

*Table 9.2* (Continued)

| S. No. | Project Stages | Proposed Resilience Strategies |
|---|---|---|
| 11. | **Project Execution** | • Quality assurance, quality control, and monitoring<br>• Preparedness for damage prevention strategies during construction stage<br>• Potential loss assessment, loss mitigation strategies and risk transfer<br>• Recurrent EWE and disaster sensitive alternative planning for construction activities<br>• Safety provisions against hazards<br>• Preparedness for prevention of damage to material, equipment, and works<br>• Disaster-resilient labour hutments<br>• Considerations for local labour deployment and material procurement<br>• Sustainable construction techniques and processes |
| 12. | **Project Handover** | • Community handover<br>• Community involvement in continuity of resilience processes<br>• Awareness and preparedness programmes for communities and stakeholders<br>• Financial risk transfer and insurance mechanisms to reduce risk with public |

The healthcare infrastructure serves to provide medical aid and emergency services and acts as a shelter during extreme events. However, these healthcare facilities have often been found to lack the resilience to absorb the impacts and continue functioning during such events. Even as the codes and standards recommend resilience and risk reduction strategies, these structures fail to respond or perform during disasters.

The healthcare infrastructure has been found to lack uniform distribution and proportionate service composition in India, as seen in the literature, case studies, and expert reviews in this book. The uneven dispersal of healthcare facilities and absence of efficient and functioning medical care in villages and remote areas puts pressure on the existing healthcare facilities in cities and towns, more so during and after an EWE. This further increases the risks to the healthcare facilities in terms of their operation, functioning, backups, staff availability, and patient intake. With the existing lack of awareness, resilience, and risk reduction strategies in various medical facilities in urban and peri-urban areas and the increased load of patients in addition to an upsurge in the event of a natural disaster, the healthcare infrastructure has a tendency to collapse under excessive distress, both in terms of structure and services.

A significant cause of such unresponsiveness is the sporadic occurrences of EWEs, which thereby leads to uncertainty and indecisiveness to invest funds in a structure that may or may not encounter such an event in its entire lifetime. Another cause can be recognised as the lack of awareness and knowledge of the need to provide resilience in the structures. As a result, the financing bodies and investors, along with the client, aim to reduce costs and direct funds to other facilities that are found more necessary or appropriate. This leads to not only increased risk in such facilities in the case of EWEs but also catches the administration, patients, staff, and other stakeholders unaware in the occurrence of such events.

Even if the existing healthcare facilities ensure backup and availability of overhead staff when needed, these may not be sufficient to cater to the exponential increase in times of emergency and trauma. Further, the equipment, machinery, number of beds, spaces, and structure may or may not be designed to handle stress and loads after a certain factor of safety. As a result, the structure and services may disintegrate when burdened with excessive demand in addition to the occurrence of an EWE. This highlights the need for more such healthcare facilities in rural/district/peri-urban areas that ensure the availability of medical and emergency care to locals in case of an upsurge in demand. Therefore, the overall purpose of this forward-looking research is to ensure undisrupted and even functioning of the healthcare infrastructure at the local level. The objective of this study has been aligned to ensure resilient and continuous services during and after the occurrence of an EWE.

The methodology for implementing risk-based resilience mitigation is described in Figure 9.2.

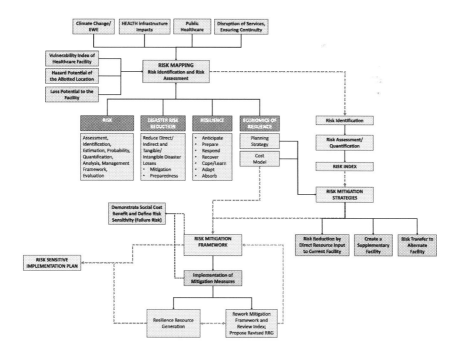

*Figure 9.2* Methodology flowchart.

### 9.3.1    *Risk mapping*

Risk mapping involves the identification and assessment of risks posed to the healthcare infrastructure, which helps the medical facilities to understand, acknowledge, and prepare for the known and unknown risks to their infrastructure and operations.

Based on the linkage of the work already presented in the preceding chapters, the linkage of risk mapping with the healthcare infrastructure is presented in Table 9.3.

This research commences with the task of risk mapping, which involves the identification and assessment of risks to initiate risk preparedness and mitigation. Various disaster risk reduction and risk resilience methodologies, frameworks, and strategies have been pointed out through the literature review. However, it will be useful to develop an index that quantifies the risk rating of any healthcare facility in terms of vulnerability to all relevant types of EWEs. The risk rating or risk index can help identify the type and amount of risks posed to the infrastructure, aid emergency planning, and assess the degree of investment to achieve resilience. This can further be used to establish benchmarks for risk reduction and ensure minimum losses.

The purpose of risk mapping and the risk index is to enhance awareness and quantify the risk potential of a healthcare facility. This research on risk mapping should aim to identify, evaluate, and monitor potential risks posed to a healthcare facility in case of an EWE.

*Table 9.3* Linkage of risk mapping with healthcare and work already done and the outcome of the identified objective

| *Healthcare Infrastructure Linkage* | *Linkage to the Work Already Done* |
| --- | --- |
| • Healthcare facilities are prone to structural, operational, and shelter risks during and after the occurrence of EWEs.<br>• Identification and assessment of risks to punctuate risk preparedness and mitigation. | • Cost model identifies the potential value losses to the healthcare infrastructure – derived from risk identification and assessment.<br>• Risk mapping aids the knowledge of the administration about risks involved and costs associated. |
| **Outcome: Risk identification and risk assessment for healthcare facility at risk** | |

### 9.3.2    *Risk index for a specific facility: hazard potential, areas of improvement, and establishing benchmarks*

A risk index identifies the degree and factor of risk involved when identifying and assessing the risks posed to a specific healthcare facility. The index is a formulated quantity that can further help establish benchmarks to minimize losses in case of an EWE.

Based on the work already presented in the preceding chapters, the linkage of a risk index with the healthcare infrastructure is presented in Table 9.4.

To assess the risks of EWEs to healthcare facilities, inputs are required from hazard potential, loss potential, and vulnerability index. It therefore becomes

*Table 9.4* Linkage of risk index with healthcare and work already done and outcome of the identified objective

| *Healthcare Infrastructure Linkage* | *Linkage to the Work Already Done* |
| --- | --- |
| • Formulation of loss potential, vulnerability index, and hazard potential into an equation that calculates the risk index of a specific healthcare facility.<br>• Used to establish benchmarks for risk reduction and ensure minimum losses. | • Value losses calculated in the study – can be used to calculate loss potential.<br>• Can be further used to formulate and benchmark risk index.<br>• Areas of improvement and risk analysis discussed in the study. |
| **Outcome: Formulation of a risk index using identified risks and vulnerability index, loss potential, and hazard potential** | |

necessary to develop the hazard potential (index), loss potential (index), and vulnerability index and formulate these into an equation that results in the risk index.

### 9.3.3 Identify risk mitigation strategies

Risk mitigation strategies help prepare the hospital administration for the upcoming known and unknown risks in terms of operation, structure, staff, and patient safety.

Based on the work already presented in the preceding chapters, the linkage of risk mitigation strategies with the healthcare infrastructure is presented in Table 9.5.

Awareness and knowledge of risks and mitigation strategies not only assist the organisations and healthcare facilities to adopt risk reduction techniques but also allow the hospital/facility/organisation to anticipate, prepare for, respond to, recover from, and adapt to any impending extreme events in terms of finances, structure, staff, and backup. Further, risk mapping also paves way for adoption of resilient strategies in the existing infrastructure and resilient design, planning, and construction in upcoming healthcare facilities.

Risk mapping and development of a risk index lead to the identification and enhancement of risk mitigation strategies that are beneficial for administration and

*Table 9.5* Linkage of risk mitigation strategies with healthcare and work already done and outcome of the identified objective

| *Healthcare Infrastructure Linkage* | *Linkage to the Work Already Done* |
| --- | --- |
| • Strategies beneficial for administration and staff for emergency planning and preparedness.<br>• Reduced losses to structure, operation, community, and lives when risk reduced through planning and resources. | • Study identifies risk evaluation and management framework through the literature – can be further used to derive mitigation strategies. |
| **Outcome: Risk mitigation strategies corresponding to risk amount and risk index to reduce EWE risk to a minimum** | |

staff for emergency planning and preparedness. This can result in reduced losses to the structure, operation, community, and lives when risk is reduced through planning and resources.

The study and proposed cost model in this book identify the potential value losses to the healthcare infrastructure, which have been derived from risk identification and risk assessment. These value losses can be used to calculate loss potential and further used to formulate and benchmark risk index. The book also identifies through the literature, the risk evaluation and management framework, which can be further used to derive mitigation strategies.

### *i    Risk reduction by direct resource input to current facility*

Input of resources directly to the healthcare facility under risk mapping reveals the degree of input required to make the infrastructure resilient and avoid maximum losses.

Based on the work already presented in the preceding chapters, the linkage of direct resource input to the current facility with the healthcare infrastructure is presented in Table 9.6.

The risk mitigation strategies can be achieved through three proposed methods, of which the first is:

**Risk reduction by direct resource input to current facility:** This method involves input of resources from government/international agencies. Shortfalls and risks found in the current healthcare facility can be reduced or eliminated with the help of such resources. Resources aimed at specific risk reduction invested in techniques for mitigation may also help reduce the amount of losses.

*Table 9.6* Linkage of direct resource input to current facility with healthcare and work already done and outcome of the identified objective

| *Healthcare Infrastructure Linkage* | *Linkage to the Work Already Done* |
|---|---|
| • Shortfall and risks found in current healthcare facility can be reduced or eliminated with input of resources from government/international agencies.<br>• Resources aimed at specific risk reduction invested in techniques for mitigation – may reduce quantum of losses. | • Cost model identifies potential value losses (tangible and intangible) to the structure, functioning, and stakeholders – can be further used and developed to evaluate total resource generation needed. |
| **Outcome: Value of resource input to ensure processes necessary to carry out reduced risks** | |

### *ii    Create a supplementary facility*

A supplementary healthcare facility, in addition to the existing hospital infrastructure under risk mapping, creates a separate entity to ensure low risk and high resilience in the process of new design, planning, and construction. This structure also works as a backup facility and helps reduce the load on the main healthcare facility.

*Table 9.7* Linkage of supplementary facility with healthcare and work already done and outcome of the identified objective

| *Healthcare Infrastructure Linkage* | *Linkage to the Work Already Done* |
| --- | --- |
| • Supplementary healthcare facility to be used in conjunction with existing facility – reduces load and provides backup.<br>• Strategies for mitigation of risks and shortcomings in existing facility also derived. | • Current study identifies the value losses in the existing structures.<br>• Can be adapted to identify risks in new facilities.<br>• Further used to evaluate and reduce risks. |
| **Outcome: Resources required to add a supplementary facility to sustain overall medical facility** | |

Based on the work already presented in the preceding chapters, the linkage of a supplementary facility with the healthcare infrastructure is presented in Table 9.7. *The second method among the risk mitigation strategies is:*

**Create a supplementary facility:** This entails addition of a supplementary healthcare facility to be used in conjunction with the existing facility, which can reduce the load and provide backup/redundancy. Further, this sustains the overall medical facility and helps determine strategies for mitigation of risks and short-comings in the existing facility.

*iii    Risk transfer to alternate facility*

Transfer of risk to an alternate facility that is resilient and can absorb impacts/ perform under load can assist the main facility to reduce risks and thereby reduce their losses.

Based on the work already presented in the preceding chapters, the linkage of risk transfer to an alternate facility with the healthcare infrastructure is presented in Table 9.8.

The third method among the risk mitigation strategies is:

*Table 9.8* Linkage of risk transfer to alternate facility with healthcare and work already done and outcome of the identified objective

| *Healthcare Infrastructure Linkage* | *Linkage to the Work Already Done* |
| --- | --- |
| • When existing healthcare facility cannot accommodate mitigation strategies for all potential typologies of risks, movable risks can be transferred to alternate facilities with a low risk index. | • Study encompasses risk evaluation and risk mitigation techniques through the literature – can be used to develop risk transfer strategies. |
| **Outcome: Transfer of risk to an alternate facility to reduce risks to current facility** | |

**Transfer risk to an alternate facility:** This can be useful when the existing healthcare facility cannot accommodate mitigation strategies for all potential types of risks. The movable risks can be transferred to alternate facilities with a low risk index.

### 9.3.4    *Risk mitigation framework (RMF): objective of RMF consistent with overall objective*

The RMF includes the strategies and methodologies to reduce and minimize known and unknown risks due to EWEs.

Based on the work already presented in the preceding chapters, the linkage of the RMF with the healthcare infrastructure is presented in Table 9.9.

Risk mapping and the development of risk mitigation strategies draw forth the need for an RMF whose objective is consistent with the overall objective of the current and future studies, i.e., to minimise losses to the healthcare infrastructure and reduce the hazard potential and risk. The RMF therefore assists the healthcare facility to strategize the mitigation of disaster risks effectively, with the help of the processes at different organisational levels and hierarchies. The RMF, a culmination of the steps of risk mapping and risk mitigation strategies, ensures informed decision-making and accountability within the organisation. However, it is necessary to ensure that the mitigation strategies identified in the RMF can be implemented through the processes identified.

*Table 9.9* Linkage of risk mitigation framework with healthcare and work already done and outcome of the identified objective

| *Healthcare Infrastructure Linkage* | *Linkage to the Work Already Done* |
| --- | --- |
| • Assists healthcare facility to mitigate disaster risks effectively, with the help of processes at different organisational levels and hierarchies.<br>• Culmination of steps of risk mapping – ensures informed decision-making and accountability within the organisation. | • Cost model entails resilience and risk mitigation strategies corresponding to value losses identified.<br>• Can be used further to quantify a risk index and develop a risk mitigation framework. |
| **Outcome: Identification and mitigation of value losses in the healthcare facilities using identification and quantification of losses** | |

### 9.3.5    *Implementation of mitigation measures*

The strategies and methodologies identified in the RMF need to be implemented to ensure that the risks are reduced and resilience is incorporated in the healthcare facility under assessment.

Based on the work already presented in the preceding chapters, the linkage of implementation of mitigation measures with the healthcare infrastructure is presented in Table 9.10.

*Table 9.10* Linkage of implementation of mitigation measures with healthcare and work already done and outcome of the identified objective

| *Healthcare Infrastructure Linkage* | *Linkage to the Work Already Done* |
|---|---|
| • Healthcare facilities to ensure processes that mitigate risks through strategies as identified in the RMF. | • Study identifies losses and allocates mitigation measures through the literature and cost model application inferences. |
| **Outcome: Identification of mitigation strategies to be implemented in healthcare facilities** | |

It must be of the utmost importance to input resources in resilient practices, which ensure not only safety of the users and the structure but also continuity of services in times of crisis. Hence, the purpose of future research is to identify and calculate the necessary inputs to achieve resilient healthcare construction. This can be ensured through resilience resource generation (RRG) and reworking of the risk index and RMF back and forth.

### *i   Resilience resource generation*

Resource inputs from various agencies can aid the resilience building and risk reduction as required in the RMF.

Based on the work already presented in the preceding chapters, the linkage of RRG with the healthcare infrastructure is presented in Table 9.11.

The specific objective of this step can be aligned to derive an adaptive framework, or the framework for RRG, for government/international bodies to supplement risk reduction strategies and extreme weather–resilient construction of the healthcare infrastructure. This ensures minimal loss of life and structure. The resultant framework enlists the overall implications to ensure continuity of services to healthcare, at various stages, up to a minimal risk benchmark, which also is a part of future research, informed by the literature and previous studies.

*Table 9.11* Linkage of resilience resource generation with healthcare and work already done and outcome of the identified objective

| *Healthcare Infrastructure Linkage* | *Linkage to the Work Already Done* |
|---|---|
| • Inputs from government and international agencies that ensure fuelling of risk mitigation strategies (structural and operational) to assuage potential risks and losses.<br>• Inputs for staff and administration to provide emergency services when required. | • Economic resilience in terms of direct and indirect, static and dynamic, identified through resilience.<br>• Cost model evaluates losses and potential areas of inputs to alleviate those risks. |
| **Outcome: Resources required to ensure resilience in the healthcare infrastructure** | |

*ii    Rework mitigation framework and review index: propose revised RRG*

Implementation of the RMF and input of resources requires verification of the risk index and risk mapping to ensure continuous improvement in resilience and risk reduction.

Based on the work already presented in the preceding chapters, the linkage of rework and review with healthcare infrastructure is presented in Table 9.12.

Back-and-forth calculations need to be conducted to check reductions in the risk index, vulnerability index, and loss potential of the healthcare facility under review. Rework and necessary changes will need to be ensured to the RMF and RRG to secure reduction of risks to a minimum.

*Table 9.12* Linkage of rework and review with healthcare and work already done and outcome of the identified objective

| *Healthcare Infrastructure Linkage* | *Linkage to the Work Already Done* |
|---|---|
| • Back and forth calculations to check reduction in risk index, vulnerability index, and loss potential of the healthcare facility under review.<br>• Rework and changes to the RMF and RRG to ensure reduction of risks to a minimum. | • Cost model identifies value losses and sets the ground for recalculation when inputs are received.<br>• Changes in RMF and RRG assist mitigation and resilience strategies. |
| **Outcome: Revised index and framework ensure minimum risks and eliminate superfluous risk** | |

### 9.3.6    *Demonstrate social cost benefit and define risk sensitivity (failure risk)*

The cost-benefit analysis of the formulated RMF and RRG involves validation to ensure that the quantified inputs have significant outputs.

Based on the work already presented in the preceding chapters, the linkage of social cost benefit with healthcare infrastructure is presented in Table 9.13.

*Table 9.13* Linkage of social cost benefit with healthcare and work already done and outcome of the identified objective

| *Healthcare Infrastructure Linkage* | *Linkage to the Work Already Done* |
|---|---|
| • Inputs to reduce risk in healthcare facilities – to be evaluated for maximum usage and benefit to society and infrastructure.<br>• Risk sensitivity and degree of input required to secure structure from failure risk. | • Social and economic benefits of inputs identified through literature study.<br>• Cost model aligns to possible failure risks and sensitivity of healthcare infrastructure to losses in case of EWEs. |
| **Outcome: Cost-benefit analysis to indicate economic benefits** | |

While the RRG framework incorporates the risks, solutions, inputs, and their amount, it needs to establish benchmarks for minimal losses (since loss cannot be zero in the case of extreme events) and demonstrate how this methodology, as well as the investment solutions, reduce risks and achieve these benchmarks. This further requires validation through cost-benefit analysis, which ensures that the investments are expected to yield the desired results in terms of the best possible costs. Additionally, the RRG framework should be able to determine the reduction in the loss potential, hazard potential, and vulnerability index, since these eventually determine the overall safety/risk potential of the structure.

The model therefore requires a back-and-forth calculation mechanism to ensure fulfilment of all benchmarks that bring the losses to a minimum. This model can also be divided into various stages and categories in terms of the budget, requirement, urgency, and areas of resource input that are aimed to be fulfilled by a particular agency or body. The economic benefits of this model also need to be enlisted and illustrated to establish the affirmative need of the model.

This RRG model, therefore, is expected to not only estimate the resource input implications of achieving resilience and risk reduction but also ensure that the healthcare facility continues to operate and does not succumb under pressure in case of an EWE.

### 9.3.7   Risk-sensitive implementation plan

It is essential that the RMF and RRG are sensitive to the risks and incorporate the same during implementation to avoid lags and unexpected losses during EWEs.

Based on the work already presented in the preceding chapters, the linkage of a risk-sensitive implementation plan with the healthcare infrastructure is presented in Table 9.14.

A risk-sensitive implementation plan to implement the RMF and RRG to align with the risk sensitivity of the healthcare infrastructure needs to be derived. Also, the risk index needs to be reviewed back and forth to safeguard the structure in terms of minimal risk.

Having developed a methodology to ensure risk mapping, resilience, and mitigation strategies, it is also found to be necessary that the execution of the RMF and RRG requires mapping of healthcare infrastructures across the country. It has been observed through the literature and expert reviews that there is an unequal and

*Table 9.14* Linkage of risk-sensitive implementation plan with healthcare and work already done and outcome of the identified objective

| *Healthcare Infrastructure Linkage* | *Linkage to the Work Already Done* |
| --- | --- |
| • Implementation of RMF and RRG to align with risk sensitivity of healthcare infrastructure. | • Cost model assesses losses that are most critical and sensitive; applies factor of sensitivity to typologies. |
| **Outcome: Risk index to be reviewed back and forth to safeguard structure in terms of minimal risk** | |

sporadic allocation of hospitals, district medical facilities, and health centres in the states as well as the country. This leads to increased distances and travel times for certain communities, thereby increasing their exposure to risk and losses in case of an EWE. The mapping, therefore, must ensure equitable distribution of critical and emergency medical care within the authorised/acceptable radius. Further, the mapping must follow land-use pattern and locations/sites that are the least vulnerable to natural disasters/EWEs.

### 9.3.8    *Reiteration of objectives as achievements*

This step assesses the objectives identified in future research and whether these are aligned and address the overall cause and objective of the study conducted in this book.

Based on the work already presented in the preceding chapters, the linkage of reiteration of objectives with the healthcare infrastructure is presented in Table 9.15.

*Table 9.15* Linkage of reiteration of objectives with healthcare and work already done and outcome of the identified objective

| *Healthcare Infrastructure Linkage* | *Linkage to the Work Already Done* |
|---|---|
| • Formulation of a risk index that is used to establish benchmarks for risk reduction and ensure minimum losses.<br>• Lay out risk mitigation strategies that reduce risk and supplement sustenance as well as operation during and after an EWE.<br>• Derivation of a risk mitigation framework to quantify and apply risk reduction and resilience strategies.<br>• Resource generation and cost-benefit analysis to reduce risk in healthcare facilities – to be evaluated for maximum usage and benefit to society and infrastructure. | • The objectives achieved in future research and the current research conducted in this book align to achieve the umbrella objective of ensuring resilience and reduced risk to the healthcare infrastructure and continuity of medical services.<br>• The research also aims to create awareness and preparedness in healthcare infrastructure authorities of impending risks and losses in case an EWE strikes. |

The study conducted in this book, including the literature review, expert opinions, and proposed cost model, can be regarded as a building block to advanced research that delves deeper into the risk assessment and resilience strategies. The healthcare infrastructure, as has been observed, is not as resilient as it is required to be. The resultant damages lead to reconstruction and losses that are not only unnecessary but are unmeasurable and avoidable. The purpose of the current as well as future research, therefore, is to avoid such losses and ensure maximum safety, security, well-being, and functioning of society and the healthcare infrastructure.

# 10 Annexures

## 10.1 Experts' opinions on EWEs and healthcare infrastructure vulnerability: transcripts

a) **Expert 1**

I. **Remarks on EWE vulnerability:** Extreme weather events, natural calamities such as earthquakes, and climate change, can render the health infrastructure dysfunctional. Unnecessary floods, such as the ones that occurred in Srinagar and south of India recently, were not planned for. It can be deduced that this is not just because of the climate change, it's also how we have developed our cities, in context of the urban planning in practice, which is done so poorly that the natural drainage patterns have been blocked, the places from where the water could have actually flown through, or which was the original natural slope. This is mostly because of the over-construction, industrialisation, and more built-up area that architects, planners, as well as clients always seek. This causes floods, and as urban planners, we don't plan for resistance, and rather keep building wherever possible or wherever we can, and for which reasons these floods and cyclones happen. Besides global warming, strange occurrences in the environment, such as forest fires in Australia, Amazon Forest, California, etc., occur, which cannot be got into control; it takes months and sometimes even more to get these under control. These natural calamities can impact all structures, and also healthcare structures.

II. **Remarks on healthcare projects' shortcomings:** To begin with, firstly, the tendering process is wrong at many levels. When we tender out for healthcare infrastructure, merit is of no significance at all. The entire tendering process is a rigged process, it's not fair anymore. What is brought on the table is not of commendable quality anymore, since it accounts other non-merit factors such as the cost input, corruption, rigged procedures, setups by some persons with influence, or money.

Secondly, when the process of tendering or selection of architects is carried out, it may not be necessary that one interview or one jury can help decide whether the selected ones would be the best consultants for the job. For selection of consultants, rather than only judging on design proposals,

DOI: 10.1201/9781003393108-10

one should actually look at past works of the consultants, because for a critical infrastructure as hospital, the designing and construction requires expertise and experience. Of course, this could pose a problem for a newcomer consultant to step into that position of work.

III. **Remarks on resilience intervention:** As mentioned previously, construction of a healthcare infrastructure is an area of expertise and experience; yet at the same time, design is only one part of the process. It would be more helpful if one visits a successful hospital previously designed/constructed by a consultant, to understand the functionality and design flow. Meeting and understanding the views of the user, the hospital management, to see how functional that hospital is, or how well it is running; because eventually design is not just about creating something that is aesthetic or looks good in a plan or an elevation, it's more about how user-friendly the project is. Whether the end users, the hospital staff, or the management or the patients are satisfied with the design and services.

Also, it is significant to ensure the involvement of hospital consultants, who can guide about the precise functionalities for someone who has not done too many hospitals, but could be a great architect. The hospital consultant becomes very useful for them. He/she can explain to the architect how the functions flow in a hospital. For instance, in operation theatre areas, there is a basic movement pattern which has to be followed from a totally unsterile area to a semi-sterile area to a 100% sterile, and then how various things are coming in.

It is also important to note that the involvement of a hospital consultant does not mean just getting a sign-off from them, it means getting a lot of input and involvement in the design process and final design. One way of doing it is for the client to have a hospital consultant – rather than the architect making a provision for one. Similar to fire consultants, hospital consultants, etc., disaster management consultants should also be a part of the design process team. Even for a situation as of now, of COVID-19 pandemic, a different set of requirements has been devised for design of hospitals. Disaster management wing should now come in-built in hospitals – which takes care of any disasters and its consequences on the hospital, which happen at any point of time.

IV. **Remarks on enhancing awareness:** Often our principal architect used to say that one should never begin a hospital with just the requirements – he always mentioned that whenever one starts with a hospital or any project, there should be a project brief. By the project brief he meant that all the stakeholders should get involved. A person who is a first-time client, who just wants to make a hospital, who may or may not be a doctor, may not understand all the aspects of getting the hospital on ground. The project brief comes in here, which has to be prepared even before the project requirements come, because requirements might mean one needs or wants a 500-bed multispecialty hospital, or sometimes the norms are laid out, or it could be a teaching hospital, depending on other norms that are available. Every hospital needs a brief, which keeps not just the client in mind, but also the hospital consultant, the architect, the disaster management expert, finance team, experts available for earthquake, for fire. These consultants bring in their own inputs for the brief. Before one sets out even to make the hospital or start designing or even drafting the requirements, a detailed project brief or project report must be drafted, just in words, where different stakeholders should be involved, through a series of meetings. This could also use the involvement of consultants who specialise in making project reports. The complete project philosophy by the client and all other stakeholders, with their ideologies incorporated – so that the client also responds better and understands that it's not just making a building of brick and mortar, but a lot of elements need to be put in. An example of this could be – sometimes a building needs more fire escapes – but the client asks to cut corners somewhere or the other, since he may not understand that it is only for the betterment of the hospital or the infrastructure. Hence, the whole team should sit together at all points of time. A project brief must be drafted, and shared with all stakeholders; this helps create a better project at the end – and more elements taken care of.

b) **Expert 2**

I. **Remarks on EWE vulnerability:** First of all, the healthcare infrastructure in India is across various hierarchies, like primary healthcare, dispensaries, general hospitals, and super-speciality hospitals. They are not balanced, in the sense that they are not developed evenly across the country, which is one major issue. When checked district-wise, one finds that in the rural areas, healthcare facilities are lacking in many places. In case of an event like flood or excessive rainfall, these facilities which are already little less in number, if they get flooded, or in case of power failure, cannot be relied upon to provide healthcare services. Because it is less in number, it becomes even more vulnerable. This is because of certain areas that might be totally without any healthcare facility.

As per the real-time location-based studies conducted by the interviewee, amongst education, water supply and other infrastructure, healthcare has been the most neglected infrastructure.

II. **Remarks on healthcare projects' shortcomings:** The main thing is that nobody has actually gone and found out that with the advancement of knowledge and health, healthcare facilities across hierarchies can be made more efficient. The facilities still have similar kind of staff and personnel who are manning the facilities. From district headquarters to tehsil headquarters, there is total apathy, with just one room in place of a dispensary or other healthcare facility. Persons who have been employed cannot operate the equipment, or the equipment is not in use, and sometimes it's not even supplied, although, now with COVID-19, there is an increased awareness and thinking. Also, there are parallel medical systems like Ayurveda and Unani, and many people try to manage with that. However, like the connecting roads, and other facilities, we don't have a balanced development perspective, and no state of art upgradation.

III. **Remarks on resilience intervention:** With respect to climate, the facilities should be tried to not be located in places which are prone to flooding. For instance, if it is a coastal area, the hospital building should be located according to sensitive land use classification. So, if there is an elevated area, or if an area is protected from exposure to storms, etc. The healthcare facilities are where the people will rush in case of emergency. Similar to doing micro-zonation for earthquakes to check safety, it needs to be identified which places are safe for congregation, similarly, hospital should be such located, while doing micro-zonation, that it should be safe in events of EWE, and should be able to accommodate in case of EWE. Hospitals, like schools, big churches or big temples, should have big congregational spaces. The connectivity to the hospital should be efficient. Normally these things are well-written, but they are not implemented, like wide roads in front, so that people do not have problem in approaching the hospital. These things should be followed without any compromise. Any encroachments must be removed, to ensure right of way and clear pathways.

IV. **Remarks on enhancing awareness:** We must make them know that these buildings are approaching, similar to school and airport, due to signage, speed breakers, and silent zones. Traffic movement and noise must be curbed. This must be done at various levels, from designs, to signage, to even putting up hoardings. The informal sector of vendors must be discouraged and removed, and such facilities must be included within the hospital designs. Further, the number of beds is a problem in the urban setup because the healthcare facilities are not sufficiently developed in suburban, districts, tehsils, and rural levels. Hence, people from these areas need to come to cities to avail healthcare services.

The areas on which the interviewee has worked and analysed, it was always observed that the healthcare infrastructure backlog is seen in various rural and suburban areas. It is therefore necessary that these facilities are strengthened at planning levels, designs.

Healthcare needs the maximum intervention, especially in rural and suburban areas. If one correlates to the risks, for instance, if there is a risk of floods, the plinth needs to be higher. If there is traffic congestion, traffic management needs to be incorporated. Scenarios must be developed to conduct simulations and develop the framework.

c) **Expert 3**

I. **Reviews on EWE vulnerability:** At this point, the vulnerability of a structure will depend on largely where it is located. This is one very important factor which needs to be considered. For example, in Delhi, it's landlocked, so rise in sea level issues don't have a consideration in the criteria, and need not be as much prioritised as flooding. The land use impact on the location of infrastructure is important. Within healthcare infrastructure, the primary, secondary, and tertiary centres need to be looked at. The vulnerability is also directly proportional to whether the healthcare infrastructure is mapped or not. Suppose we have a plan for a city where we actually map the healthcare infrastructure, then the vulnerability will reduce. But if the healthcare structures are randomly allocated, it is a skewed criterion. Therefore, land use, location, and the geographic location of the city itself, are significant factors to look into the vulnerability of healthcare infrastructures.

Secondly, whether the healthcare infrastructure is connected, and the way it is connected with each other. For example, if secondary clinics or hospitals are connected in some way or the other, with the main ones. That does not necessarily imply road or physical connectivity, it also means connected through a network. For instance, if a particular clinic gets a patient, and the patient needs critical care; and during an extreme event, such as a flood, the clinic was the nearest healthcare facility. A connectivity where doctors can talk to each other, or a digital connection, through which some expert advice can be provided, can reduce the vulnerability. Ambulance services are also significant, but in case of an extreme event, like a flood, it will be difficult for the ambulances to reach. When critical care is required, in an instance such as a collapse of a building because of flood, there is a major surge of affected people, in case of informal populations or slums, where the homes are not well constructed, only the tertiary clinics or health facilities will be available.

In coastal areas, everything is highly vulnerable. The healthcare infrastructure is even more vulnerable. It would be helpful to draw a vulnerability index, using which a prioritisation activity can be conducted, such as the parameters or attributes of planning that increase or affect the vulnerability of healthcare infrastructure.

In a peri-urban area, the populations are highly vulnerable and affected, when a disaster strikes. Hence, the vulnerability of healthcare infrastructure should also be made proportionate to the socio-economic aspect of the society, and how outreach to these vulnerable populations is invested in. In case of development of a cost model, these would be the intangible losses. Estimation of populations that are vulnerable, and the demographics of the city, which implies the kind of populations that are likely to be affected the most. Further, the kind of healthcare infrastructure is there in the land use plan, and whether there is healthcare infrastructure in the planning process, or if it is just allocated; yet the proportion needs to be mapped as well.

II. **Remarks on healthcare projects' shortcomings:** Usually, construction is aligned with the bylaws and standards, so there should be standards for critical infrastructure. For hospitals and clinics, construction standards definitely exist, which have to be complied with. The critical aspect of healthcare infrastructure, for instance, in a city, all the primary, secondary and tertiary facilities are mapped, and the most critical facilities out of these should be identified. Further, it must be checked if those critical facilities are complying with a certain standard. In a 50-year or a 100-year storm, those critical infrastructures that were identified based on the demographics, would need to comply with these standards for critical infrastructure. Hence, the question can go reverse in this context – do we have suitable standards for critical healthcare infrastructure?

Shortfalls can be identified only if the compliance levels are known. One has to go backward and see (a) what construction standards are being followed; (b) are there construction standards for identified critical infrastructure, which would mean that healthcare facilities would need detailed design protocols. For instance, the road leading to such facilities would need to comply with those standards.

A random sampling can be carried out, to find out the compliance levels of critical infrastructure, and their connectivity from vulnerable populations. This would help make an assessment of shortfalls. The authorities that give certificates for the healthcare facilities to function must ensure compliance check.

III. **Remarks on resilience intervention:** Structural standards and quality of materials are very important. A desk review of an extreme weather event, such as Cyclone Fani 2019, to review the healthcare infrastructure that Odisha has, which was deemed critical. From here, it can be checked backwards to identify their structural and compliance standards. The decision-making criteria also need to be looked at, for instance, what critical infrastructure means, if the structure is designed to withstand a certain degree of disaster, definition of the disaster and the vulnerability in a region, and use the decision-making pyramid from the Technical Assistance report by ADB. The report considers the vulnerable populations, their livelihood losses, and their time of recovery post-disaster. This gives an idea of the extent of vulnerability. Further, the resilience index and vulnerability index will give an insight on the characteristics that are needed for measuring the tangible and intangible losses.

IV. **Remarks on enhancing awareness:** Awareness can be increased by intense consultation. One major shortfall in the planning and designing system is that the practitioners fail to understand who they are designing for, which are the consumers. Group discussions, during the planning and construction phases, must also include the most important stakeholders, who are the persons for whom it is being designed, who get affected, and who get benefitted.

Various types of consultation techniques exist, which the practitioners often fall short of. It is important to get the right persons and consultants on board. In addition, in designing a space that is focussed on the service for the public and will be used by the public, the persons and communities which are likely to visit these facilities must be consulted. During a disaster; the facility must continue functioning, it should keep performing during and after the disaster also. To achieve this, apart from structural stability, the people within the facility make a difference. The staff, administrators, medical practitioners, must be consulted, and must understand what critical infrastructure is; that the facility that they are working in is a critical facility. Different grades of consultation, not just the people, but also the ones who are running the facilities should be interacted with.

## d) Expert 4

I. **Reviews on EWE vulnerability:** Firstly, it depends on the geographical condition of a hospital. For instance, in a seashore area, there are cyclones and extreme rains that can cause flooding, and the hospitals are vulnerable. Also, extreme in temperature is quite a discomfort for the patients. Not all hospitals have air conditioning, maybe a few rooms are air-conditioned, but the rest are normal rooms, which get affected by the weather. So, hospitals are, in general, at a disadvantage. As doctors, we do not plan according to the extreme weather events, we just give it to the architect, who designs the hospital, and we do not think much towards the design aspects of the hospital.

To build a hospital, the director/doctor would not approach a regular architect. We would approach a professional who knows how to design a hospital. There are a few firms in Gujarat, whose job is to only design hospitals. Yet, it has been observed that they do lack a very professional expertise to design a hospital.

II. **Remarks on healthcare projects' shortcomings:** Firstly, the architects do not consider the patient aspect of designing a hospital. Whenever a patient is admitted in a hospital, he must feel comfortable. Most of the hospitals are stuffy and uncomfortable. They are not airy and breathable. We do not see a lot of greenery. It's usually just blocks that have rooms within rooms. The hospital, especially the patient rooms, should have natural light and natural ventilation.

Secondly, for the process of tendering, the location of the hospital is important, if it is located in a crowded or a commercial area, or a quiet area. Quieter areas, preferably a little outside of the city are desirable. Within the hospital, it is preferred to be less crowded. Air circulation, planning aspect, and the heat and temperature aspects are significant in a hospital.

III. **Remarks on resilience intervention:** In case of floods, building the foundation a little higher is preferred; no underground parking or storage, since the basements are usually flooded. A surge in cyclones has been observed in Gujarat, Odisha, and Maharashtra lately. For this, the structure should be sturdy, the position and orientation of the building should be such that it is least affected by the extreme winds.

IV. **Remarks on enhancing awareness:** There is a lack of awareness in doctors, in case of building a hospital. Majority of the big hospitals, in big cities and metropolitans, have builders and corporates involved in building the hospital. Hence, the doctors never get involved, and often do not have much idea on how to build or design the spaces in hospitals.

To increase awareness among practitioners and clients alike, they can be brought together in seminar, conferences, fairs, etc. Such meetings highlight the different components of hospital building and design, like construction, material, type of building, and costing. These conferences were not common earlier, but have become more frequent and popular lately. Otherwise, it is best to hire a healthcare specialist, who already knows how to design the hospital. This is not a hotel, or any other commercial structure; however, some architects only focus on maximising the rooms and floor areas, and do not concentrate on the patients' comfort, natural lighting, and ventilation as much.

# Index

accountability 21, 110, 111, 139, 164
accumulation 5, 125
adaptation 13, 22, 25, 27, 48, 51, 63, 64, 72, 87, 88, 103, 104, 114, 117, 120, 127, 136
administration 12, 95, 121, 133, 134, 159–161, 165
affordability 80, 81, 105
agriculture 6, 9, 16, 27, 50, 52, 53, 56–58, 60–62, 72
agri-income 54
Amphan 58
anomaly 5
anthropogenic 3, 5, 8, 23, 86, 107, 153
assessment 43, 45, 65, 72, 75, 103, 106–110, 120–122, 129, 134, 136–139, 143, 150, 152, 153, 156, 158, 160, 162, 164, 168
authorities 8, 21, 30, 44, 45, 67, 69, 70, 94, 106, 168
avalanches 7, 9

behavioural 85, 87, 132
benchmark 134, 161, 162, 165
beneficiaries 19
Bittner 129–131, 134
breakdown 11, 22, 60
build-back-better 40, 42, 71
built-environment 104
buttress 87
bylaws 1, 88

calamity 36, 44, 68
capacity-building 38
carbon 3, 5, 8, 14, 23, 94
cascading 14, 51, 64, 108
casualties 3, 43, 56, 58, 59, 61, 62, 129, 148

catalyst 143, 150
catastrophe 66, 99, 107, 126, 137
causative 109
CDC 96, 100
CDRI 105
CEEW 13, 24, 122
climate-resilient 64, 113, 122
Climatology 5–7, 25
cloudburst 54, 61
coastal 5, 7, 8, 10, 11, 71, 107
co-benefits 72, 112
co-dependent 29
collaboration 18, 35, 76, 83, 99
collapse 22, 40, 54, 59, 62, 93, 107, 129, 139, 158
communication 18, 20, 37, 38, 46, 53, 55–58, 60, 61, 83, 85, 86, 94, 96, 97, 111, 120, 134
communities 3, 9, 10, 16, 18, 19, 43, 45, 64, 65, 71, 79, 83, 85–88, 94, 95, 99, 100, 102–105, 118, 119, 121, 123, 127, 128, 134, 137, 138, 141, 151, 154, 156, 158, 168
compliance 30, 36, 111, 142
comprehensive 8, 12, 17, 34, 39, 43, 67, 69, 80, 93, 94, 109, 113, 128, 130, 136, 149, 150
Congregational 157
consequence 13, 29, 34, 54, 55, 59, 71, 109, 133
conservation 112, 157
construction 1, 7, 15, 22, 24, 28–30, 34, 41, 44–46, 50, 59, 64, 66, 82, 88, 89, 91, 96, 98, 100, 104, 105, 107, 121, 136, 158, 161, 162, 165
contamination 4, 61, 94
Contextual 156, 157
cost-effectiveness 120, 128

countermeasure 96
critical infrastructure 1, 3, 11, 12, 21–24,
    28–31, 34, 44, 45, 49, 50, 52, 53, 71, 72,
    91, 93, 99, 101, 102, 112–114, 122, 124,
    128, 131, 151, 152, 154
cyclone 5–7, 13, 25, 33, 53, 56, 58, 71, 102

decentralised 76, 84, 113
decision-making 30, 37, 84, 110, 111, 164
demographic 70, 79, 82
destruction 5, 7, 13, 14, 23, 71, 82, 95, 127,
    152
devastation 6, 7, 59, 66, 86
development-environment 3, 25
DFID 128, 138
disaster-prone 66
diversification 128, 132
drainage 29, 55, 59, 62, 83, 107, 113, 146
droughts 3, 5–7, 9, 10, 12, 14, 34, 51, 62,
    68, 86, 108, 125
DRR 71, 103–106, 157
dynamic 1, 38, 96, 114, 116, 132, 165
dysfunction 2, 3, 64, 148

earthquake 13, 32, 33, 41, 45, 47, 100, 106,
    121
ecological 3, 5, 9, 15, 97, 102, 103, 117,
    122, 134
econometric 143
economics 43, 103, 124, 134–136, 152,
    154
ecosystem 27, 34, 50, 102, 105
emergencies 25, 33, 34, 64, 73, 85, 90, 98,
    100, 107, 120, 129, 131
emphasis 34, 70, 79, 82, 83, 117, 136
encroachment 55, 59
endemic 95
environment 2–4, 14, 20, 23, 24, 27, 28,
    42, 50, 63, 72, 96, 105, 122, 128, 133,
    134, 151, 153
epidemic 33, 47, 59
equilibrium 12, 22, 31, 32, 36, 37, 40, 41,
    46, 54, 57, 65, 67, 81, 87, 91, 97–99,
    102, 120, 127, 133, 143–145, 147, 149,
    158, 159
equitable 16, 18, 76, 168
essential 11, 14, 23, 31, 38, 43, 64, 65, 68,
    77, 80, 94, 99, 107, 113, 145–148, 154,
    167
estimation 28, 30, 108, 109, 121, 133,
    135–138, 140, 143, 144, 147, 148
evacuation 9, 23, 34, 39, 64, 100, 117, 128,
    157

evaluation 33, 37, 47, 80, 106–108, 110,
    111, 116, 121, 129, 130, 136, 152–155,
    157, 161–163
EWE 2, 13, 14, 16, 23, 27–32, 38, 41,
    43–46, 71, 82, 87–89, 92, 93, 96–100,
    104, 105, 107, 121, 126, 127, 131, 133,
    134, 136, 137, 144, 149–154, 156–161,
    167, 168
exacerbate 63, 93
ex gratia 148
extreme weather event 4

facilitate 19, 74, 85, 113, 129, 137
famines 95, 108, 125
Fani 53, 71
fatalities 3, 6, 7, 31, 32, 54, 55, 62, 66, 71,
    121, 133
feasibility 68, 157
financing 19, 69–71, 81, 110, 124, 128,
    134, 154, 157, 159
Firefighting 94
fiscal 75, 106
flooding 3, 7, 9, 32, 34, 35, 51, 55, 57, 59,
    66
forecasting 33, 47, 66, 68, 128
framework 3, 11–13, 17, 20, 25, 34, 36,
    42, 44, 64, 67, 70, 72, 83, 102–106, 110,
    111, 113, 121, 123, 129, 131, 134–136,
    138–140, 143, 149, 150, 152, 153, 161,
    162, 164–168
fundamental 21, 37, 76, 77, 105, 113–114
funding 20, 69, 88, 112, 128

GDP 79, 125–127, 142, 143
global 3, 5, 10, 11, 13, 15, 20, 21, 24, 28,
    29, 31, 41, 45, 47, 50, 66, 72, 75, 83, 89,
    102, 105, 122, 128, 131, 141, 151, 152,
    154
GoI-UNDP 66
governance 12, 17, 20, 21, 34, 78, 84,
    104–107, 111, 139, 142
grassroots 18
guidelines 25–27, 30, 34–36, 39–42, 44,
    64, 67, 84, 88, 89, 122, 137, 139, 150

habitat 23, 27, 50
haphazard 3, 68
harbinger 3, 4
havoc 62, 64, 71, 154
hazard 7, 8, 13, 30, 32, 35, 36, 43, 45, 69,
    71, 82, 99, 107, 110, 122, 128, 131, 138,
    139, 141, 160, 161, 164, 167
hierarchy 2, 31, 36

hospital 24, 29–40, 45–47, 53, 61, 71, 72, 75, 85, 87, 89, 97, 98, 100, 106, 107, 121, 127, 129–131, 133, 134, 136, 142, 145, 148, 149, 161, 162
Hudhud 56
humanitarian 104, 125, 128, 141
hurricanes 86, 134
hydrological 6, 117
hygiene 55, 56, 94, 95
Hyogo 17, 102, 103, 106, 129, 139

illness 62, 94–96
incentives 81, 127
indicators 19, 37, 74, 76, 81, 120, 121, 139, 141, 142, 152, 153, 156
Indo-Gangetic 10
infections 32, 55, 56, 80, 83, 95
infrastructures 2, 14, 23, 44, 45, 88, 97, 153, 154, 167
intangible 30, 43, 44, 74, 105, 121, 125, 133–136, 142, 144, 150–154, 162
interdependencies 24, 83, 113
Intergovernmental 3, 24, 72
interventions 1, 23, 36, 74, 110, 119, 128, 136
investment 12, 23, 30, 43, 64, 65, 71, 76, 125, 126, 132, 134, 151, 153, 154, 160, 167
IPCC 7, 8, 10, 24, 72, 119

jeopardise 20, 92

Kotrupi 54

landslides 5, 7, 9, 23, 32, 54, 59, 68, 107, 119
life expectancy 80–82
livelihood 4, 7, 56, 105, 128, 132
load-bearing 97
low-carbon 119, 123, 156
low-income 105, 126, 135
low-risk-exposure 128

machine-learning 8
macro-economic 53, 126, 132
manifestations 13, 49, 51, 64, 117
man-made 11, 36, 86, 108
mapping 29, 30, 41, 73, 75, 90, 160–162, 164, 166–168
meteorological 6, 8, 68, 117, 122
methodology 14, 71, 87, 136, 137, 143, 152–154, 159, 167
micro-economic 132

micro-zonation 30, 156
MoHFW 76, 79, 83, 84, 89
mortality 10, 15, 17, 34, 75, 79–82, 106, 119
multi-hazards 13

National Health Policy 41, 74, 75, 84, 89
NDMA 34, 35, 106, 122
NDMP 34
negligence 31, 82, 88

OECD 80, 112, 113, 122
outbreak 47, 48, 59, 89, 100
overwhelmed 26, 94

pandemic 76, 86
paradigm 21, 42, 66
paradox 2–4, 24, 25, 151
paramedical 99, 130
Plan-Do-Check-Act 113
policies 14, 17, 27, 33, 34, 41, 42, 44, 46, 67–70, 74, 75, 80, 83, 87, 106, 111, 136, 139, 151
post-disaster 37, 95, 128, 132, 143, 150
pre-disaster 68, 70, 95, 126
preparedness 2, 8, 17, 30, 31, 33–40, 42, 46, 47, 48, 66, 67, 69, 71, 97, 98, 100, 103–106, 112, 115, 134, 139, 151, 152, 157, 158, 160–162, 168
protocols 44, 93, 95, 99
PTSD 33, 96
PVI 141, 142

qualitative 110, 136, 137
quantification 87, 109, 120, 137, 138, 141, 143, 144, 150, 152, 153, 164

rationale 49, 101, 130
recommendations 25, 31, 113
recoverability 114, 115, 121
recurrent 9, 31, 54, 71, 158
redundancy 3, 88, 91, 92, 96–102, 104, 115, 121, 144, 152, 153, 157, 163
region-specific 28, 45
rehabilitation 17, 35, 37, 95
resilience 1–3, 12–14, 17, 20, 22–26, 28, 30, 36, 37, 40, 42–46, 48–51, 69–73, 82, 88, 89, 91–93, 96–98, 100–106, 112–124, 128, 129, 131, 132, 134–144, 150–154, 156–160, 162, 164–168
resourcefulness 96, 104, 121, 144
response 6, 17, 22, 23, 28, 31, 34–39, 45, 50, 66–72, 86–88, 93, 94, 99, 100, 103,

104, 109, 112, 126, 128, 132, 139, 141,
  151, 153
risks 6, 7, 13, 14, 21, 22, 24, 43, 51, 64,
  67, 72, 87, 102, 104–112, 114, 116,
  119–121, 127, 128, 132, 136, 137, 139,
  143, 149, 152–154, 156–158, 160–168
robustness 67, 96–98, 104, 114, 115, 121,
  143, 157
rural-urban 20

sanitation 15, 16, 20, 21, 35, 56, 58, 60, 64,
  72, 76, 77, 79, 80, 84
SDG 16–19, 24, 76, 90
SDMP 36, 37
SFDRR 12
snowmelt 7
socio-economic 4, 10, 11, 23, 27, 63, 64,
  69, 78, 83, 142
stakeholders 45, 87, 104, 111, 116,
  157–159, 162
strategies 3, 13, 22, 64, 65, 75, 80, 82,
  86–88, 110, 117, 119, 122, 123, 132,
  134, 151–154, 156–158, 160–168
susceptibility 140, 141
sustainability 4, 15, 16, 18, 19, 21, 45, 46,
  103, 119, 142, 156, 157

TB-HIV 83
temperature 3, 5, 6, 8, 9, 22
transformation 20, 119, 142
tsunami 7, 33

undisrupted 29, 159
unsustainable 3, 107
urbanisation 4, 17

value-based 142, 150
variability 8, 10, 22, 62, 64, 114
vulnerability 2, 9–11, 13, 14, 21, 23,
  24, 26, 28–31, 33, 36, 42, 43, 66,
  69, 70, 72, 74, 88, 99, 102–104,
  107, 110, 114, 127, 129, 131,
  139–142, 151, 154, 156, 157,
  160, 161, 166, 167

water-borne 34, 52, 83, 89, 95
waterlogged 52, 57
wildfire 9, 119
winds 5, 10, 22, 56, 58

Yamuna 59

zones 30, 33, 59

Printed in the United States
by Baker & Taylor Publisher Services